World War II
on the Big Screen

World War II on the Big Screen

450+ Films, 1938–2008

Doris Milberg

McFarland & Company, Inc., Publishers
Jefferson, North Carolina, and London

LIBRARY OF CONGRESS CATALOGUING-IN-PUBLICATION DATA

Milberg, Doris.
    World War II on the big screen : 450+ films, 1938–2008 / Doris Milberg.
        p.   cm.
    Includes bibliographical references and index.

    ISBN 978-0-7864-4740-4
    softcover : 50# alkaline paper ∞

    1. World War, 1939–1945 — Motion pictures and the war.
2. Motion pictures — United States — History — 20th century.
I. Title. II. Title: World War two on the big screen.
D743.23.M55   2010
791.43'6584053 — dc22   2009052812

British Library cataloguing data are available

©2010 Doris Milberg. All rights reserved

No part of this book may be reproduced or transmitted in any form or by any means, electronic or mechanical, including photocopying or recording, or by any information storage and retrieval system, without permission in writing from the publisher.

Front cover: John Wayne in *The Longest Day*, 1962 (20th Century-Fox/Photofest); at top film ©2010 Shutterstock

Manufactured in the United States of America

McFarland & Company, Inc., Publishers
   Box 611, Jefferson, North Carolina 28640
     www.mcfarlandpub.com

To Ted,
whose love, patience and encouragement
have sustained me
throughout the creation and birth of this book;
and to the films depicting a proud era
in our history. Their beat goes on.

Table of Contents

Preface	1

Part I. 1938–1945

One — Prelude to War: Fact and Fantasy	7
Two — Scarlett and Rhett, Hitler and War	15
Three — A Tenuous Peace in America	20
Four — The Road to War: December 7, 1941	28
Five — American Mobilizes	38
Six — War Themes: The Making of a Legend	56
Seven — Praise the Lord and Pass the Propaganda	80
Eight — Soldiers in Greasepaint	90
Nine — The Longest Day	96
Ten — The Road to Victory	114

Part II. Après la Guerre: War-Related Films

Eleven — In the Wake of War	131
Twelve — The Best Years of Our Lives	141
Thirteen — The End of the Forties: A Time of Darkness	148
Fourteen — A Changing Scene, a Changing Society: The Fifties and Sixties	152
Fifteen — Time Marches On: The Seventies and Eighties	175

Sixteen — The End of a Century   193
Seventeen — The Dawning of a New Century   198

Epilogue   205
Selected Bibliography   207
Index   209

Preface

In researching this book, I found it fascinating to note the number of films about World War II that are still being produced today, decades after the cessation of hostilities — which only goes to prove that although "War is Hell," to quote famed nineteenth century war hero William Tecumseh Sherman, it is still one hell of a screen subject.

World War II on the Big Screen is not merely a compendium of World War II films. The book is the chronicling of an era in which dictatorship and enslavement were pitted against democracy and freedom.

The motion pictures discussed in the pages that follow can, of course, be seen and enjoyed as separate entities, but put into the context and events of the times, they serve to give the moviegoer of today a clearer understanding of that gone but never-to-be-forgotten part of our nation's history.

Since a book listing all of the war-related films that have been produced before, during and since World War II would fill several thousand pages, I have chosen those motion pictures, major and minor, which, to my way of thinking, best convey the thoughts, moods and events of the era. I hope that the reader will get a true feeling for these important years in the life of our nation.

Much of the book's material is concerned with the period beginning in 1938 and ending in 1945. The story of the events that occurred in Hollywood and the films which were produced during this era are placed against the larger backdrop of a world in crisis.

During the last years of peace, the social whirl of the rich and famous was in full swing and much of the gossip in Tinsel Town revolved around producer David Selznick's search for the perfect Scarlett O'Hara, the fiery heroine of *Gone with the Wind*, Margaret Mitchell's sweeping saga of the Civil War. Only a few films revolved around the global headlines Americans were digesting along with their morning coffee.

America was officially, if not politically, neutral in 1939, the year of Germany's march into Poland. As more and more of Europe began to quake under the jackboots of Adolf Hitler's Wehrmacht, however, the pace in Hollywood began to quicken and more films were produced which were definitely anti–Nazi in tenor and had, as their twin themes, patriotism and preparedness.

After Pearl Harbor and our own entrance into the conflict, the propaganda machines really began to churn. For the duration of the war, commercial films, documentaries and shorts extolling our armed forces and articulating our reasons for fighting were cranked out almost on an assembly line basis. Many of the documentaries and shorts were produced by special service units of the military under the direction of several then-familiar names, among them Frank Capra, George Stevens, William Wyler and John Huston. These filmmakers undertook the task of bringing the war to the people on our home front.

And speaking of the home front, civilian Hollywood banded together as never before and, in an unparalleled effort, pushed temperament and ego aside and gave of their time, their money, their energy, their hearts and, in the case of actress Carole Lombard, a life.

The number of bond drives, USO camp shows and hospital visits in which Hollywood personalities participated, is a matter of record. A good example of this is the Hollywood Canteen, which opened its doors in October of 1942. Members of the armed forces stationed in the area could always go to the canteen for an evening of good food and even better entertainment served up by some of their all-time film favorites.

In short, to paraphrase England's Prime Minister Winston Churchill, this was filmdom's finest hour.

As the face of the war was altered, the films made about it reflected these changes. The vividness of emotions that motion pictures brought to audiences in theaters throughout the nation was probably Hollywood's greatest achievement during those trying times. The images that the motion picture industry presented may not always have reached the heights of realism, but the movie capital gave the public and the millions who still view these old films today, an increased awareness of the era's global events. (In some productions, however, there is also a sense of adventure which has not always reflected the true brutality of armed conflicts.)

And then, three years and eight months after the attack on Pearl Harbor, it was all over and Johnny and Janie came marching home again. *World War II on the Big Screen* goes on to deal with many of the films released soon after the end of the war which mirrored the problems confronting our nation as it returned to a peacetime standard. The final chapters and epilogue take us through the ensuing decades, trying to define the ongoing fascination with World War II and its aftermath.

Many of the motion pictures discussed in the book can be seen by the reader through the magic of television, video cassette and in some cases DVDs. Those who lived through the war are able to reflect upon an unwanted, but glorious period in their lives. For younger generations, the viewing of the films of World War II is a lesson in our nation's history, a look at our last "popular war."

Hollywood is the sum total of its parts and it is to be hoped that you, the reader, will be transported back to those hectic and exciting days when the world of make believe suddenly had to face reality.

Part I

1938–1945

Chapter One

Prelude to War: Fact and Fantasy

During the late 1930s, many people searched for an escape from a decade of hardship and strife. Years of widespread economic depression, unemployment, breadlines and abject poverty followed the stock market crash of 1929. Those who could look beyond their own problems, however, had seen the beginnings of another kind of hardship. By 1933, while President Franklin Delano Roosevelt was taking steps to shake this country loose from its malaise, Adolf Hitler, the Austrian chancellor of Germany, was embarking upon a far different course, one which he believed would lead to global domination by his adopted land. Instead, twelve years later, his evil machinations led to a funeral pyre amongst the ruins of Berlin and a world that would never again be the same.

In those years of the threadbare thirties, Hollywood and the motion picture industry played an important role in boosting the morale of the nation. Americans saw such classics as *It Happened One Night, Cavalcade, The Thin Man, Mutiny on the Bounty* and several musicals starring the team of Fred Astaire and Ginger Rogers. These films not only entertained, they poured money into Hollywood's coffers. This in turn led to the maintenance of a privileged class of people whose antics and lifestyles titillated the average American. The romance of Clark Gable and Carole Lombard, the on-again, off-again marriage of Errol Flynn and the tempestuous Lili Damita, the slugfests of the "Battling Bogarts," Bogie and his actress wife Mayo Methot — plus, of course, anything pertaining to Hollywood's royal couple, Douglas Fairbanks and Mary Pickford, were only a few of the gossipy tidbits devoured by a celebrity-hungry populace.

While this was taking place, Chancellor Hitler had become

"Führer." This Austrian upstart, a vagabond who had lived in the mean flophouses of Vienna, had traveled to Germany, became a citizen and joined the German army when World War I began. With the end of the war and the Treaty of Versailles, the provisions of which most Germans considered harsh and unjust, the time was ripe for an upheaval. And the Austrian took every advantage of the situation.

He joined a small group of National Socialists and, with his mesmerizing stare and raging harangues, soon became the leader of the party and a force to reckon with. The National Socialists became the majority party in the German Reichstag (the elected legislative body of the country) and, with the death of the aged head of state, Paul von Hindenberg, hero of World War I, Hitler declared himself Führer.

Under his leadership, all phases of German life, social, cultural and economic, were now dictated by his National Socialist Party and, as the slogan went, "The party is Hitler and Hitler is the party." It soon became clear that his special scapegoats were to be the Jews. Hitler's theory of a "master race" did not include the Jews of Germany or, for that matter, of any other country.

His tentacles reached into the cream of Hollywood society. By 1935, a half-decade before the release of Charlie Chaplin's devastating satire *The Great Dictator*, all films made by the "Little Tramp" were banned in Germany. The reason given? "Herr Chaplin is not pure Aryan." In 1938, it was also decreed that music written by Jewish composers could only be played if the songs were identified as having been written by "pure Aryans." As the year ended, Joseph Paul Goebbels, Hitler's minister of propaganda, confiscated, in the name of Der Führer, all movie houses owned by Jews. The stated objective was to remove these people from any connection with the German film industry. (This was the case with all Jewish-owned businesses.) The minister also had a hand in the production of films and ultimately, many of the biggest names in Berlin saw the handwriting on the wall, fled their country, came to America and gave of their talents: writers, musicians, producers, directors, actors.

Hitler and his ally, the Italian dictator Benito Mussolini, were also busy on other fronts. While the newly crowned Edward VIII renounced the British throne for Walis Warfield Simpson, the woman he loved, Hitler occupied the Rhineland, thus negating the Versailles Treaty, and the Italians occupied Ethiopia.

Another sinister figure loomed on the horizon: Spain's Francisco

***The Great Dictator*:** Is it any wonder that Charlie Chaplin's films were banned in Germany even before the war began and in all of occupied Europe during the war?

Franco. The Spanish Civil War began in 1936 and ended in 1939, just scant months before the German invasion of Poland. Thousands saw the conflict in term of good against evil, of Fascism and dictatorship versus Republicanism and freedom under a constitutional monarchy. Aided and abetted by his German and Italian counterparts, General Franco's Fascist armies defeated the pro–Loyalists. This bloodbath, in which hundreds of thousands of human beings perished, has since been referred to as the prelude to World War II.

Nineteen thirty-eight marked the last full year of world peace. Hitler proclaimed the political and geographical union of his native Austria with Germany (the "Anschluss") and the partition of Czechoslovakia. British Prime Minister Neville Chamberlain returned to England after his meetings with the German dictator. His mood was hopeful as he solemnly stated that the talks had brought about "peace in our time."

With this in mind, it is easy to comprehend the reasons as to why the Hollywood of 1938 did not want to deal with the growing Nazi menace. It was not considered politic, with Hitler on the rampage, to produce anything that would enrage Der Führer. Also, for the better part of the decade, America's foreign policy was one of neutrality tending towards isolationism; escapist entertainment was the order of the day. A few intrepid moviemakers, however, both here and abroad, did throw caution to the wind and some classic films resulted. In retrospect, one of the more interesting productions released in 1938 was not filmed in Hollywood — it was of Russian origin.

What makes the Russian production *Alexander Nevsky* so fascinating is that its historic theme was repeated in real life during the winter of 1941, three full years after the film's release. Directed by Serge Eisenstein, it tells of the attack upon Russia by the Teutonic hordes of Germany in the year 1242 and the subsequent repulsion of these armies by the forces of Prince Alexander Nevsky. The epic drama parallels Hitler's invasion of the Soviet Union, one of the great blunders of the war on the Nazi dictator's part, and culminates in a great ice battle, many of which the soldiers of 1941, ill prepared for the Russian winter, faced.

A few films of the thirties took their inspiration from the daily headlines. The conflict in Spain was the backdrop for 1937's *The Last Train from Madrid* and for *Love Under Fire*, the first released by Paramount, the second by Twentieth Century–Fox.

Last Train stars Dorothy Lamour, Lew Ayres, Olympe Bradna and

Gilbert Roland. It is a topical drama of a group of disparate people trying to leave the Spanish capital in the wake of war. Though the words "Republican" and "Fascist" are not mentioned in the film, audiences read between the lines and the production, though lambasted by the critics for being cliché-ridden, did fairly well at the box office, with Ayres and Bradna taking acting honors, he as a journalist and she as a girl who is shot before the train reaches Valencia. Also featured in the cast are future stars Anthony Quinn and Robert Cummings.

Love Under Fire is an attempt at comedy-drama starring Don Ameche as a Scotland Yard detective and Loretta Young as a jewel thief (who is not what she appears to be) caught in Madrid in the midst of the conflict. After Ameche proves Loretta innocent, the two escape from Spain and make their way back to England. Others in the cast are Frances Drake, John Carradine and Sig Ruman. The trite Fox film did not make an impression upon audiences.

Blockade (1938) from United Artists pairs the ever-popular Henry Fonda with England's Madeleine Carroll, with Leo Carrillo and Reginald Denny prominently featured in the supporting cast. It was another of Hollywood's contributions to the international situation, but a bland one. The plot involves a peace-loving "Spanish" farmer who takes up arms to defend his homeland; it is more of a love story than anything else and makes no mention of either Franco or Fascism. The most interesting aspect of the movie was the publicity given it at the time of its release. A disclaimer was issued which read, "Care has been taken to prevent any costume of the production from being accurately that of either side in the Spanish Civil War. The story also does not attempt to favor any cause in the present conflict."

These films showed the nations of the world that the events taking place in Europe could no longer be ignored. More and more filmmakers were learning this lesson. One production starring a few of Hollywood's brightest stars brought the Nazi menace even closer to the American public: *Three Comrades* (1938), a MGM release based upon a best-selling novel by the famed Erich Maria Remarque, is set in post–World War I Germany and stars Margaret Sullavan, Robert Taylor, Robert Young and Franchot Tone. The story, basically a romantic one, does touch upon the rise of the "brown shirts," Hitler's storm troopers, and depicts the street riots which the Nazi movement used in the takeover of the land of Goethe and Schiller.

Remarque, whose blockbuster anti-war novel *All Quiet on the Western Front* had been made into an Academy Award–winning film in 1930, did not write the screenplay for *Three Comrades*. Instead the task fell to the popular F. Scott Fitzgerald. Several telling scenes in Fitzgerald's treatment did not reach the screen, including one in which several well-known books, Remarque's among them, are burned. Much of the film's political content was blunted by censorship and the fear of exacerbating conditions in Europe, but it remains nevertheless a haunting and thought-provoking motion picture.

Spy tales have always been fodder for filmmakers. Axis agents had been at work in Europe and in the United States long before the invasion of Poland and the subsequent bombing of Pearl Harbor. Two films, one British and the other American in origin, took advantage of this fact of life: Britain's production is a fanciful bit of fiction, the American film is based upon reality.

The Lady Vanishes: Michael Redgrave (left), Margaret Lockwood and Paul Lukas are discussing the disappearance of an elderly governess during a train ride in pre-war Europe.

Take one part suspenseful plot and one part delicious humor, lace it with sly over-tones of political propaganda and the result is *The Lady Vanishes*. A masterful Alfred Hitchcock thriller made in England, the film pits Margaret Lockwood and Michael Redgrave against Nazi spy Paul Lukas in the hunt for a kidnapped British agent, played by Dame May Whitty, who is on the same train as the trio. Whitty is carrying vital information for the British government which she has encoded into a melody. At the climax of the film, a bemused Lukas sees his quarry cross the border into Switzerland, while Lockwood and Redgrave meet up with the old woman in London. The all–British supporting cast includes Cecil Parker, Googie Withers, Basil Radford and Naunton Wayne. Much of the humor of the film is supplied by Radford and Wayne, playing two proper Englishmen who feel inconvenienced by the imminence of war.

There have been two versions of this story produced thus far, the second one made in 1979 with Elliott Gould and Cybill Shepard in the Redgrave-Lockwood roles and the ever popular Angela Lansbury in the Whitty role. The Hitchcock film, however, is the better by far, with the rotund director's touch evident throughout. (The famed director was actually the second choice on this project, whose original title was *Lost Lady*. "Hitch" stepped in when the other filmmaker proved unavailable. A classic resulted.)

During the early 1930s, Warner Bros. had been in the forefront of realistic drama. Social themes such as the Depression and the criminal element had been an important part of the studio's output. In the last years of the decade, however, a new "criminal element" surfaced in its films.

Led by its energetic head, Jack Warner, the studio undertook a project titled *Confessions of a Nazi Spy* (1939). The film deals with the actual discovery of a Nazi espionage ring operating along the eastern coast of America. The screenplay was based on a book written by Federal Bureau of Investigation agent Leon Turrou, taken from the files of the Bureau without the approval of the then-chief J. Edgar Hoover. Starred are Edward G. Robinson as an FBI agent, Paul Lukas and Francis Lederer as naturalized American citizens turned Nazi spies, and George Sanders as a Gestapo agent. Others in the cast include Joe Sawyer, Sig Ruman and Dorothy Tree.

The German government was strenuous in its attempts to have the production cancelled. Hitler's *chargé d'affaires* in Washington, Hans

Thomsen, delivered a blistering message to Cordell Hull, the secretary of state, denouncing the film as "pernicious propaganda" whose role was to poison relations between "our two countries."

It was daring for the studio to continue production. Rumor has it that Warner and Edward G. Robinson were receiving threatening letters but, with the tacit approval of President Roosevelt, the film was completed in 1938 and released in the spring of 1939.

Interesting in content and ambitious in intent, these films only touched the surface of what would engulf the world a few months later. But most Americans were not really concerned with events taking place outside of their land. They were finally seeing a light at the end of the long dark tunnel created by the Depression. The affairs of foreign nations were of little moment. That the Czechs and the Austrians were losing their independence was not as important to the average American as was the abdication of a king and the search for Scarlett O'Hara.

Chapter Two

Scarlett and Rhett, Hitler and War

Nineteen thirty-nine dawned with a deluded Neville Chamberlain still speaking about a peaceful world and a voice from England's political wilderness, Winston Churchill, dissenting with the prophetic "You have gained shame and will get war."

An astute Adolf Hitler, taking advantage of the English and French aversion to making waves, occupied Czechoslovakia, renounced an agreement made with Poland and signed a non-aggression pact with his Soviet counterpart, Josef Stalin. A secret clause of this pact called for the division of Poland, which was the next item on Der Führer's wish list of acquisitions.

Popular opinion in France and England was changing, however, and the leaders of these countries were soon forced to reverse their politics and their policies. They now declared that the territorial integrity of Poland would be preserved at all cost.

In another theater of operations, the Japanese warlords were on the march. As early as 1931, they had overrun the large section of Northeastern China known as Manchuria, but their appetites for the twin aphrodisiacs of power and expansion had not been appeased in the ensuing years. The rest of China, divided and torn by civil war, was easy prey for the Sons of Nippon. So were the smaller, militarily important islands which dotted the Pacific Ocean.

While Hitler was gobbling up parts of Europe, and while the Japanese were occupied with China and at the same time casting covetous eyes on Pacific islands not within their sphere of influence, the minds of Americans were on other things. Though tuned into events abroad, the greater part of the nation still preferred to avoid entering into what

George Washington had called "entangling alliances." Not many of its citizens believed, as did President Roosevelt, that their generation had a "rendezvous with destiny."

Nineteen thirty-nine saw no real changes in Hollywood. It was a year of marriage, divorce, gossip and the appearance of several promising newcomers including William Holden, Dana Andrews, Linda Darnell and a dark-eyed girl named Phyllis Isley who later changed her name to Jennifer Jones. Other young hopefuls getting their feet wet as studio contract players were Esther Williams and Kathryn Grayson at MGM, and Rita Hayworth and Glenn Ford at Columbia.

The gossip columns were full of news about the impending divorces of Betty Grable and former child star Jackie Coogan, and fiery Mexican beauty Lupe Velez and Johnny "Tarzan" Weissmuller. Also beginning separation proceedings were raven-haired Brenda Marshall (who later married William Holden) and the first Mrs. Orson Welles, who shed the twenty-five-year-old "Boy Wonder" (so-called due to his sensational *War of the Worlds* radio broadcast of the previous year) after a six-week stay in Reno. Welles later married and divorced screen goddess Rita Hayworth. On a more romantic level, popular British leading man Brian Aherne married Joan Fontaine and Clark Gable finally tied the knot with longtime love Carole Lombard. The Gable-Lombard nuptials occurred in the midst of the filming of *Gone with the Wind* and was a publicist's dream.

Not that David Selznick's production needed any more publicity. For months, the burning question in the film capital (as well as the rest of America) had been who would play Scarlett O'Hara. Clark Gable was everyone's choice for the role of Rhett Butler. As the star was under contract to MGM, Selznick had to bargain with studio mogul Louis B. Mayer. (L.B. was the producer's father-in-law.) But business is business, and besides needing Gable, Selznick was in need of ready cash. In the deal of the century, for Gable and a dollar amount totaling $1.25 million, MGM received the distribution rights to the film plus half its profits. The other parts were up for grabs.

The Scarlett Sweepstakes resembled a horse race in which some of filmdom's favorite fillies ran neck and neck for what all of Hollywood considered the plum part of the decade. A partial listing of the actresses tested for the role of Margaret Mitchell's spirited belle was a page out of Hollywood's "Who's Who" during the thirties: Bette Davis, Joan Ben-

Two. Scarlett and Rhett, Hitler and War

nett, Katharine Hepburn, Paulette Goddard, Margaret Sullavan, Loretta Young, Lana Turner and Jean Arthur, just to name a few.

When the smoke cleared (just as the "burning" of Atlanta was being filmed), it was a dark "horse," British beauty Vivien Leigh, in town with Laurence Olivier (her lover and soon to be husband) who emerged victorious. She was a client of Myron Selznick, David's agent brother; Myron had brought Vivien to the studio. There and then, David Selznick had his Scarlett. Leslie Howard, Olivia de Havilland and Hattie McDaniel (the black actress would be the first of her race to win an Academy Award) were assigned the other major roles.

Nineteen thirty-nine was a banner year for the motion picture industry, a year which saw the release of some of the greatest films ever made. But this euphoria did not extend to the world at large.

On September 1, Hitler's armies invaded Poland and by the third of the month, both England and France were at war with Germany. At first, hostilities were muted in what later became known as the "phony war," but this state of affairs lasted only a short time.

Before discussing the war genre, an interesting film can be mentioned. It was not related to the war in any sense, yet the production did have something to do with the war. Actor Robert Montgomery had gone from Hollywood to England in 1939 to make *Busman's Holiday,* a mystery based on a novel by Dorothy Sayers. With the outbreak of war in 1939, he went back to Hollywood, but returned to London in 1940 when, despite the threats of air raids, the studios there resumed filming; the movie was released later that year.

As can be seen by the release of such films as *Busman's Holiday,* not many films had as their theme the events taking place abroad; the majority of those that had any relationship at all to the war which was just beginning were being produced in England and were mainly spy melodramas. Only one film, made in America in 1938 and released in early 1939, touched upon the actual war brewing and this occurred only at the end of the film.

Idiot's Delight, from MGM, stars Clark Gable and Norma Shearer and is the tale of two ex-vaudeville performers who rekindle an old romance on the eve of World War II. Comedic overtones throughout the film overshadow the bombs that fall at its climax. The production also features Edward Arnold, Charles Coburn and Burgess Meredith and was based upon the hit play by Robert E. Sherwood which had starred popular stage stars Alfred Lunt and Lynn Fontanne. More interest was focused on the singing and dancing "talents" of Clark Gable than on any other aspect of the film.

Warners' *Espionage Agent* (1939) is the story of an American diplomat who falls in love with a spy. Starring Joel McCrea, Brenda Marshall and Jeffrey Lynn, the film followed in the wake of *Confessions of a Nazi Spy* and preceded by one year one of the best spy melodramas of all time, *Foreign Correspondent*, in which McCrea again played the hero. Caught in the middle of the two, though its message is about the potential effects of espionage in America, *Espionage Agent*. is not remembered by too many fans, if at all.

Universal's entry into the espionage drama came in 1940 with *Enemy Agent*. Richard Cromwell stars as a draftsman mistakenly taken for a spy by government agents. At film's finale, the good guys have caught the bad guys and also manage to get a-hold of plans vital to the construction of a secret army bombsight.

Q Planes (released in America as *Clouds Over Europe*), *The Lion Has Wings* and *Ten Days in Paris* (seen in America as *Spy in the Pantry* and *Missing Ten Days*) were shot in England and are of interest mainly due to their stars. An improbable story of a ray that helps spies to steal planes during test flights, *Q Planes* stars Ralph Richardson and Laurence Olivier as (respectively) the slightly daft intelligence agent and the pilot who finally catch the villains in action. Popular English actress Valerie Hobson provides the love interest for Olivier in the role of Richardson's reporter sister. Handling a serious subject with comedic overtones, this movie is somewhat far-fetched, but the performances are good and it is, all in all, an entertaining effort, if not a major one.

The Lion Has Wings, released in this country by United Artists in 1940, is a documentary-style drama that traces the events leading up to the war. Produced by Alexander Korda, it co-stars Merle Oberon and the busy Ralph Richardson and contains much newsreel footage. The film, made in ten days, sets out to prove that the Lion (England) has the Wings (the air power) to protect itself from any invasion to its shores.

The last film of the trio, *Ten Days in Paris*, stars Rex Harrison. The elegant Englishman plays a young man who wakes up in a Paris nursing home with a bullet wound to his head. This has caused him to suffer a complete loss of memory regarding his movements over the previous ten days. He subsequently learns that he has been involved in trying to prevent a munitions train, with a time bomb aboard, from penetrating the Maginot Line (a zone of French fortifications erected along the French-

German border prior to World War II). This, he soon finds out, he has accomplished in true heroic cinematic style.

While the British film industry was thus engaged, a minority in Hollywood protested the making of films of a political nature. It charged that the movie capital was being one-sided in its approach to the international situation. Several people in this group were especially verbal while the non-aggression pact between Hitler and Stalin was in effect. With the invasion of Russia during the summer of 1941, there was a sudden change of attitude.

The majority of moviemakers in Hollywood, however, felt the need for preparedness and for American intervention into the war. Twentieth Century–Fox mogul Darryl F. Zanuck, in the forefront of this group, while preparing to make more anti-fascist propagandistic films which he believed were in the public interest, was quoted as saying, "If you charge us with being anti–Nazi, you are right."

Despite this schism and despite the premature death of the legendary Douglas Fairbanks, Sr., at the age of fifty-six, 1939 ended on a high note for Hollywood, the movie industry and especially for producer David Selznick. Though beset by a myriad of problems, including the use of three directors, plus a controversy over the word "damn," *Gone with the Wind* was completed before the end of the year. The premiere took place in Atlanta on December 14, 1939. General Sherman and his troops may have created a stir by marching into Georgia during the 1860s, but so did Selznick as he and *his* troops landed at the Atlanta airport that December.

Among the dignitaries and celebrities attending the gala were author Margaret Mitchell, the mayor of Atlanta, newlyweds Clark Gable and Carole Lombard, Scarlett herself, Vivien Leigh, and Olivia de Havilland (Melanie in the film). Reports emanating from the Georgia capital chased every other story off the front pages of the nation's leading newspapers.

Nevertheless, the war overseas was escalating dangerously and menacing all who believed in freedom and democracy.

Including Americans.

The decade's final months saw the beginning of the end of the America her people had once known, the end of an age wherein the fictional story of a dashing captain and a Southern belle was big news and a young girl named Dorothy pursued the American dream somewhere "Over the Rainbow."

Chapter Three

A Tenuous Peace in America

Events taking place during the early part of 1940 brought about a great change in the thinking of many Americans. By year's end, those sympathizing with the Allied cause felt it only a matter of time before their nation entered into the war. There were still, however, strong isolationist elements hell-bent upon a policy of strict neutrality. These groups found the perfect spokesman for their cause in Colonel Charles Lindbergh, who in 1927 had succeeded in making the first non-stop solo flight over the Atlantic Ocean to Europe. "Lucky Lindy" had a profound impact upon the average citizen via newspapers, movie newsreels and, even more importantly, over the radio.

As a medium, radio was in its golden age; most Americans were avid radio fans and spent hours glued to their crystal sets. A twist of the dial brought to the listener a potpourri of sounds: musical, comedic and dramatic. Radio was a "theater of the mind," a private theater in which people could visualize what they were hearing and paint their own pictures of the spoken words coming out over the ether waves.

Radio brought the realities of the international situation into homes across the nation. War bulletins reached the public on a daily basis. The Columbia Broadcasting System News Department was staffed by some outstanding correspondents of the day, among them Edward R. Murrow (people who lived during that era will recall his stirring "This Is London" broadcasts during the Blitz); William L. Shirer, who had been in Germany reporting on the rise of the Nazis; and roving correspondent Charles Collingwood. These men and their fellow journalists put into sharper focus the latest happenings from abroad for people who were still telling themselves "this is their war, not ours."

Three. A Tenuous Peace in America

The "Sitzkrieg," or "phony war," lasted only for a short while. By spring of 1940, Germany had conquered Belgium, the Netherlands and Luxembourg. The occupation of Paris was accomplished in June and within a few days, the French were calling for an armistice.

The surrender of France took place in the forest of Compiegne, a small city on the River Oise. The terms of the armistice were signed in the same railroad sleeping car in which Germany had been given its surrender terms in 1918. Hitler's gaze of malice mixed with triumph was not lost on the reporters who were there.

A "changing of the guard" of a somewhat different nature than usual took place in Great Britain when the diffident Neville Chamberlain gave way to the larger-than-life Winston Churchill as prime minister. "The Battle of Britain" was just about to begin and all that Churchill could offer his beleaguered countrymen was a policy of "blood, sweat, toil and tears."

In 1939, President Roosevelt had stated that America would remain neutral, but one year later, the nation was moving closer and closer to the Allied cause. By June of 1940, the War Department had released surplus arms to England and in September of that year, fifty destroyers were being transferred to that country as part of the "Lend Lease" bill enacted by Congress. These factors, plus events abroad, did not auger well for the United States.

Hollywood's economy felt the tremors of war much earlier than did the greater part of the nation. Though America was ostensibly neutral, several films coming out of the movie capital were definitely not. Due to the increase of anti–Fascist sentiment, American motion pictures were officially banned in all German-held territories and there was a tightening of the foreign markets in Asia. To add to this depressing scenario, Americans themselves were not going to the movies as before and domestic revenue was also down; box office grosses were at their lowest in over a decade. Studio heads announced a curtailment in production and the industry adopted a policy of watchful waiting.

Hard hit too was the sizable British colony in Hollywood. All Englishmen of draft age working in the film capital were summoned home as soon as their last commitment was ended. The situation of the mother country was grave indeed. Only one bright spot shone through the dark clouds of despair: England had suffered a stunning defeat at Dunkirk, but with the cooperation of both civilian and naval craft, the bulk of the Allied forces (over thirty-five thousand men, mainly British, some French) was evacuated from the French seaport. This was a major strategic blunder on Hitler's part.

At a mass meeting in Hollywood, transplanted Englishmen, not members of the armed forces, reaffirmed their devotion to the land of their birth and pledged to serve it in any capacity. In attendance were such favorites as Ronald Colman, Brian Aherne, Charles Laughton, Laurence Olivier, Cary Grant, Ray Milland and Basil Rathbone.

A committee headed up by character actress Dame May Whitty and famed boogie-man Boris Karloff arranged for the evacuation of sixty English children during the height of the London blitz. The usually thrifty Cary Grant underwrote the expenses for this venture by donating a large part of his salary from his latest film, *The Philadelphia Story* (1940).

Much of Hollywood, however, maintained its usual frenetic pace. Celebrity marriages, romances and divorces grabbed the headlines. William Powell married the much younger MGM contract player Diana Lewis, Jane Wyman said "I do" to Ronald Reagan (this union would last eight years, leaving the field clear for Nancy Davis and Reagan's rise to the presidency of the United States), and Vivien Leigh became Mrs. Laurence Olivier. Of the three unions, only the Lewis-Powell lasted "till death do us part."

Lana Turner tied the knot with bandleader Artie Shaw. A few months later, she was single again and in love with singer Tony Martin, but the two did not marry. Joan Crawford divorced Franchot Tone and vowed never to walk down the aisle again, but she did, two more times. And love, with a wedding ring in the forecast, was in the air for young singers Judy Garland and Deanna Durbin (both marriages ended in divorce).

But frivolities aside, as the months went by, and as the news from Europe went from bad to worse, more and more *reel* action began to imitate *real* action. A look at some of the year's war-related output proves the point.

Arise, My Love (1940) is set at first against the backdrop of the Spanish Civil War and then shifts to the start of World War II. Starring Claudette Colbert as a reporter and Ray Milland as a pilot who meet in Spain and fall in love, the film also features Walter Abel as a harried editor trying to get a newspaper out amidst all the confusion.

The production was strongly interventionist in theme and did a brisk business at the box office. A *Variety* review read in part, "Paramount has brought forth a film of absorbing romantic interest, proving that love will find a way through the hazards of air raids, torpedo attacks and enemy invasion." An Oscar was awarded the film in the category of Best Original Story.

Torpedo attacks figure in *Escape to Glory* a 1940 Columbia film which stars Constance Bennett, Pat O'Brien and Alan Baxter. A British freighter, carrying an interesting group of passengers returning to America, is attacked by a German sub at the outbreak of the war. One passenger on the ship is an alcoholic; another is a district attorney traveling with a female companion. Also on board are a convicted murderer and a German doctor. How this disparate group of people copes with the situation at hand is the basis of the story. By film's end, the sub is destroyed.

Fiction followed fact: During those early days, a German submarine would indiscriminately attack whatever ships it could, wreaking havoc in its wake. Undersea warfare would soon figure mightily as the conflict raged on. Americans read their newspapers, went about their business, listened to radio reports and were glad to be uninvolved.

Wanting to shake more of his fellow countrymen out of their isolationist tendencies, James Roosevelt, son of the president, bought the rights to an English film titled *Pastor Hall*. This virtually forgotten movie is based on the life of Pastor Niemoller, who in 1934 was shot for his anti–Nazi activities. Given the times, the subject and a cast unknown to most Americans, it is easy to see why the production did not fare well in the States. The film was released under the United Artists banner.

Two Hollywood dramas, however, caught the mood of a Europe in turmoil; one became a hit for MGM. *The Mortal Storm* (1940) stars Margaret Sullavan, James Stewart, Robert Stack, Robert Young as a young Nazi and, in a role light years away from his *Wizard of Oz* portrayal, Frank Morgan. The script was a timely one, dealing with a German family torn apart by the rise of Hitler. The film's most effective moments take place as friend is pitted against friend, brother against brother and father against child. The climactic scene as young lovers Stewart and Sullavan attempt an escape to the Swiss border is unforgettable: She is fatally wounded, he survives. (Dan Dailey, who would later appear in movies as a song and dance man, makes his screen debut in this production.)

Four Sons, a 1940 Twentieth Century–Fox release. features Don Ameche and Eugenie Leontovich. Like *The Mortal Storm*, *Four Sons* is the story of family dissension in pre-war Europe; this time, the action unfolds in Czechoslovakia. An anguished mother (Leontovich) watches as her family is torn apart: It is brother against brother as two opt for the cause of National Socialism, one remains a loyal Czech and one emigrates to America. Only the mother and the naturalized American are alive at film's end. The Fox film did not do as well financially as did *The Mortal Storm*, which boasted the star power that the other film lacked.

And speaking of star power, two box office favorites in 1940 were Robert Taylor and Norma Shearer. MGM producer-director Mervyn LeRoy cast them in the film version of *Escape*, based on a best-selling novel of the day. An American civilian searches for his mother (played by Nazimova) in the Germany of 1938–39 and is aided by an American-born countess, myopic at first in not wanting to see what is happening in her adopted homeland. Conrad Veidt co-stars as a German officer in love with the countess. While the novel is vague as to the locale of this intriguing plot, the movie is not and its scenes in a concentration camp naturally incensed Der Führer. His ban on films coming from the United States was enforced even more strongly.

Also in 1940, Taylor made a film titled *Flight Command*, which co-stars Walter Pidgeon and Ruth Hussey. The plot tells of the trials and tribulations of a cadet trying to graduate from the navy's flight academy. The film benefits from the cooperation of the Navy Air Corps for its flying scenes.

Another film favorite of the day was Joel McCrea who starred in one of the best of the spy film genre. *Foreign Correspondent* (1940) is an action-packed suspense thriller with McCrea, an American reporter covering pre-war London, becoming involved with Laraine Day, Herbert Marshall, George Sanders and a Nazi spy ring. The intrepid newsman is sent to Amsterdam to cover a conference during which he witnesses the shooting of a Dutch statesman. Back in London, he begins to investigate and is almost pushed off the top of Westminster Abbey by a killer for hire played by Edmund Gwenn (who would win an Oscar for his portrayal of Santa Claus seven years later). Now continuing his investigation with a vengeance, he unmasks the head of a spy ring, survives a bombing and delivers a ringing speech in favor of American intervention in the just-beginning war. The plane crash at the finale shows direc-

Three. A Tenuous Peace in America

Foreign Correspondence: Reporter Joel McCrea is interviewing Albert Basserman on the subject of a forthcoming peace conference.

tor Alfred Hitchcock as a forerunner of the disaster films so popular during the 1970s and 1980s. Curiously enough, the film was a favorite of German propaganda minister Goebbels in spite of its pro–Allied stand.

A hit in the spy genre, *Night Train to Munich*, a 1940 British production released by Twentieth Century–Fox in this country, concerns the rescuing of a Czech scientist and his daughter, played by Margaret Lockwood, from the clutches of the Gestapo. Rex Harrison is top-cast as a part-time song plugger-cum-government agent assigned to accomplish this feat. Out to thwart these efforts is a Gestapo agent enacted by Paul Von Hernried. Soon after the release of *Night Train to Munich*, the Austrian-born actor changed his name to Paul Henried, emigrated to Hollywood and became a popular leading man.

The film's thrilling climax finds Harrison, Lockwood and the father in a ski lift taking them to Switzerland and freedom, while Nazi Von Hernried is left to face the consequences of failure. Supplying a bit of humor in the proceedings are Basil Radford and Naunton Wayne, who reprise their *Lady Vanishes* roles of a cricket- and golf-loving pair of Englishmen.

Escape from the enemy was a popular theme in 1940, and even Norwegian ice skater Sonja Henie got into the act. *Everything Happens at Night*, from Twentieth Century–Fox, made in 1939 and released in the early part of 1940, is a comedy with a rather serious theme. Like Margaret Lockwood in the previously discussed film, Henie is the daughter of a famous person, this time a political commentator, fleeing the Nazis. Her leading men are Ray Milland and Robert Cummings, playing rival reporters who come to her aid. Cummings gets Sonja, but Milland gets the scoop. Miss Henie's skating is held to a minimum in favor of the plotline, but like all of the skater's movies during those years, it made money for the studio as well as for the very astute Sonja.

The Man I Married (1940), produced by Twentieth Century–Fox production chief Darryl Zanuck himself, is an interesting film about an American woman who marries a German-American and accompanies him on a visit to his native land. To her horror, she sees him falling for Hitler's doctrine. She wants to take their small son and leave her husband. The latter will not allow this, but at film's end, the wife is aided by her anti–Nazi father-in-law, who makes the startling revelation that his wife was Jewish. Francis Lederer (seen in *Confessions of a Nazi Spy* as a German-American who betrays his adopted land) and Joan Bennett are the stars, playing husband and wife.

It was the inimitable Charlie Chaplin, however, who made the oft-seen and most lasting of the anti–Fascist films, *The Great Dictator* (1940), which was released by United Artists, the very company he had co-founded with Mary Pickford, Douglas Fairbanks, Sr., and director D.W. Griffith in 1919. In his dual portrayal of a ghetto Jew and Hynkel, the maniacal dictator of a mythical country, the brilliant Charlie mimics Hitler's ranting oratory, exposing and satirizing Fascism for what it was doing to the people of Europe.

Although Chaplin used sound fully for the first time in this production, two of its best sequences are without dialogue: the barber (Charlie) shaving a customer to the strains of Liszt's "Hungarian Rhapsody" and the diabolical Hynkel (Charlie again) using a globe as a balloon in a solo ballet as he contemplates world domination.

Jack Oakie had the role of a lifetime lampooning the Italian dictator Benito Mussolini and was Oscar-nominated for his performance.

The film was also nominated (but lost to Alfred Hitchcock's *Rebecca*), as was Chaplin in the categories of Acting (James Stewart won for *The Philadelphia Story*) and Original Screenplay. The six-minute finale in which Chaplin preaches peace and democracy was considered politically naïve by many, including the critics, but "The Little Tramp" was invited to recite the speech at President Roosevelt's birthday gala.

The people of America at this point in time were holding onto a tenuous peace. How were they to know that 1940 was to be their last full year of the status quo and that not until the summer of 1945 would the lights go on again all over the world.

Chapter Four

The Road to War: December 7, 1941

America's grip on peace was more tenuous than ever at the beginning of 1941, for although still neutral in thought, she was becoming far less so in deed. President Roosevelt called for a "world based upon four essential freedoms — freedom of speech, freedom of worship, freedom from want and freedom from fear." It was clear that the schemes of a World War 1 corporal named Hitler could not be a part of this world.

By March, "Lend Lease," which authorized our sale of vital military materiel to anti–Axis countries, had become law. In August, FDR and Churchill met in New Foundland and issued the "Atlantic Charter," a document which outlined the principles for a postwar world. What is remarkable about the conference is that it took place at all: The United States was not at war, yet its leader was meeting and talking about war aims with the head of a belligerent nation.

The news from abroad was more ominous than ever. Still on the rampage and flushed with victory, Hitler's goose-stepping Wehrmacht sought new triumphs, and several of the smaller countries felt the dictator's wrath. Next in line were the Balkans. By spring of 1941, Yugoslavia had surrendered to the oppressor (a fragment guerrilla resistance under the opposing forces of the Communist Tito and the non–Communist General Mihajlovic continued to fight) and tanks were entering the Greek capital of Athens. The picture in Europe was bleak indeed.

And then, on June 22, in a sensational about-face, Hitler invaded Russia. Abrogating the Russo-German non-aggression pact signed in 1939, the operation, code-named "Barbarossa," originally conceived as

Four. The Road to War: December 7, 1941

a short-range blitzkrieg campaign, endured for the remainder of the war and is considered by many historians the fatal blow for the Third Reich.

Somewhat nearer to home for America, the battle of the Atlantic was heating up. In October of 1941, the *Reuben James* became the first United States warship to be sunk by the German submarines patrolling the waters of that ocean. More than two hundred enlisted men and officers lost their lives as the vessel went down to its watery grave. It had been assigned to help protect a British convoy sailing to the west of Iceland.

By this time, we were at war in all but the legalistic sense of the word. In declaring that part of the Atlantic where the *Reuben James* went down an American Defense Zone, Roosevelt was hoping to preserve the technical "neutrality" of the United States.

Important events were also taking place in the Pacific. Japan, via the Tripartite Pact of 1940, was firmly entrenched in the Axis camp and the friction between it and this country was mounting steadily. By the end of 1940. the militaristic General Hideki Togo was prime minister of Japan; his plan for his country included the expansion of her influence throughout the Pacific and the seizure of the island groups strategically important to America, which he considered his country's foremost enemy.

The possibility of an attack upon our naval base at Pearl Harbor was reported to the State Department as early as January of 1941 by Ambassador Joseph Grew. By November, we had cracked the Japanese secret code which spoke of an impending attack, but amazingly enough, though Japan's moves in the Pacific were denounced, and an embargo placed on trade with her, nothing was or would be done about these reports until it was too late.

Though many in the motion picture industry felt sure that war was imminent, life went on in normal fashion for most Hollywoodians. Honeymooners included Bette Davis and her fellow New Englander, Arthur Farnsworth; also Lucille Ball and her Cuban band leader Desi Arnaz. Errol Flynn became a father and Joan Crawford adopted a baby girl (Christina would grow up to write the devastating *Mommie Dearest* about her famous mother).

Tinsel Town's hottest romance and subsequent marriage paired Cary Grant and Woolworth heiress Barbara Hutton. Town wags dubbed them "Cash and Cary," although after their divorce, Hutton maintained that Cary was the only one of her husbands who had not married her for her money.

Everything considered, however, the prevailing mood in Hollywood was more serious than usual, especially in the English community. Several of its younger members, among them David Niven and Richard Greene, were already in the British Armed Forces and the older Brits kept busy raising funds for their country's war effort.

Production-wise, with war clouds looming over the country. many filmmakers began to take on more serious themes: Hollywood's 1941 output included several anti–Nazi and patriotic plotlines.

One of the most poignant productions of the era was *So Ends Our Night* from United Artists. Based upon a novel titled "Flotsom" by Erich Maria Remarque, this 1941 film tells the compelling story of a group of homeless people fleeing the German regime. The cast includes Margaret Sullavan and Glenn Ford as a Jewess and a half–Jew, both refugees who fall in love, and Fredric March in the role of a German national who could live comfortably in the land of his birth by espousing the Hitlerian philosophy, which he does not. The three meet in Austria, but are pursued from country to country as each is conquered when the Nazis march in. March's character risks his life by returning to Germany to see his dying wife, whom he has had to leave behind. It is March who gives the best performance and provides the film with its most emotional moments. Sullavan and Ford get to Switzerland and marry. The excellent supporting cast includes Frances Dee, Erich von Stroheim, and Sig Rumann.

Paramount came out with *Hold Back the Dawn* (1941), another story about the flight of refugees from Nazi-occupied Europe. This time, most of the action takes place in Mexico. Charles Boyer portrays a desperate man trying to get into the United States. He pretends to fall in love with an American schoolteacher, played with great warmth by Olivia de Havilland, in order to marry her and come to this country lawfully. In the interesting beginning to the picture, Boyer, who has come over the border illegally because he has fallen in love with his wife who is in the hospital, tells his story to director Mitchell Leisen on the Paramount lot in hopes of selling it. The cast includes Paulette Goddard, Walter Abel and Rosemary De Camp.

Oscar nominations went to the film, de Havilland and the writing team of Charles Brackett and Billy Wilder. The latter knew what he was writing about as he had spent time in Mexico as a refugee.

At the beginning of the Nazi rise to power, director Fritz Lang, a

Four. The Road to War: December 7, 1941

Jew, was offered a prestige job in German films by none other than Joseph Goebbels, who controlled the industry. Seeing the handwriting on the wall, however, by 1936, Lang had emigrated to America and was plying his trade in Hollywood. He made several intriguing films during the next decade; one of the most interesting of these is *Man Hunt*, a Twentieth Century–Fox 1941 release.

Walter Pidgeon stars as a big game hunter from London on vacation in Bavaria who stalks Hitler for the sport of it. A Gestapo agent learns about this and pursues him to England, whereupon Pidgeon becomes the quarry. The exciting finale has Pidgeon killing the Nazi. Featured in this gripping cat-and-mouse tale are Joan Bennett as the woman who befriends him, losing her life in the process, a menacing George Sanders as the Nazi agent sent to kill him, John Carradine and Roddy McDowall.

Another excellent anti–Nazi film is the English-made *Pimpernel Smith* (1941). Its star, Leslie Howard (who also produced and directed), had previously played in a period piece titled *The Scarlet Pimpernel*; this time he is the modern-day version of that character. Instead of rescuing victims of the French Revolution, he helps people flee the Nazis. His role is that of an offbeat, mild-mannered professor of archaeology who engineers the escape of important people headed for concentration camps. He is aided by a group of American students who had previously not known of his exploits. He must also contend with a wily German officer (played by English character actor Francis L. Sullivan) who is trying to stop the professor from accomplishing his task. Almost caught near the German border, he escapes in a thick fog, calling out the prophetic words, "We'll be back."

Howard was a favorite with American audiences and the United Artists release was well-received on these shores. (It was rumored sometime later that the actor died while on a mission for the British government.)

An all–English cast, including Howard, Laurence Olivier, Raymond Massey and Anton Walbrook, can be seen in the British-made *The 49th Parallel*, shown in America in 1941. The story of six survivors of a German submarine sunk off the coast of Canada who face a hostile group of French-Canadians, the production is action-packed and performances are first-rate.

Even more fascinating is what actually happened a few months after the film's release. Fact took over where fiction left off. Eight Nazi saboteurs (four in a group) were simultaneously landed by submarine off the coasts of Long Island, New York, and Florida. Like the movie characters, the real saboteurs were caught before they could do any harm.

The theme of Warner Bros.' *Underground* also had an interesting premise for the movie-goers of 1941. The story, set in wartime Berlin, pits brother against brother in a battle of ideologies. Jeffrey Lynn plays a wounded soldier and Philip Dorn is an underground leader. The soldier is pro–Hitler until he unwittingly becomes responsible for his brother's death. Now seeing the Nazi "cause" as it really is, he takes the fallen hero's place as a leader in the Resistance.

As in *Underground*, things are not what they seem. Three locations, London, Lisbon and New York, form the backdrop for *International Lady*, a United Artists 1941 production. George Brent is a American government agent posing as a lawyer, leading lady Ilona Massey is a German agent posing as a singer, Basil Rathbone is a Scotland Yard man posing as a music critic and Gene Lockhart, a fifth columnist, is supposedly a loyal American. Miss Massey appears on Lockhart's radio show, with her songs containing coded messages giving vital information to saboteurs about American materiel going to England. Brent and Massey fall in love, but at film's end he must arrest her. (Secret information encoded in a song had been used more famously in *The Lady Vanishes*.)

For the armies in North Africa, the war was a never-ending series of battles. By 1941, the fighting was not going well for the Allies. Field Marshal Erwin Rommel was enjoying the halcyon period of his military career. His tactics had the British Eighth Army on the run; there seemed to be nothing that the "Desert Fox" could not accomplish.

The African campaign is the background for *Sundown* (United Artists), a 1941 film wherein an Arab trader's adopted daughter (who turns out to be English) aids the British in repelling invading Germans from a desert outpost while falling in love with its commander. Starred are Gene Tierney and Bruce Cabot as the lovers, with George Sanders as an officer on the outpost who is suspicious of Tierney's character.

The Army was not the only British branch of the military represented in films made during the months before Pearl Harbor. Twentieth Century–Fox's Darryl Zanuck, who felt that America's entrance into the war was only a matter of time, paid tribute to England's gallant fliers with *A Yank in the RAF*. To insure the production's success at the box

Four. The Road to War: December 7, 1941

A Yank in the RAF: Cocky American pilot Tyrone Power (far right) joins the RAF and soon comes face to face with the realities of war and John Sutton as Wing Commander Mortley. Actor on left is unidentified. Actual combat footage was used in the film.

office, he used two of the studio's top personalities, Betty Grable and Tyrone Power. The plotline has Power playing a cocky, conceited American civilian pilot who joins the Royal Air Force, meets his former girlfriend (Grable, of course) in London and becomes a hero at the finale. (The script had Power dying, but because of his popularity with film fans, the ending was changed.) The movie is greatly enhanced by the use of actual newsreel footage of both aerial dog fights and of an event which had recently taken place: the evacuation of Dunkirk.

Dangerous Moonlight, a British film released by RKO in 1941, tells the tale of a concert pianist who escapes from Poland, joins the Polish unit of an RAF fighter squadron and loses his memory during the Battle of Britain. Music and the love of a young woman restore him to health. Starred are Anton Walbrook, Sally Gray and the beautiful "Warsaw Concerto."

The RAF was also represented in a documentary titled *Target for Tonight*. The production puts the audience into the cockpit of a bomber as it sets off for Germany. Detailed also is how such raids were planned during World War II. The film, shot in England, has a cast consisting entirely of Royal Air Force personnel.

Almost documentary in style is *Convoy*, a film made with the cooperation of the British Admiralty. The screenplay depicts life aboard an English cruiser on duty in the North Sea. The final reel is a confrontation between the cruiser and a German battleship. Outgunned, the vessel holds out until rescued by friendly forces. The all–British cast includes Clive Brook, John Clements and two actors who would make their mark in Hollywood, Michael Wilding and Stewart Granger.

Six years after his screen debut, Errol Flynn was still one of the more popular stars in the Hollywood firmament. Warner Bros. teamed Flynn with the durable Fred MacMurray in a production titled *Dive Bomber*. The film, made with the cooperation of the United States Naval Air Corps, has Errol playing a naval surgeon who devotes himself to aviation medicine after an injured airman dies on his operating table (the pilot had "blacked out" after going into a power dive). Though the obligatory love scenes are pure Hollywood (Alexis Smith is the lady enamored of "Doctor" Flynn), the air scenes and those filmed in the laboratory are quite good. The film was well received by both critics and fans, although anyone seeing it probably found it hard to believe Errol Flynn spurning the advances of a pretty girl.

Another branch of the armed forces was represented in 1941's *I Wanted Wings*, a Paramount release made with the cooperation of the Army Air Force. Filmed on location in Texas, it tells a tale of three men of differing backgrounds who meet at aviation school and go through the training that will earn them their wings. Starred are Ray Milland, Wayne Morris and William Holden.

There are two interesting aspects to the film: the debut of diminutive Veronica Lake and the fact that the story's action parallels the actual training program of a group of cadets stationed on the site of the film's location. Miss Lake's "peek-a-boo" hair style delighted moviegoers, but was a hindrance once the war started with Rosie the Riveter going to work in a factory wearing her hair over one eye. Rosie soon pinned up her tresses, as did the blonde Veronica.

During the 1940s, Bud Abbott and Lou Costello, discovered for

Four. The Road to War: December 7, 1941

radio by singer Kate Smith, also carved out lucrative screen careers for themselves. Signed by Universal Studios in 1940, they were riding the crest of a popularity wave. The movies they made were a mixture of their zany visual comedy and music supplied by such well-known singers as Ella Fitzgerald, Dick Powell, Martha Raye, Ginny Simms and the Andrews Sisters (Maxene, Patty and LaVerne).

Both *Buck Privates* and *In the Navy* team the boys with the singing sisters. The first film was a major one for Bud and Lou and for their studio: It sky-rocketed the duo to third place in the national film popularity polls, behind Mickey Rooney and Clark Gable, and made money for the movie company.

The plot involves Bud and Lou finding themselves trapped in an induction center and in the army. Highlights in the film take place when Maxene, Patty and LaVerne sing two of their all-time hits, "Boogie-Woogie Bugle Boy of Company B," which was Oscar-nominated as Best Song of the Year, and "I'll Be with You in Apple Blossom Time." The winning song had a more somber theme, as will be seen shortly.

In the Navy has crooner Dick Powell, a few years away from a startling career move which turned the aging juvenile into a first-rate dramatic actor-producer-director, playing a radio singer who joins the navy to get away from his over-adoring public. Abbott and Costello are two of the sailors he meets. Although Bud and Lou engage in some hilarious antics, it is Powell and the Andrews trio who make the film one of the better wartime comedies to come out of Universal.

The boys again switched services for *Keep 'Em Flying*. This time they are aviation mechanics in the Army Air Corps, up to their tool boxes in shenanigans. Martha Raye is featured in a dual role — as if one Martha Raye, she of the large mouth and raucous comedy style, is not enough. This film did not fare well at the box office; it was the fourth release in ten months for the comic duo, and to some, their routines were becoming tiresome.

While *In the Navy* has Dick Powell joining up to escape show business, Paramount's *Caught in the Draft* (1941) stars Bob Hope as a movie personality who is drafted into the army, courtesy of the Selective Service Act; try as he might, he cannot get out of it. Known on radio as "Rapid Robert" for his fast way with a quip, Hope milks his role of the gun-shy recruit who faints at the sight of blood, aided and abetted by Eddie Bracken (his chauffeur) and Lynne Overman (his agent) who have been drafted into the same unit. By film's end, however, Dorothy Lamour, as his colonel's daughter, turns Bob into both a reluctant hero and an ever-lasting husband.

At the time that *Caught in the Draft* was produced, draft-dodging was a topic that America could sit back and laugh at, but a few months later, the Selective Service Act was a reality and no laughing matter.

A peaceful Sunday afternoon in December was shattered with the news that the American base at Pearl Harbor had been attacked by forces of the Japanese Empire. A day later, President Roosevelt made an emotionally charged speech to a joint session of Congress, also broadcast over the radio, which began, "Yesterday, December 7, 1941, a date which will live in infamy." Roosevelt called for a declaration of war on Japan, and three days later, America *was* at war, not only with the Far Eastern nation, but also with its Axis partners Italy and Germany.

By the time the Academy Award festivities for 1941 took place in February of 1942,* the U.S. had been at war for over two months. The previous year's Best Actor, James Stewart, in an Army Air Corps uniform, was one of the presenters.

Among the also-rans in that Oscar Derby was what many have arguably called the best film ever made, *Citizen Kane*. Though Orson Welles, its producer-director, co-writer and star, vehemently denied it, its story of an eccentric publishing tycoon was a thinly disguised portrait of then powerful publisher William Randolph Hearst. Hearst failed to prevent the film's release, but with many well-placed friends in the industry, he blocked its getting a number of well-deserved Oscars. Welles did, however, share one with writer Herman Mankiewicz for Best Original Screenplay.

How Green Was My Valley (1941), starring Walter Pidgeon, Maureen O'Hara, Roddy McDowall and Donald Crisp, about a Welsh mining family at the turn of the century (a premise far removed from anything connected with Welles or with war), was chosen Best Film; its director John Ford and character actor Crisp were also honored as Best Director and Best Supporting Actor. Joan Fontaine and Gary Cooper won the major acting awards, the former for her role in *Suspicion* and the latter for his performance in the title role of *Sergeant York*, as the pacifist who,

---

*At first, with things looking quite grim in the Pacific, the Academy thought of canceling the ceremony, but then decided to proceed.

Four. The Road to War: December 7, 1941

against his convictions, went to war in 1917 and emerged a hero. Cooper had been the choice of the real Alvin York when the latter sold the film rights to his life story. Best Supporting Actress honors went to Mary Astor for *The Great Lie*.

The most interesting award for a public reeling from the shock of Pearl Harbor was the one for Best Song. With Paris declared an open city and occupied by the Germans, Oscar Hammerstein II had penned a poignant lyric and Jerome Kern had set it to music. "The Last Time I Saw Paris" was introduced by blonde actress Ann Sothern in a MGM film titled *Lady Be Good*. The song won Oscars for its co-writers, a second for Kern (number one came in 1936 for "The Way You Look Tonight," from *Swing Time*), a first for Hammerstein.

It is an old adage in the entertainment industry that the show must go on. The awards took place as scheduled, but did so in a subdued atmosphere. America, of course, was at war, and almost immediately, this fact struck at the very heart of the Hollywood community: Only a month before Oscar night, one of its brightest lights had been snuffed out in the name of patriotism.

Chapter Five

America Mobilizes

As 1942 began, producer Alexander Korda and director Ernst Lubitsch were certain that they had a surefire hit on their hands. *To Be or Not to Be* is a black comedy about the efforts of a hammy Polish theatrical troupe to thwart the Nazis. The United Artists release takes place in Warsaw on the eve of the 1939 German invasion; as the troupe, led by that "great Polish actor" Josef Tura and his wife Maria (Jack Benny and Carole Lombard), prepares for a performance, they learn that their beloved land has been invaded. The next scene shifts to a shelter below the theater. Maria joins the Resistance and learns that there is a traitor who is going to give the Gestapo the names of key people in the Polish Resistance. The jealous Tura, at first unaware of his wife's participation in the movement and suspicious of her comings and goings, also becomes involved. They outwit the Nazis and fly to freedom. Robert Stack, Lionel Atwill and Stanley Ridges head a fine supporting cast.

Benny had the role of a lifetime playing Tura and Lombard matched him line for line as Maria. Like Maria, the lovely and gifted Carole was soon galvanized into action. Like other Americans, she had heard the broadcast of December 7. Like many Hollywood stars, she realized that millions of dollars needed to be raised and that she could do her bit by making personal appearances and by selling bonds.

The blonde star, a native of Indiana, was at the peak of a career which had begun in the 1920s. First seen in Mack Sennett comedy shorts, she soon graduated to leading roles and established her versatility in both comedy and dramatic roles. Her list of leading men included the elite of Hollywood: William Powell, to whom she had been married in the early thirties, John Barrymore, Bing Crosby, Fred MacMurray, Fredric

Five. America Mobilizes 39

To Be or Not to Be: Jack Benny (center) and Carole Lombard (nestled next to him) as Joseph and Maria Tura, who head a Polish group of Shakespearean actors in Warsaw and outwit the Gestapo to escape to England. Charles Halton (glasses), Tom Dugan (mustache) and Lionel Atwill are to the left of Benny and Robert Stack is to the immediate right of Lombard.

March, James Stewart and Clark Gable. By 1939, she was Mrs. Gable and, as the new decade dawned, her future had never looked brighter.

In January of 1942, Carole headed a war bond rally taking place in Indianapolis. It was a huge success and a personal triumph for the actress, but triumph turned to tragedy as her Hollywood-bound plane crashed into a Nevada mountain peak. When the wreckage was cleared, a diamond earring was found, one of a new pair given her by her husband.

Like Lombard in *To Be or Not to Be* who joins the Polish Resistance after the fall of Warsaw, so Elisabeth Bergner joins the French Resistance movement after the fall of Paris in *Paris Calling* (Universal, 1941). She meets and falls in love with an American pilot (Randolph Scott) and kills her former lover turned traitor (Basil Rathbone, who was equally at home playing heroes as well as villains as will be seen shortly). It was in this film that European star Bergner made her American film debut.

On the war front, things looked quite gloomy for the Allied effort during the early part of the year. Manila fell to the Japanese and General Douglas MacArthur, the American commander in the Far East, retreated to the Bataan Peninsula, also a part of the Philippines island chain. After heroic resistance at Bataan and at Corregidor, the MacArthur-led forces surrendered and the general was ordered to Australia. To make matters worse, American Marines suffered a stunning defeat at Wake Island. The British, too, were having their share of hard luck during the first months of the year as the crown colony of Singapore was occupied by the forces of Japan.

On the other side of the world, the news was scarcely better. American were reading about the razing of the Czechoslovakian village of Lidice by the Nazis in retaliation for the assassination of Hitler's top bully boy in that country, Reinhard Heydrich. Nearer to home, German submarines were in action along our eastern seaboard. The submariners called it "the happy time": In "wolf packs," they prowled at will and struck with impunity, sinking merchant ships carrying needed supplies and impeding the Allied war effort. German saboteurs were also landing along our coastlines, but most were apprehended before any real damage could be done. On the West Coast, the scare of a possible invasion by the Japanese caused a panic which resulted in the forcible relocation and internment of many innocent Japanese-Americans.

Towards the end of the year, however, America was on the offensive in the Pacific. Our vocabulary now included the names of some hitherto little-known islands, among them the Gilberts, the Marianas, and Guadalcanal in the Solomons. Fierce fighting erupted in the seesaw battles which bore their names. Major boosts to American morale were a victory at Midway and a raid over Tokyo, the capital of Japan, by seven hundred bombers under the command of General James Doolittle. (The 1944 MGM film *Thirty Seconds Over Tokyo*, starring Spencer Tracy, Robert Walker and Van Johnson, chronicles this event.)

America was also taking the offensive in Europe as the first contingent of GIs landed in Iceland en route to the strife-torn continent. Some lived to tell the tale, others did not.

Battles between the British and the Afrika Corps under Field Marshal Rommel had resulted in a calamitous state of affairs. The German forces were advanced almost to the gates of Cairo and control of the Suez Canal, the vital link between England and her Asian-Pacific possessions. But then almost miraculously, the tide changed in favor of the British. The leadership of the charismatic General Bernard Montgomery and the audacious fighting of the British Tommies stopped Rommel at El Alamein. "The Desert Fox" would be the subject of several movies, played by such noted actors as Erich von Stroheim and James Mason.

Hollywood reflected these events in both film production and in the loss of several of its most popular leading men. With America now joined in the fight, 1942 saw such movie heroes as Tyrone Power, Victor Mature, Robert Taylor, Dan Dailey, Ronald Reagan, William Holden, Henry Fonda, Robert Montgomery and James Stewart in real-life uniform. By August of that same year, the "King" himself, Clark Gable, at the age of forty-one, had also taken the oath as an army private.

Male stars above draft age or medically deferred included Gary Cooper, Bing Crosby, John Garfield, Fred MacMurray, Spencer Tracy, Fred Astaire and James Cagney, plus naturalized citizens Cary Grant and Ray Milland. A few new faces loomed on the cinematic horizon — faces which would soon become familiar to a movie-hungry public: Van Johnson, Robert Walker and Peter Lawford. Besides their regular film work, these stars joined with their female counterparts in donating much of their off-screen time to war work — USO tours, camp shows and hospital visits.

By mid–1942, most of the stars in Hollywood had made personal appearances all over the country to promote the sale of war bonds and this, combined with a September bi-coastal radio program, helped raise millions of dollars on the nation's behalf. Soon after this gigantic undertaking, the Hollywood Canteen opened its doors. The driving forces behind this project were Bette Davis and John Garfield. The price of admission? A uniform. From the start, the Canteen did a brisk business. Seven nights a week, sandwiches, coffee, cigarettes and, above all, lots of great entertainment were served up to lonely members of the armed forces far away from home.

The stars gave their all for those giving *their* all. On any night of the year, GIs could eat sandwiches served them by Hedy Lamarr, dunk doughnuts in coffee poured for them by Jane Wyman, or watch Edward G. Robinson wield a broom and dance to the music of Benny Goodman, Harry James and other great music-makers.

The USO was another organization which catered to the needs of the transient service personnel who were swelling the ranks of the film capital's population. Actress Yvonne DeCarlo, in her book *Yvonne: An Autobiography* (St. Martin's Press, 1987), gives her impressions of Hollywood during those turbulent years:

> With the USO and the Canteen located within a block of each other, the strip between Hollywood and Sunset Boulevard swarmed with military personnel passing through on their way to unknown destinations. Honky tonk bars sprang up, storefront photo galleries, pinball parlors, midway-type arcades, rifle ranges; the old restaurants were packed with new business and new places opened to profit from the overflow. The wartime business boom was on.

Though the movie moguls saw the need for escapist film fare during this first year of the war, they nevertheless increased their output of films which reflected the global situation. *United We Stand* (Twentieth Century–Fox, 1942) is a documentary which goes into the history between the two world wars. Narrated by Lowell Thomas, a popular newscaster of the era, it emphasizes the rise of the National Socialist Party, the Japanese attacks on China, the failure of the League of Nations and the lack of unity among the free nations, all of which led to the outbreak of World War II.

Once war had been declared, embassies of Axis countries were closed down, their diplomats were declared persona non grata and known enemy agents were rounded up by the FBI.

Espionage has always held a strange fascination for most people, its practitioners being involved in much derring-do and danger. During the early years of the war, Americans became very spy-conscious. Typical posters of the times read, "A slip of the lip can sink a ship," "Bits of CARELESS TALK are pieced together by the ENEMY" and the terse "A careless word — Another cross." With the success of such films as *Confessions of a Nazi Spy* and *Foreign Correspondent,* Hollywood saw the advantages of making more in the genre.

In *Secret Agent of Japan* (Twentieth Century–Fox, 1942), Preston Foster is a night club owner in Shanghai who learns that Japanese spies are appropriating property and abusing the people of the city. He teams up with a British agent (Lynn Bari) and they report the Axis activities to their respective governments.

Humphrey Bogart had an enormous hit in *The Maltese Falcon*

(thanks to George Raft, who had turned down the part because he did not want to work with a neophyte director named John Huston). This convinced Warner Bros. that the actor had a whole new career as a movie hero. Two of his 1942 releases had spy motifs; in one of them, *Across the Pacific*, he is reunited with Huston as well as his co-stars of *The Maltese Falcon*, Mary Astor and Sydney Greenstreet. Intrigue is the chief element of the film. Playing a "disgraced" military man who is really on a secret mission, he thwarts the attempts of Greenstreet to gather information about the Panama Canal for the Japanese. In the midst of filming, Huston was called up for active duty, and Vincent Sherman took over.

Like *Across the Pacific*, *China Girl* (Twentieth Century–Fox, 1942) takes place in the months before Pearl Harbor. George Montgomery plays a newsreel cameraman who has worked in Burma and China. Because he has a book containing military information regarding Japanese plans, he is imprisoned. He escapes to Mandalay and meets a beautiful Chinese girl (Gene Tierney). Together they dodge Japanese spies and give the information to the American government. Also seen in the film are Lynn Bari, Victor McLaglen, Alan Baxter, Myron McCormick, and Philip Ahn.

Lloyd Nolan is a hero of a different sort in the Twentieth Century–Fox film *Manila Calling* (1942). He plays the leader of a group of Americans on Mindanao (the second largest island in the Philippine chain) who continues the fighting after the Japanese have captured the island. Among those with him are a singer (Carole Landis) who refuses to be evacuated and a telephone engineer (Cornel Wilde). The men build a short wave radio and send out vital information on Japanese troop movements until enemy soldiers close in and wipe them out.

In *Across the Pacific*, Sydney Greenstreet is trying to obtain information about the Panama Canal. Also taking place before Pearl Harbor in 1941 is *Submarine Raider* (Columbia, 1942). In this purely fictional film, Marguerite Chapman has some information about the Japanese plans in Hawaii which she learns after her yacht has been attacked by what will shortly become the enemy. Left afloat in the sea, she is picked up by an American submarine and an unsuccessful attempt is made to warn American forces at Pearl of the impending attack. Along with Chapman, John Howard is starred as the sub commander, with other roles going to Bruce Bennett, Forrest Tucker and Larry Parks.

Little Tokyo U.S.A. is another film in the spy genre. Preston Foster stars as a policeman who, just before the attack on Pearl Harbor, tries to prove the existence of an espionage ring in the Japanese section of Los Angeles. He is framed on a phony murder charge, but with the aid of his reporter girlfriend (Brenda Joyce) exposes the ring. After the bombing at Pearl, Californians were afraid that the Japanese would attack their state. This led to the decision to place the Japanese population of California in internment camps for the duration of the war. True-life footage of Japanese-Americans being herded out of L.A. provides *Little Tokyo U.S.A.* with its "happy ending."

All Through the Night is a spoof on the gangster film with a twist. This time Humphrey Bogart is a Broadway racketeer who, with his gang of characters, breaks up a Nazi spy ring. The saboteurs planning to blow up a battleship in New York Harbor are led by Conrad Veidt and Judith Anderson. Bogart's "henchmen" include such unlikely "heroes" as Jackie Gleason, Phil Silvers and William Demarest, all of whom play up the film's comedic aspects. "Bogie" also manages to have a romance with Kaaren Verne, cast as an unwilling accomplice of Anderson and Veidt. Her father has been in a concentration camp and is being kept alive because of her cooperation. When she finds out that her father is not alive, she comes to the aid of Bogart and his "boys."

As the war raged on, Conrad Veidt, a talented actor of German descent, was kept increasingly busy playing both Nazis and men devoted to the Allied cause. In an interesting film titled *Nazi Agent*, released by MGM in 1942, he essays a dual role, that of a fanatic Nazi diplomat and his twin brother, a naturalized American citizen loyal to his adopted country. When the diplomat is accidentally killed by his twin in a struggle, the latter takes his place and anonymously aids the Allied cause. A B movie, it proved popular with the public who would hiss and boo Veidt.

Espionage films with Allied agents defeating the enemy were very popular. One film released by MGM, a comedy with music, and two from Universal, are just more examples of the genre.

MGM's *Ship Ahoy* (1942) stars dancer Eleanor Powell as the star of a show on board a Puerto Rico–bound ship; Powell is tapping out Morse Code messages to the Allies. Zany Red Skelton mistakenly thinks she is a spy on the Axis side. By film's finale, he has realized that Powell is a true blue American. Also on board are Virginia O'Brien and Bert Lahr.

The music is supplied by the Tommy Dorsey Orchestra. Tommy's vocalist at the time was a skinny kid from Hoboken, New Jersey, named Frank Sinatra.

Madame Spy (Universal, 1942) casts Constance Bennett as an American counter espionage agent who becomes, for her job, involved with Axis agents. Don Porter is second-billed as a reporter romantically linked with Miss Bennett, while John Litel plays the leader of the Nazi ring.

Via special effects, Jon Hall becomes the *Invisible Agent* in the 1942 Universal film of the same name. Injected with a chemical that makes him invisible, he is able to obtain vital information for the Allies. Saboteurs have devised a scheme to bomb New York City. Aiding our intrepid hero is Ilona Massey as a counter espionage agent for the Allied cause. The fanciful film's cast includes Peter Lorre, Sir Cedric Hardwicke and J. Edward Bromberg as the villains. *Invisible Agent* was nominated for an Oscar for Special Effects.

Robert Cummings was a minor leading man when tapped for the lead in *Saboteur* (Universal, 1942). His everyman type of image blended well with the story of an aircraft mechanic enmeshed in the web of intrigue spun by director Alfred Hitchcock. Suspected by the law of setting the Los Angeles factory in which he works on fire, he is also pursued by the enemy agents responsible for his predicament. On the run, he crosses the country and, in the process, meets Priscilla Lane, who aids him in unmasking the culprits. One gets away, but in the film's finale, which takes place atop the Statue of Liberty, the nefarious evil-doer, played with menacing stealth by Norman Lloyd, gets his comeuppance, or in this case, his "comedownance." This scene is considered a masterpiece of the genre.

Two spy films made for Universal at about this time proved entertaining to the public. Both feature Basil Rathbone and Nigel Bruce in their most popular roles: Sherlock Holmes and the ever-faithful Dr. Watson.

In the business of filmmaking, occasional liberties are taken with the written word; the Holmes-Watson film series went even further by seesawing between the 1890s of the Arthur Conan Doyle stories and the 1940s.*

Sherlock Holmes and the Voice of Terror takes place in Britain at the

---

*In the films, the Watson character is bumbling. Not so in the Conan Doyle stories.

height of the Blitz. A disembodied radio voice has been aiding the Nazis by giving them classified information. Holmes is called in by a committee of statesmen to find the traitor. Less than halfway into the film, the audience realizes that the "voice" is a member of the committee, but everyone has a good time finding him. In the supporting cast are some well-known character actors of the 1940s, including Reginald Denny as the spy, Thomas Gomez and Henry Daniell.

Sherlock Holmes and the Secret Weapon (made in 1942, released in early 1943) pits Holmes and Watson against that basest of villains, Professor Moriarity, played by Lionel Atwill, who has been aiding the Nazis. This time, the evil one is after a bombsight which has been divided into four parts, each segment entrusted to a different scientist.

The Lady Has Plans (1942), from Paramount, stars Paulette Goddard as a war correspondent stationed in Lisbon, which was a wartime mecca for spies of every nationality. She may or not be working for the Axis. It is up to Ray Milland to find out. How will he know? The enemy agent has a tattoo on her back. It turns out that Miss Paulette is a true blue American; she and Milland team up to catch the lady with the plans. In support of the two stars are Margaret Hayes (the true miscreant), Albert Dekker, Roland Young and Cecil Kellaway.

Alan Ladd, a bit player, had recently come into his own in the role of a cold-blooded killer in Paramount's *This Gun for Hire* (1942). He meets a blonde singer (Veronica Lake, a blonde, even shorter than the diminutive Ladd) and becomes involved with fifth columnists out to do harm to the United States. The master villain is Laird Cregar. (Vastly overweight, Cregar went on to make a few more motion pictures and would die at the age of twenty-eight as a result of crash dieting.)

Ladd also appears in a 1942 war-related comedy drama playing the title role in *Lucky Jordan*, a con man reluctantly in the armed forces who outwits a Nazi spy ring. Cast opposite the actor is Helen Walker as an army welfare worker to whom Ladd becomes attracted. Also in the film are Marie McDonald, Lloyd Corrigan and Sheldon Leonard. The latter, for many years a gangster on the radio and in the movies, later became a television mogul, instrumental in producing several hit shows.

Another comedy in the spy vein is 1942's *My Favorite Blonde*, a Paramount production. Bob Hope plays a vaudevillian, a straight man for a trained penguin, who meets beautiful Madeleine Carroll on a train between theater dates. She is a British spy, trying to escape a band of

Nazis headed by George Zucco and Gale Sondergaard. Hope and friend help the young lady out of her predicament.

Several American productions of 1942 have European settings with resistance to the enemy as their common theme. Columbia's *Commandos Strike at Dawn* takes place in Norway. The film stars Paul Muni as a widowed fisherman in love with an Englishwoman played by Anna Lee. After the Nazi invasion, she and her diplomat father return to England. When Nazi officials occupy his village, Muni's daughter is taken hostage. He escapes to England and leads a raid on his town to destroy a nearby airfield. The mission is a success, his daughter is saved, but Muni dies.

RKO's *Joan of Paris* stars French actress Michelle Morgan as a woman who sacrifices her life so that five Allied airmen in occupied France can escape capture by the Gestapo. Paul Henried is the flier with whom the doomed girl falls in love. Both stars made their American film debuts in this motion picture. Also in the cast is Alan Ladd playing a small role as another of the fliers, Thomas Mitchell as a sympathetic priest and Laird Cregar as a sinister Nazi official.

Another 1942 film taking place in occupied Paris is *Reunion in France* from MGM. Joan Crawford portrays a Frenchwoman whose fiancé (Philip Dorn, giving the only good performance in the movie) is ostensibly a Nazi collaborator. Unbeknownst to Mlle. Crawford, however, he is, in reality, an important member of the French underground. Into this mishmash comes John Wayne as a downed American pilot whom our heroine helps to escape. The most apt description of this potboiler came from a reviewer of the era: "*Reunion in France* is the Joan Crawford version of the fall of France."

Two years later, Paramount took the theme of a downed pilot in occupied France and called the story *Till We Meet Again*. While on the run, the flyer, played by Ray Milland, meets a nun who aids him in escaping the Germans. Co-starred with Milland is Barbara Britton. Supporting the two stars are Walter Slezak, Lucille Watson and Konstantin Shayne.

Avoiding the Gestapo was the theme of three other 1942 releases. Unfortunately, not too many people were able to outwit the Nazis and the films lack the realism necessary for them to be credible, but each in its own way is original and entertaining.

The best of them is *The Pied Piper* (Twentieth Century–Fox), which is about a crotchety old English gentleman caught in France at the outset of the German invasion. He finds himself saddled with a group of children trying to get to England. Monty Woolley plays the title role to perfection and he is surrounded by a first-rate supporting cast including Anne Baxter, Roddy McDowall and Otto Preminger, the latter as the Nazi official with whom Woolley must match wits. Warm and sentimental, the film was a surprise hit at the box office and received an Oscar nomination, as did Woolley. The production lost to the blockbuster *Mrs. Miniver* and the actor to James Cagney for his portrayal of showman George M. Cohan in *Yankee Doodle Dandy*.

The very popular Cary Grant stars with Ginger Rogers in *Once Upon a Honeymoon*, a curious and original mix of comedy and drama from RKO. American burlesque queen Ginger marries a baron (Walter Slezak) whom she thinks is aiding the Allied cause — but he is really a high-ranking Nazi official. Enter Cary as an American radio correspondent. The first half of the film has Cary telling the skeptical bride about her husband, and the last half has them both trying to elude him. An interesting postscript to this production was that neither star would relinquish top billing, so it was decided that half of the advertising would feature the lady's name first and vice versa for the other half.

Dana Andrews played a role similar to that of Grant in *Berlin Correspondent* (Twentieth Century–Fox). Using a pre-arranged code, Andrews' character attempts to communicate vital information to the free world in his seemingly innocent broadcasts. He is aided by the father of a Gestapo agent (Virginia Gilmore). The latter is unaware of her father's activities, and switches her allegiance when she discovers that her father has been arrested and is about to be executed. The reporter, the girl and her father escape after surviving many tight situations. In an important role is Martin Kosleck, who was the quintessential Nazi in several films made during the war.

United Artists released *One of Our Aircraft Is Missing* in 1942. Six British airmen are forced to evacuate their plane and parachute into occupied Holland. The film, made in England, traces the attempts of the men to get back to their home base while avoiding capture by the enemy. In this, they are aided by some heroic Dutch Resistance members. The film proved to be a hit in both Britain and America and was nominated for a Best Original Screenplay Award. Featured in the cast are Eric Portman, Peter Ustinov, Bernard Miles, Roland Culver and Googie Withers.

Filmed with the cooperation of the British government, *Eagle Squadron* (Universal) takes place in England, where a group of American pilots join the RAF in fighting the Luftwaffe. They are also instrumental in locating a mysterious German plane wreaking havoc along the coast of France and hijacking it. Robert Stack, Eddie Albert, Jon Hall, John Loder, Leif Erickson and Edgar Barrier are the pilots while Diana Barrymore, daughter of John and aunt to Drew, provides the love interest for Stack.

Ronald Reagan is also in the air for *International Squadron* (Warner Bros., 1941). He is a cocky, restless pilot who, after ferrying planes to England, decides to join the RAF. After being responsible for the deaths of two other airmen, he redeems himself by going on a suicide mission. Featured in the cast are William Lundigan, Reginald Denny and Cliff Edwards; the latter was the voice of Jiminy Cricket in Walt Disney's *Pinocchio*.

The setting for *Desperate Journey* (1942) is also the European continent. This time the action takes place in Germany. Five downed American bombardiers are on the run, but the predictable end of the film finds our intrepid heroes well on their way to London, freedom and more feats of daring. But what else can be expected when Errol Flynn is top-cast in the film? Co-starred with the dauntless one as two of the other escapees are Ronald Reagan, in his second teaming with his fellow Warner Bros. contractee (the first was the 1940 production *Santa Fe Trail*) and veteran character actor Alan Hale. Released at the same time that Flynn's famous rape case hit the headlines (he was acquitted), the film did excellent business at the box office and many cheered when the handsome star's name appeared in the credits.

Flynn was not the only "hero" of World War II. If we are to believe many of the commercial films which came out in the early 1940s, John Wayne was another soldier/sailor/Marine/pilot who almost single-handedly won out over the enemy every time. His 1942 flag-waver *Flying Tigers*, from Republic Pictures, fictionalizes the very real group of pilots assembled in China by General Clare Chennault. Though the story is basically about the conflict between Wayne and his hot-headed friend and fellow pilot, enacted by John Carroll, and there is a tepid love story involving Anna Lee, several scenes are excitingly portrayed on the screen and hint at the important role the Tigers played in defeating the Japanese.

The war in the Pacific is also the theme of 1942's *A Yank on the Burma Road*, an MGM film starring Barry Nelson and Laraine Day. Its true significance lies in the fact that it was released only seven weeks after the attack on Pearl Harbor. The central character is an American trucker in the Philippines, out for the money he can make, whose patriotism comes to the fore upon hearing of his country's entrance into the war. The production was a "B" effort at best, one reviewer of the era called it "glib humbug."

Not so Paramount's *Wake Island*. With a cast including Brian Donlevy, Robert Preston, Macdonald Carey and Oscar-nominated William Bendix, the film tells the harrowing and stirring saga of the bitter defeat suffered by Marines at Wake during the war's early years. Virtually taken from the headlines of the day and realistically portraying the courage of a group of Americans fighting for every inch of soil on the strategic

Wake Island: U.S. Marines (from left) Macdonald Carey, Robert Preston and Brian Donlevy man a machine gun trying to hold Wake Island against stronger Japanese forces. The film received four Academy Award nominations.

island, the film was a big hit in 1942, artistically and propaganda-wise. It received an Oscar nomination, as did its director John Farrow.

Gung Ho (Universal, 1943) tells the fictionalized story of a real raid which took place on Makin Island in the Pacific theater of war in 1942. It describes the preparation of a Marine Raider battalion for the mission and how many lose their lives in recapturing the island from the enemy. Randolph Scott heads a cast which includes Alan Curtis, Noah Beery, Jr., J. Carrol Naish, Rod Cameron and, in a bit part, a young man named Robert Mitchum.

Via the movies, Randolph Scott also "traveled" to the Atlantic theater of war for *Corvette K-225* (1943). He stars as the commander of an escort warship of the British and Canadian naval forces known as corvettes. Crossing from Canada to England, the vessel is attacked by sea and by air, but does accomplish its mission. In the cast are Andy Devine, Ella Raines and *Gung Ho* veterans Noah Beery, Jr., and Robert Mitchum (the latter would become a major star in 1945).

Another film heralding our men at sea is *The Navy Comes Through* (RKO, 1942). Pat O'Brien, George Murphy, Jackie Cooper and Desi Arnaz are part of the crew of an old freighter in the Atlantic which gets to accomplish such deeds as blowing up a bomber, sinking a sub and capturing a German supply ship and using it against the enemy. A bit fanciful, but profitable for the studio.

The setting for *Ship with Wings* (1942), a British film released by United Artists, is a German-controlled Greek island. Stationed in the area is a British aircraft carrier. One of its men volunteers to destroy a German dam and is killed in the attempt. Heading the all–English cast are John Clements, Ann Todd, and Leslie Banks. The production contains some excellent aerial photography and shows the military importance of aircraft carriers.

Not neglecting the home front, MGM produced two films that proved to be effective pieces of propaganda. *Joe Smith, American* stars Robert Young as an aircraft factory worker with specialized knowledge of a new bombsight. Enemy agents kidnap him, but Joe does not tell them anything. He escapes and leads the FBI to his captors. The film was released during the spring of 1942 and though it did not make for high-powered viewing, it nonetheless helped to define what Americans were fighting for. Young's wife is played by Marsha Hunt and his son by Darryl Hickman.

The War Against Mrs. Hadley (1942), starring Fay Bainter, deals with the complacency of many Americans who think they can ignore what is happening all around them. By the final reel, Mrs. Hadley, a wealthy, pampered society matron, has been made to realize that the survival of her way of life cannot be separated from the defense of the democratic ideal. Supporting Miss Bainter are Edward Arnold, Van Johnson and Spring Byington.

Also on the home front, actor Lew Ayres was making news. "Dr. Kildare," so popular in the 1930s, had suddenly become *persona non grata*: Early in 1942, while many of the major and minor stars were joining the armed forces, Ayres was making a suspense mystery titled *Fingers at the Window*. He then announced that he was a conscientious objector. Fans were shocked at the news, but applauded when the army sent him overseas for Medical Corps duty where he distinguished himself.

England had been defending the ideals of democracy for more than two years before the United States entered the war. Three important films released in 1942 paid tribute to the gallantry of the English people and the trials and tribulations they faced on a daily basis.

Journey for Margaret, an MGM production, made a big star of a little girl named Margaret O'Brien. The diminutive actress, whom legend says (and she has never refuted this in any interviews) could cry on cue, portrays a victim of the London blitz who is adopted by an American war correspondent (Robert Young) and his wife (Laraine Day). They have lost their expected baby and welcome the frightened little girl and another child, a boy, into their home and into their hearts.

While Americans were getting their information via reports by Edward R. Murrow and other radio newsman, the British people were actually living this nightmare of continuous bombings. Many of them would never awaken. *Mrs. Miniver*, also from MGM, proved to be the blockbuster of the year. The poignant story, taken from a novel by author Jan Struther, shows how a "typical" English family copes with the horrors of war. The film captured the hearts of everyone who saw it. The gentle humor and strength exhibited in the screenplay was a tribute to a beleaguered civilian population and had a great effect on the American public's feelings towards their English cousins. Prime Minister Winston Churchill is purported to have said, "This film has helped Britain more than a whole flotilla of destroyers could."

Mrs. Miniver: Greer Garson (holding Christopher Severn)and Walter Pidgeon (embracing Clare Sanders) play a married couple striving for some sort of normalcy during the London Blitz.

British-born Greer Garson and her frequent co-star of the 1940s, Canada's Walter Pidgeon, are eloquent as the Minivers and the supporting cast includes veterans Dame May Whitty and Henry Travers plus newcomers Teresa Wright, Richard Ney and Helmut Dantine. The last named is seen in the small but showy role of a downed German pilot who confronts Mrs. Miniver in her own kitchen. Though at times somewhat melodramatic and possibly a bit unrealistic (although the 1941 landing of Rudolf Hess in a Scottish hayfield was full of melodrama and would never have been believed had it not actually happened), the film won five Academy Awards: Best Picture, Screenplay, Director (William Wyler), Actress (Garson) and Supporting Actress (Wright).

The excited Greer's speech at the Academy Awards ceremony went on for quite a while (but not as long as has been implied in the folklore of the movie capital), causing one wag to make the comment that her acceptance had more lines in it than her role as Mrs. Miniver. The red-haired star couldn't have cared less. Not only honored by her peers, she was a brand new bride to boot. Her husband, Richard Ney, had played her eldest child in the film. The marriage was of short duration.

In Which We Serve was completed in 1942 but ran into censor problems in America with the Hays Office. The British producers at first would not allow the film's distribution in this country. After no small amount of haggling over the use of certain phrases, the production premiered here in January of 1943. Though ostensibly about a destroyer, the HMS *Torrin*, which had been torpedoed off Crete in 1941, the real essence of the film lies in the stories of her crew members. Written, directed and starred in by Noël Coward, this tribute to the British navy was a tremendous hit and, like *Mrs. Miniver*, had great propaganda value during those early years of the forties. Besides Coward, the excellent all–English cast includes John Mills, Richard Attenborough (who would go on to become an outstanding film director), Michael Wilding (who became one of Elizabeth Taylor's husbands), Celia Johnson and Kay Walsh. The film was Oscar-nominated, as was Coward for his original screenplay. Neither film nor its creator won, but the latter was voted a certificate by the Academy Board of Directors commending him for his "outstanding achievement."

As 1942 ended, Allied forces landed along the North African coast. Warner Bros. moved the release date of one of its productions to coincide with this event and also with an upcoming meeting between Roo-

Five. America Mobilizes 55

In Which We Serve: **Noël Coward (center) and unidentified actors are survivors who cling to a raft in the Atlantic after their destroyer has been sunk. Like *Mrs. Miniver*, the film was a big hit and had great propaganda value during the early part of the war.**

sevelt and Churchill. Stalin had been asked to join the two leaders but had demurred, saying that he could not leave his country while several major military operations were taking place.

The locale of both film and conference was an exotic city in Morocco. The film would one day eclipse the importance of the conference and would make legends of two of its stars.

Chapter Six

War Themes: The Making of a Legend

The fame of the film *Casablanca* (1942) has grown to epic proportions with the passage of time. We may forever misquote certain of its lines (for example, "Play it, Sam, play 'As Time Goes By'" has evolved into "Play it again, Sam"), but the romance and the intrigue of the screenplay still get to us.

The making of the movie is, in itself, a fascinating bit of folklore. Based on a play that had never been produced, *Everybody Comes to Rick's*, the Warner Bros. production was to have starred Ronald Reagan, Ann Sheridan and Dennis Morgan. Fortunately, for the studio and for filmgoers, the roles went to Humphrey Bogart, Ingrid Bergman and Paul Henried.

The film captured the immediacy of a wartime situation: the plight of refugees and their attempts to obtain exit visas to neutral Portugal and freedom. This, intertwined with the story of the most celebrated lovers since Rhett Butler and Scarlett O'Hara, made *Casablanca* a classic for the ages. Rounding out the cast were Claude Rains, Conrad Veidt, Sydney Greenstreet, Peter Lorre and Dooley Wilson, each contributing memorably to the film's success.

The production made international film favorites of Bogart and Bergman plus a standard of the lovely ballad "As Time Goes By," sung by Wilson as Sam. The song was not a new one, having been written in 1931, but not until Wilson's rendition of it in Rick's Café did it have everyone in thrall.

Two endings were shot, one in which café owner Bogart winds up with Ingrid, the other with resistance leader Henried "getting the girl."

Casablanca: From left, an unidentified officer, Claude Rains, Paul Henried, Humphrey Bogart and Ingrid Bergman have come to an impasse over a letter of transit out of Casablanca. Who will get to Lisbon? Ronald Reagan was penciled in for the role played by Bogart, but wiser heads prevailed.

The latter was used and the final fade-out sees "Bogie" walking into the distance with the opportunistic Vichy policeman Renault (played to sardonic perfection by Rains) and commenting, "Louie, I think this is the beginning of a beautiful friendship." (At the end of 1944, Henried starred in *The Conspirators* in the role of a guerrilla leader, not too unlike his *Casablanca* character of Victor Lazlo. This time the setting is Lisbon and his leading lady is Hedy Lamarr. Peter Lorre and Sydney Greenstreet head the supporting cast.)

Roosevelt and Churchill proved to be the best press agents that Jack Warner could have wished for. Between the North African landings and the Casablanca talks, the studio reaped the largest promotional bonanza since Selznick's *Gone with the Wind*. The film was a huge hit and garnered three Academy Awards: Best Picture, Director (Michael Curtiz) and Screenplay (Howard Koch and the Epstein brothers, Julius and Philip).

The meetings in the Moroccan seaport were among the most important of the war: Under consideration were proposals for the invasion of Sicily, an island off the southern coast of Italy, and for landings on European soil via the English Channel. Also emerging from the talks was a declaration which called for the "relentless waging of war" until the enemy agreed to an unconditional surrender.

Nineteen forty-three saw American bombers in raids over Germany and the surrender of Hitler's forces at Stalingrad. By mid–September, Italy had capitulated; Benito Mussolini was no longer its leader. At year's end, in Teheran, Roosevelt, Churchill and Stalin were in agreement over Channel invasion plans and were looking towards a decisive 1944.

The war was still taking its toll of Hollywood's male population. Mickey Rooney was classified 1-A (fit for service), Henry Fonda was assigned sea duty and Jean-Pierre Aumont, newly married to exotic actress Maria Montez, left the film capital to join the Free French Army. Actors Robert Preston, Gilbert Roland and Bruce Cabot headed for overseas duty with Air Force Intelligence. A new star, however, was on the horizon in the person of Gregory Peck. Signed by RKO in 1943, the young actor made his screen debut in *Days of Glory*, a 1944 paean to the Russian partisans engaged in guerrilla warfare against their Nazi enemies.

Despite the war, many Hollywood personalities found time for love and marriage. Dorothy Lamour, Paramount's "Sarong Girl," became engaged to an army captain — her marriage to William Ross Howard would last until his death — and Rita Hayworth began to date Orson Welles, whom she married a few months later. (This merger was of short duration.) Being seen together were Betty Grable and orchestra leader Harry James, plus Charlie Chaplin and the teenaged daughter of playwright Eugene O'Neill. Both couples married — the Grable-James wedded bliss lasted for twenty years, and the May-December romance of Chaplin and his Oona lasted until the death of the "Little Tramp" in 1977.

Other marriages taking place in 1943 did not outlive the decade. Among the brief unions were those of Hedy Lamarr to British actor John Loder, Ann Sothern to MGM contract player Robert Sterling, and Ginger Rogers to Jack Briggs. During the halcyon period of Ginger's wedded bliss, she was a camp follower, living near the base at which her Marine husband was stationed. (Several comedies using this theme were produced during the war years.) One jarring note which occurred amidst all these nuptials taking place was the divorce of Judy Garland from composer-orchestra leader David Rose.

Nineteen forty-three was a banner year for filmmaking and a good part of the Hollywood output was devoted to war-related subject matter. More World War II films were made that year than at any other time in the history of the movies. These productions showed the many faces of war: the grim realities of battle, views of the home front (not all dramatic), the thrills and chills of spy-chasing and espionage.

They Came to Blow up America, from Twentieth Century–Fox, stars George Sanders, equally adapt at playing heroes and villains in his long career, as an American agent of German parentage. Taking the place of an American Nazi, held by the FBI, Sanders goes to Germany and enrolls in a school for sabotage, He joins a group going to America with the avowed intent of committing acts of sabotage, but upon arrival in this country, they are promptly arrested. Other members of the cast include Anna Sten, Ward Bond and Sig Ruman.

The Spanish Civil War provided the backdrop for two interesting films released during the second full year of the war. *The Fallen Sparrow* (RKO) is a murky drama in which American volunteer John Garfield, returning from Spain after enduring many months of torture in a fascist prison, takes on a Nazi spy ring based in New York. Maureen O'Hara, in one of her few unsympathetic roles, and Walter Slezak are the enemy agents and the two acquit themselves in fine fashion, but it is Garfield as the reluctant hero, a part he played so well in many of his movies, who carries the plotline.

For Whom the Bell Tolls (Paramount), based upon the novel by Ernest Hemingway, stars Gary Cooper and Ingrid Bergman as two disparate people who meet and fall in love during the turbulent days of the war in Spain, just before the outbreak of World War II. He is an American who joins a band of partisan fighters opposed to Franco. Bergman's Maria is a part of the group. A strong cast of supporting players is headed by Akim Tamiroff and Greek actress Katina Paxinou. Although Cooper, Bergman and Tamiroff were nominated, it was Paxinou, as a tough-minded guerrilla fighter, who picked up an Oscar as Best Supporting Actress.

A sidelight to the casting of the film is that the original choice for the feminine lead was actress-dancer Vera Zorina. As legend has it, Zorina did not photograph well in the close-cropped hair style that the part called for. Bergman did, and so the lovely Swedish import landed another plum role.

The French underground is the subject of *Paris After Dark* (Twentieth Century-Fox), with George Sanders starred as a doctor able to go about his job with no restrictions when he is actually a leader of the resistance movement. In key roles are Philip Dorn and Brenda Marshall. The film's director, Leonide Moguy, was a Frenchman who escaped from France after the German occupation.

Appointment in Berlin (Columbia) stars George Sanders again as a good guy, a British Secret Service agent who becomes a staff member of a German radio station. Ostensibly broadcasting anti-British propaganda *à la* Lord Haw Haw (a real-life British traitor), in reality his messages contain much vital information. He does not survive at the end. Sanders' character is somewhat similar to Dana Andrews' in *Berlin Correspondent*, but the latter does not die.

Five Graves to Cairo: Erich von Stroheim (left) as Field Marshal Rommel, his adjutant Peter van Eyck and Franchot Tone posing as a German spy pore over a map, but only Rommel knows the whereabouts and meanings of the "five graves."

Six. War Themes

Some other intriguing spy dramas emerged during the year. One of the best is *Five Graves to Cairo*, a Paramount release. Starring Franchot Tone and Anne Baxter, with German-born director Billy Wilder at the helm, the film is set at a small desert hotel in Egypt. A British Tommy (Tone) staggers into the lobby scant minutes before the arrival of the fabled Field Marshal Erwin Rommel (portrayed by Erich von Stroheim). The story then has Tone assuming the guise of a Nazi spy while trying to decipher the secret of "the five graves" to which Rommel is constantly alluding. How his mission is accomplished makes for highly enjoyable, albeit highly improbable viewing.

We continue along the coast of North Africa for our next foray in the world of the war-related film.

An operetta becomes a war film?

In 1929, *The Desert Song*, with music by famed composer Sigmund Romberg, was filmed with John Boles as the mysterious Riff leader who leads Moroccan natives against some evil Arabs. It was the first all-talking, all-singing operetta to come to the screen. In 1953, the film was remade with Gordon MacRae as the leader of the Riffs who defeats the nomadic army of an evil sheik (played by Raymond Massey).

In between the two, in 1943, the Brothers Warner came up with the idea of having the head of the Riffs lead his men against a Nazi attempt to lay a railway line between Dakar and the North African coast. Dennis Morgan plays the mysterious hero of the Riffs, an American veteran of the Spanish Civil War whose aim is to thwart the German mission. Heading the cast of supporting players are Bruce Cabot, Gene Lockhart, Curt Bois and Faye Emerson, the latter at one time the wife of Elliot Roosevelt, the son of the president.

Leaving North Africa, we travel to Europe for MGM's *Above Suspicion*, which stars Fred MacMurray as an Oxford professor who, while honeymooning on the continent, is asked to track down a missing Allied agent for the British Secret Service. Joan Crawford is Fred's bride and willing accomplice. The supporting cast includes Conrad Veidt, this time on our side, and Basil Rathbone as a Nazi out to stop the newly married couple.

It was the end of an era for Crawford: She had been with MGM for seventeen years. She would go on to her greatest triumph at Warner Bros., as we will soon see. On a much sadder note, *Above Suspicion* was the last film for Veidt, who suffered a fatal heart attack shortly after completing his role.

English actor Robert Donat plays an Allied spy on a dangerous mission in *The Adventures of Tartu*, an MGM production. He is sent into Nazi-occupied Czechoslovakia to blow up a poison gas plant. This the intrepid Britisher does, after many harrowing attempts. Featured in the cast are Valerie Hobson and Glynis Johns, two well-known British actresses of the era.

Another of England's imports to the United States was John Sutton. In *Tonight We Raid Calais*, the British Intelligence officer he portrays, like Donat in *Tartu*, is flown into Europe, this time to blow up a munitions plant in occupied France. He is captured before the mission is completed, but others who take his place bring about the desired results. Appearing with Sutton are Lee J. Cobb, Annabella and Howard Da Silva.

George Montgomery is not flown into Europe intentionally in the Twentieth Century–Fox production *Bomber's Moon*—he crashes in Germany and is imprisoned along with a "Czechoslovakian" played by Kent Taylor, who is secretly a German spy. With the help of the underground, the two escape and make for the coast. The spy is killed before he can expose those who have helped in the escape. The pilot steals a German plane and flies to England.

As super-sleuth Sherlock Holmes, the aforementioned Basil Rathbone crosses over to the Allied side for *Sherlock Holmes in Washington* (Universal). He and the everpresent Dr. Watson (Nigel Bruce) journey to our nation's capitol to retrieve some highly important microfilm from a nest of Nazi spies. What they've been searching for has been hidden in a book of matches and, needless to say, many cigarettes are lit before the dynamic duo reaches their objective.

In a humorous vein, *They Got Me Covered*, a Samuel Goldwyn production, stars Bob Hope as a foreign correspondent based in Russia who is so busy having a good time on his expense account that he neglects to report a singular occurrence—Hitler's invasion of Russia. Fired, Hope and his long-suffering girlfriend (Dorothy Lamour) decide that the only way to make amends is to nab some enemy agents. This is done amidst much hilarity. Otto Preminger is suitably sinister as the head of the spy ring and adds just the right touch to the comedy, which did quite well at the box office.

Besides what was happening in Russia, heavy fighting was going on in several places all over the globe, and the resultant loss of life was tremendous. Several films produced during the year paying homage to the men and women of the armed forces had as their locales the steamy jungles of the Pacific Islands, the icy waters of the Atlantic, the shifting sands of the African desert and various towns and villages on the European mainland. Most of these epics were fictionalized accounts, filmed on Hollywood soundstages and/or at nearby locations. The battles portrayed, however, were all too real. Though the cast members were well-known celebrities, they served to bring to those at home some of the urgencies and horrors of the dramas being played out thousands of miles away.

Crash Dive (Twentieth Century–Fox) was made with the cooperation of the Navy Department and several scenes were filmed at the submarine base in New London, Connecticut. Tyrone Power portrays an executive officer on a sub commanded by Dana Andrews. Much of the story revolves around the rivalry for the affections of Anne Baxter, but mutual respect for each other comes with a raid on a German naval base. Being the bigger star in the Hollywood firmament, Power gets the girl. In the fine supporting cast are James Gleason and Dame May Whitty.

From submarines, we come to destroyers. Edward G. Robinson stars as a World War I veteran who wangles himself a place on a *Destroyer* (Columbia). Constantly complaining about how much better things were done in his day, he alienates the rest of the crew, but finally redeems himself by saving the day when the ship goes into action in the Pacific Ocean. Appearing with Robinson are Glenn Ford, in love with Marguerite Chapman (Robinson's daughter), Edgar Buchanan, Leo Gorcey and Regis Toomey. (One year later, going against his tough guy image, Robinson played a meek, middle-aged man for Columbia in *Mr. Winkle Goes to War*. Inducted into the army, the reluctant ex-bank clerk becomes a hero when in the South Pacific he drives a bulldozer into a foxhole which has been concealing a nest of enemy soldiers.)

We think of servicemen as strong and virile, somewhat in the mold of some of the actors who portrayed them in the movies. A typical example of this is Robert Taylor, who stars in *Stand By for Action*, a 1942 MGM production. His role is that of a Harvard grad who is subordinate to an officer (grittily played by Brian Donlevy) who has come up from the ranks. They clash until Taylor learns the realities of war. In the cast are Charles Laughton as the admiral who watches the metamorphosis, Chill Wills, Walter Brennan and Marilyn Maxwell. This was not a major hit for Taylor.

Action in the North Atlantic (Warner Bros.) pays tribute to the men of the Merchant Marine. During the early part of the war, German submarines ran rampant over Allied shipping in the choppy waters of the North Atlantic. Our merchant seamen battled mightily to keep convoys and supplies afloat. Humphrey Bogart and Raymond Massey play prototypes of these gallant men. When their ship is separated from the rest of the convoy, it is up to them to get it and its crew members safely back to port. Featured in the fine supporting cast are Alan Hale and a young actor billed as Bernard Zanville, who later changed his name to Dane Clark and enjoyed a lengthy career in movies and on television.

Sahara (Columbia) is a realistic enactment of the desert warfare which took place during the North African campaign of 1942. Besides the advancing German armies, Allied soldiers also had to battle the elements: sand, blinding windstorms, sand, oppressive heat and still more sand. The film stars Humphrey Bogart, this time playing the commander of a tank named "Lulubelle." The action unfolds during the halcyon days of the Afrika Korps, just before the fall of Tobruk. A small group of Allied soldiers under Bogart stumbles onto an abandoned well and must defend it from an attacking motorized army battalion. Featured in the cast are Bruce Bennett, Lloyd Bridges, J. Carrol Naish and Dan Duryea.

A second film portraying the battle for the hostile terrain of the North African desert is *The Immortal Sergeant* (Twentieth Century–Fox). Veteran character actor Thomas Mitchell is excellent, the title role of the battle-hardened non-com, while Henry Fonda matches him line for line as an inexperienced corporal who must take command of the advance patrol when his superior is killed. Interspersed via flashback is a romance between Fonda and Maureen O'Hara. *The Immortal Sergeant* was inspirational in tone and typical of much of the film fare released during the early 1940s.

One of the finest documentaries to come out of the North African campaign is the British-made *Desert Victory*, which details the defeat of Rommel's forces by the British Eighth Army under Bernard Montgomery. During the making of this on-the-spot sixty-minute film, four cameramen died and another seven were wounded. Heroics, of course, were not confined to campaigns against the forces of Germany. The conflict in the Pacific was the setting for some very fine films released throughout the war. *Air Force* (Warner Bros.) is an exciting piece of material about the "life" of a flying fortress named "Mary Ann" from the time she leaves San Francisco on December 6, 1941, to her arrival in Hawaii on the following day and the subsequent actions in which she is involved until she is severely damaged in the battle of the Coral Sea. Directed by Howard Hawks, a World War I Air Corps veteran, and featuring a cast headed by John Garfield, Arthur Kennedy and Gig Young, the film, which was sanctioned by the Air Force. is a realistic portrait of air power in wartime. Hawks shot the film in Tampa, Florida, and was given the use of a real flying fortress. Integrated into the production is some actual newsreel footage of the Battle of the Coral Sea.

The shooting of *Bombardier* (RKO) was to have started in 1941, but it didn't get off the tarmac until 1943, the reasons being the advent of Pearl Harbor and the loss of personnel to the armed forces. The story about the men who drop bombs over enemy territory with deadly accuracy stars Pat O'Brien, Randolph Scott, Eddie Albert and Robert Ryan, with Anne Shirley providing the love interest. The exciting finale has Scott dying to insure the success of a bombing mission over Tokyo.

Leaving the air, we come to our next group of films, also set in the Pacific theater of war. *Bataan* (MGM) recounts the last days of a group of soldiers fighting on the Philippine peninsula after the fall of Manila who attempt to hold off advancing Japanese forces so that the main body of Allied troops can escape. The interesting all-male cast includes Robert Taylor, George Murphy, Lloyd Nolan, Robert Walker and Desi Arnaz. Although fictional in characterization and shot in typical Hollywood style, *Bataan* depicts what actually occurred during some of the darkest days of the war and, as realistically as possible, portrays a group of men waging a losing battle.

The infamous "Death March" came as a result of the Bataan surrender. The Japanese forced their captives, both American and Filipino, to march to various prison camps. Thirst, oppressive heat, lack of food and dysentery were their "companions." Those who could not continue the march were bayoneted and killed while those who tried to help their comrades suffered the same fate. Several thousand prisoners never reached their destinations and more died in the camps, victims of starvation, torture and disease.

Wallace Beery had been with MGM since the beginning, appearing in one of that studio's first productions in 1924. Almost twenty years later, in 1943, the studio cast the veteran star in *Salute to the Marines*,

Bataan: Robert Taylor (left) and Lloyd Nolan are part of a small contingent of American soldiers and Filipino natives who, after the fall of Bataan, try to hold off the advancing Japanese so that others can escape. Only one man lives at film's end.

an action thriller set in the Philippines at the outset of the war. His role is that of a sergeant-major who struggles to get his family away from the fighting before the Japanese attack. Fay Bainter and Marilyn Maxwell play his wife and daughter. Others in the cast include William Lundigan, Reginald Owen, Ray Collins and Keye Luke.

The year before, the Marines had been represented in *To the Shores of Tripoli* (Twentieth Century–Fox). The most interesting aspect of the film is that it was made with the cooperation of the Marine Corps and that various scenes were shot at the base in San Diego and also at sea with the Pacific fleet. John Payne stars as a brash recruit who is taught by a veteran sergeant (Randolph Scott) to have respect for the service. Maureen O'Hara plays a navy nurse with whom the now humbled Payne falls in love.

Several Oriental actors made a good living in war-related films. A case in point is *China*, a 1943 Paramount project which stars Alan Ladd. He plays a salesman in China interested only in making money until Pearl Harbor turns him around and he joins a band of Chinese guerrillas. Loretta Young supplies the romance and William Bendix is the loyal buddy. Orientals in the cast include Philip Ahn, Victor Sen Yung and Iris Wong. Ladd joined the armed forces soon after the film was released.

Throughout the conflict, thousands of women served their country in varying capacities as part of our armed forces. Nowhere were they of more value than as combat nurses on the battlefields. These brave "angels of mercy" came as close to the actual fighting as it was possible to be and had a first-hand view of the horrors of war. They bandaged wounds, saw men writhing in agony, and closed the eyes of human beings who would not live to see another day. Two 1943 films describing the courage and determination of the nurses on Bataan were released within weeks of each other.

Paramount's *So Proudly We Hail!* stars Claudette Colbert, Paulette Goddard, Veronica Lake and, in his film debut, Sonny Tufts. This is the latter's finest hour on screen: His character is warm, honest and eminently real. Though Goddard was Oscar-nominated, the most interesting performance is Lake's. *Sans* her famed "peek-a-boo" hairdo, the actress excels as the widow of a serviceman cut down at Pearl Harbor. At film's end, she seals her fate with a bomb that takes several of the enemy with her. Featured prominently is George Reeves, who later became typecast, until his untimely death, as television's Superman. Others in the cast include Barbara Britton and Walter Abel.

Cry "Havoc" takes place on an island in the Pacific theater of war. MGM's all-female cast includes Margaret Sullavan and Fay Bainter as army nurses, remnants of a decimated unit, who recruit and command a group of disparate American volunteers headed by Ann Sothern, Ella Raines, Marsha Hunt and Joan Blondell. The last and most poignant scene depicts the fear and apprehension of this small but brave band of women as their hands are raised in surrender to their Japanese captors.

A year later, Universal paid tribute to the lesser known contribution of the opposite sex in *Ladies Courageous*, the story of the women who flew needed airplanes overseas. Those who did this dangerous job were called WAFs, pilots of the Women's Auxiliary Ferrying Service. The WAFs were mainly unheralded and did not get the credit they so richly deserved. Loretta Young stars as an officer in the service; others under her command are Diana Barrymore, Geraldine Fitzgerald, Evelyn Ankers, and June Vincent. Philip Terry and David Bruce are two of the men in the girls' lives. The action speeds up when one of the girls, who has some personal problems, nearly wipes out the unit when she crashes a plane.

A *Bataan*-like all-male cast is featured in *Guadalcanal Diary* (Twentieth Century–Fox), another in the series of battlefront dramas. The action again takes place in one of the more strategic areas of the Pacific, this time the island of Guadalcanal. As the scenario unfolds, a group of Marines are shown as they endure life in boot camp, in a foxhole, on jungle patrol, in hospitals and on the enemy-infested beaches. The players include such Hollywood veterans as Preston Foster, Lloyd Nolan, William Bendix and Anthony Quinn. The film was considered most realistic and was successful at the box office.

Another 1943 production about this sector stars the Pacific Ocean and a submarine named the *Copperfin*. With Cary Grant as captain, plus John Garfield, Alan Hale and Dane Clark as crew members, the sub starts out on a top-secret mission — *Destination Tokyo*. The information they need to collect is crucial to an American bomber attack upon the Japanese capitol city. Though the story is fictional, the raid in question is not: Led by General James Doolittle, Americans manning the bombsights served to bring the war to the Japanese mainland and gave a needed boost to United States morale at a time of great stress. Newsreel footage, interspersed with the fictional lives of the sub's crew, add to the authentic feel of this Warner Bros. production, made with the cooperation of the War Department.

The same year, debonair Cary switched over to a more light-hearted venture in *Mr. Lucky*, released by RKO. He gives a sparkling performance as a con man who is reluctant to serve his country. He needs money to launch his gambling ship and decides to swindle the American War Relief Society to raise the necessary funds. To paraphrase a ballad of the 1930s, love walks in in the person of Laraine Day; she reforms him and brings out his latent patriotism. His ship becomes a transporter of medical supplies rather than a floating casino. A cast of well-known character actors, including Paul Stewart, Charles Bickford and Gladys Cooper, helped to make the film a big success, earning a tidy profit for the studio.

A combination of flight, fancy and Spencer Tracy went into the making of *A Guy Named Joe*, an MGM production. Tracy, the consummate actor, portrays a dead pilot "assigned" by his heavenly supervisor to help fellow aviator Van Johnson both in the air and on the ground. Things heat up when the very much alive Johnson falls for the very much alive Irene Dunne to the consternation of the very much dead Tracy. That the premise was hokey did not concern the viewing audiences — the film was a big hit.

Production halted when Johnson was seriously injured in a motorcycle accident. Tracy refused to have the young redheaded actor replaced — thereby gaining a lifelong friend — and filming resumed as soon as Johnson was sufficiently recovered.

Fantasy did not extend to the grim realities of what was taking place at home and abroad. Americans were facing the war's impact amid draft laws, shortages and the rationing of food and essential goods. But although threats of Japanese air raids which never materialized threw a scare into many West Coast residents, leading to the internment of many innocent Japanese-Americans, the average citizen had to go to the movies to get an idea of what life was like under enemy rule. War-torn Europe provided the setting for several films released in 1943.

Gene Kelly, known primarily as a dancer, made several non-musical appearances for MGM. One highly dramatic film in which he appears is *The Cross of Lorraine*, with Jean-Pierre Aumont co-starred. The plotline deals with a group of French soldiers who at first believe German promises of an honorable armistice. Winding up in a prisoner of war camp, they soon realize the duplicity of their captors. Also in the cast are Peter Lorre as a sadistic German sergeant and Hume Cronyn as an informer.

Kelly's MGM bosses, having lost several leading men to the armed forces, realized his potential and cast him in other non-musical roles during the war years. *Pilot #5* features Gene, Franchot Tone and Marsha Hunt in a potboiler about an idealistic flier (Tone) who is killed on a suicide mission for which he volunteered. Via flashbacks, Kelly relates the story of his doomed friend. It is soon revealed that Tone had become involved with a fascist group. When he finally saw the light, he exposed his former friends, but at the cost of a flourishing career. Joining the Air Corps to continue his struggle against fascism, he crashed his plane into a Japanese aircraft, destroying it as well as himself.

Hangmen Also Die! and *Hitler's Madman* were out within a few months of each other in 1943. The first named, which was released by United Artists, focuses upon the assassination of Hitler's chief henchman in Czechoslovakia, the sadistic Reinhard Heydrich, and the hunt for his slayers. Brian Donlevy stars as a doctor working for the Resistance in Prague, who is the actual killer and on the run. Anna Lee and three-time Oscar winner Walter Brennan are featured in the cast as a history professor and his daughter who give Donlevy refuge. The film was produced, directed and co-written by Austrian-born refugee Fritz Lang, whose sure hand created the proper amounts of terror and tension. Due to the cooperation the production received from the Czech government, the film was lauded for its accuracy. It was a sad time in that country's history.

Hitler's Madman, from MGM, features John Carradine as Heydrich and goes further with the story than does the Lang film and culminates in the infamous razing of Lidice, the small Czech village which the Nazis suspect of harboring those involved in the assassination. The film's subject was taken from the headlines of the day and American audiences were once again shown the excesses of the totalitarian governments with which their country was at war.

Czechoslovakia is also the setting for Paramount's *Hostages*. A story of the Czech underground movement, it stars Luise Rainer, Paul Lukas, William Bendix, Katina Paxinou, Oscar Hololka and Hans Conreid. The routine wartime melodrama is interesting in the fact that it marked the end of the acting career of Luise Reiner. She had not appeared on screen for five years after winning two Academy Awards for her second and third movies, the first in 1936 for *The Great Ziegfeld* and the second in 1937 for *The Good Earth*.

Six. War Themes

The theory of a "master race" had as its core a belief in Aryan superiority. The Nazis worked diligently to imbue young German minds with this fanaticism. The prototypes of this "master race" were tall, strapping men and women with blond hair and blue eyes. Most of the Nazi hierarchy did not fit this description.

Hitler's Children (RKO) is a vivid account of the actual youth movements (or Hitler Jugend) which existed throughout Germany before and during the war. The film stars Bonita Granville playing a girl marked for sterilization because of her anti–Nazi beliefs and her refusal to bear children for the Reich; Tim Holt is the German officer who loves her. Caught in the maelstrom of events, the two have sealed their fate. The horrors of anti–Semitism and sterilization of non–Aryan women are realistically recreated and the production, due to the topical nature of the material, was a hit at the box office. The cast includes Kent Smith as Granville's father, Otto Kruger, Hans Conreid and Lloyd Corrigan.

Unlike *Hitler's Children, Hitler's Madman* and *Hangmen Also Die!*, which are all based upon fact, *This Land Is Mine* (RKO), *The Moon Is Down* (Twentieth Century–Fox), *Edge of Darkness* (Warner Bros.) and *The North Star* (Goldwyn), all released in 1943, are works of fiction. Nevertheless, many of the characters portrayed in them are representative of the real people who so stoically bore the brunt of the Nazi onslaught.

This Land Is Mine stars Charles Laughton as a timid French schoolmaster who shows his own personal bravery in the face of the tyrannical takeover of his village by the enemy. Laughton, under the guidance of director Jean Renoir, a new arrival to American shores, turns in a finely honed, understated performance and is surrounded by a fine cast which includes Maureen O'Hara, George Sanders and Walter Slezak. The film is a fine character study showing how different personalities will react under unnatural conditions: Sanders collaborates with the enemy, thinking that this is the way to peace and security, while Laughton and O'Hara realize that the only way to attain these goals lies in the youth of their nation learning from the past in order to plan for the future.

The Moon Is Down and *Edge of Darkness* both depict the courage of Norwegians during the Nazi invasion and occupation of their country. The similar plots each center on a town and the conflict between its people and their uninvited visitors. The town offers many forms of resistance, resulting in death on both sides. The players in the first film are

Sir Cedric Hardwicke, Lee J. Cobb, and Henry Travers. Based upon a John Steinbeck novel, it did poorly at the box office. Many at the time, including Twentieth Century–Fox head Darryl Zanuck, felt that this was due to the waning of public interest in war films. This is only partially true; *Edge of Darkness,* the Warner Bros. version of Norway under siege, did quite well financially. The difference lies in the casting of each film. The acting in *The Moon Is Down* could hardly compete with the likes of Errol Flynn, Ann Sheridan, Walter Huston, Ruth Gordon and Judith Anderson. People flocked to watch the magnetic Errol, newly acquitted of rape charges, heroically lead his fellow "Norwegians" in the fight against the Nazis while making love to his beautiful leading lady Sheridan, who had just had separated from her husband, actor George Brent.

Like *The Moon Is Down,* and *Edge of Darkness, First Comes Courage,* a Columbia release, also takes place in Norway. Merle Oberon is a courageous Norwegian who befriends a German officer in hopes of obtaining information from him which will get to London via a doctor friend of hers. Brian Aherne co-stars as a British commando who, because of the danger involved in her activities, wants her to go to England with him, but she will not leave.

Back to Mr. Flynn, who kept his star status in spite of, or maybe *because of* the publicity he had garnered. Just after completing *Edge of Darkness,* he starred in *Northern Pursuit.* In this film, he is a Canadian Mountie who pretends to have Fascist sympathies in order to apprehend a group of German saboteurs. In the midst of shooting, the star collapsed and was hospitalized. A week later he was back and filming resumed. The supporting cast includes Julie Bishop, Helmut Dantine, and Gene Lockhart.

At the beginning of 1944, Errol was given a new contract which had several perks in it, including, choice of scripts, a say in production and a percentage of any profits that would come out of the film. The first film made under this "sweetheart" contract was *Uncertain Glory.* The actor plays a Frenchman bound for the guillotine. With the aid of a detective (Paul Lukas), he escapes and joins the Resistance.

The wartime love affair between Russia and the United States was in full bloom when *The North Star* (a.k.a. *Armored Attack*) was released. Anne Baxter, Dana Andrews, Walter Huston and former child star Jane Withers head a strong cast in the Lillian Hellman–scripted tale which glorifies the Russian peasantry and the guerrilla tactics of a small village pitted against the forces of evil. Some time later, with the emergence of the Cold War, this motion picture proved to be an embarrassment to the United States and to the people who made it. In an interesting turn of events, Hellman was Oscar-nominated, as was Aaron Copland for the film's music score. Neither won.

Another film, *Mission to Moscow,* proved to be a source of embarrassment to the Warner Brothers, a production that studio head Jack Warner years later wished he had never made. It stars Walter Huston and is based upon the experiences of Joseph E. Davies who had served as our ambassador to Russia. At the time of the film's release, it was looked upon as a link between two nations. The postwar view of the production was, however, quite different; *Mission to Moscow* was then thought to be the whitewashing of a regime of excesses while giving Americans an overly idealistic view of Russia.

Idealistic pictures of the American home front were also among Hollywood's output for 1943. These films were either unabashedly sentimental, unabashedly comedic or unabashedly patriotic.

The Human Comedy was writer William Saroyan's contribution to domestic U.S. morale. Mickey Rooney, the focal point of the film, is a Western Union messenger who must sometimes deliver the dreaded telegram from the War Department beginning with the words "We regret to inform you that— " which many real families were receiving at the time of this MGM release. Rooney's performance is one of restraint, a far cry from his boy-girl musicals with Judy Garland, and he was Oscar-nominated, as were the film and director Clarence Brown. Actor Frank Morgan registers strongly as the senior telegraph operator after whom Rooney's character wants to pattern himself. The supporting cast is a movie buff's dream: Marsha Hunt, James Craig, Fay Bainter, Van Johnson, Donna Reed, Barry Nelson and, in a bit part, Robert Mitchum.

Don Ameche and Frances Dee are the recipients of a such a telegram from the War Department in *Happy Land* from Twentieth Century–Fox. Mixing sentiment, drama and fantasy, the film, somewhat of a tearjerker, has Ameche, with the aid of a ghostly relative, taking a journey into the past and reliving some of the happy and memorable moments in the life of his now dead son. Parents who had suffered similar losses, and who displayed gold stars in their windows, could readily identify with this gentle and unassuming, albeit Hollywood, look at life and death in small town America.

Also on the home front, millions of Americans heeded the call of their country and made immeasurable contributions to the war effort by their work in factories and shipyards all over the country to get out the materiel needed by our armed forces in defeating the enemy. Defense plant workers were the central characters in three films to be discussed here: two were released in 1943, the third a year later.

In *Tender Comrade* (1943) an RKO pull at the heartstrings, Ginger Rogers plays a serviceman's wife who takes a job in a defense plant when her husband (Robert Ryan) is sent overseas. She rents a house with some co-workers (Kim Hunter and Ruth Hussey among them), all of whom are service wives and all of whom show varying degrees of patriotism and equally varying degrees of love for their men. The film is a flag-waver, full of sloppy sentiment and patriotic jargon, much of it spouted by Ginger when she is notified that her husband has been killed in action. It is not one of the star's shining moments on screen, and years later, she made some unflattering comments about the film.*

A second film about war plant workers, RKO's *Gangway for Tomorrow* (1943) stars Margo as a French refugee, Robert Ryan as a race car driver and John Carradine as a hobo among a group of five working in a munitions factory. As they ride to work, via flashback, each relates private details about themselves. The film shows the human connections between people who are thrown together, this time in a war atmosphere.

A Paramount entry, *I Love a Soldier* (1944), stars Paulette Goddard as a San Francisco defense plant welder who is averse to marriage until she meets a GI on leave (Sonny Tufts). The problems they face make up the bulk of the film. It would take Samuel Goldwyn's *The Best Years of Our Lives* (1946) to focus more realistically and forcefully on the problems of soldiers and their wives during and after the war.

As has been mentioned, however, not all films about the home were full of pathos and bathos. Comedy and music also played a part in the year's war-related output. Americans eager for some light entertainment to draw their attention away from the daily headlines were enchanted by *The More The Merrier* (1943). This delightful comedy from Columbia,

---

*In a six-part documentary about the RKO Film Studios, which was aired over the Arts and Entertainment Television Network in the 1990s, Ms. Rogers was shown denouncing *Tender Comrade*, more or less labeling it leftist propaganda. The film's director Edward Dmytryk and its writer Dalton Trumbo, were later part of the famous "Hollywood Ten," who, during the McCarthy era, were listed as subversive.

set in wartime Washington D.C., spoofs the housing shortages which were part and parcel of life in large American cities during the war. Veteran actress Jean Arthur portrays a government worker who rents out half of her Washington apartment to elderly Charles Coburn. The cherubic Coburn, who walked off with a Best Supporting Actor award for his performance in the film, turns right around and rents half of his half to Joel McCrea. When Arthur meets up with McCrea, the finale becomes predictable, but by then, who cares? *The More the Merrier* was produced by George Stevens, his last project before entering the service. Later, under his guidance, some of the finest documentaries of the war would be made.

The locale of *Government Girl* (1943) is also wartime Washington. The film is supposedly comedic, but it actually pinpoints the then-serious problem of war profiteering. Some Americans made a fortune via the black market (selling scarce items at a huge profit) and via the sale of strategic war materials to the government at inflated prices. Olivia de Havilland plays secretary to Sonny Tufts, an honest industrialist who almost gets caught up in a scandal which is not of his making. The humor of the film is forced and in no way compares with the charm of the Arthur-McCrea-Coburn opus. Olivia had not wanted to do the film in the first place, but was loaned to RKO by David Selznick, who in turn, had obtained her services from her home studio, Warner Bros. Though the feisty actress showed her distaste for the film while making it, the venture was a profitable one for RKO.

While many Americans were beginning to shy away from films showing the starkness of battle, they did not tire of musicals, whatever their connections with the war. What 1943 audiences both at home and abroad craved were morale boosters, and several films released at the time filled the bill.

Fred Astaire's contribution to the war effort for the year 1943 was *The Sky's the Limit*, a successful production from RKO. In an Astaire musical, the plot is usually secondary to the dance numbers and this film does not break the mold. Fred, a war hero on leave in New York City, meets and falls for an ambitious photographer (Joan Leslie) who has no time for romance. Of course, the predictable ending finds Fred and Joan in a clinch. "Shining Hour" and one of the great saloon songs of all time, "One for My Baby and One More for the Road," brilliantly sung and danced by Mr. A. are the production's highlights. "Shining Hour" was

Oscar-nominated, but lost to "You'll Never Know" from *Hello Frisco, Hello*. Featured in this lightweight, entertaining film are humorist Robert Benchley and Robert Ryan.

Alice Faye, who sang "You'll Never Know" into Oscar immortality, is spotlighted in the Twentieth Century–Fox production *The Gang's All Here*. The threadbare plot of a wartime Romeo engaged to one girl, but in love with another, is merely an excuse to get on with a show which includes songs by Faye, hip-swinging by Brazilian star Carmen Miranda and specialty numbers by "King of Swing" Benny Goodman. The film, however, is mainly remembered for its choreography by the legendary Busby Berkeley, who during the 1930s had created some great dance numbers for several Warner Bros. musicals, including *42nd Street*.

Though the film marked Faye's adieu to the movie musical before leaving the screen for motherhood and radio work, the blonde actress did make a foray into the dramatic field with *Fallen Angel* in 1945. After this appearance, she did not return to the screen until 1961 and the third time around for *State Fair*.

Nineteen forty-three was the year during which a few multi-star extravaganzas contributed to the nation's morale. In some cases, these contributions were also financial.

The year before, Paramount had released *Star Spangled Rhythm*. The slim plot has sailor Eddie Bracken, thinking that his father (Victor Moore) is a big shot at Paramount, invite some of his pals to see the movie studio. Dad is really the studio gateman. Under prodding by telephone operator Betty Hutton, the reluctant Moore poses as the head of the studio. A show is put on for the sailors including almost everyone on the lot. Among the luminaries are Bing Crosby, Bob Hope, Ray Milland, Franchot Tone, Mary Martin, Fred MacMurray, Alan Ladd, Jerry Colonna and Eddie "Rochester" Anderson. A highlight of the film is when three glamour girls of the era, Paulette Goddard, Dorothy Lamour and Veronica Lake, perform a novelty number titled "A Sweater (Goddard), A Sarong (Lamour) and a Peek-a-Boo Bang (Lake)."

This Is the Army (Warner Bros., 1943) stars future Senator George Murphy, Joan Leslie and future President Ronald Reagan, plus an assortment of actors and extras actually in the army at the time of filming. This rousing tribute to a branch of the military, taken from the popular stage hit of the same name, features some Irving Berlin classics of the war years, including the humorous "Oh, How I Hate to Get Up in the

Morning," sung by a uniformed Berlin himself, "This Is the Army, Mr. Jones," the wistful "I Left My Heart at the Stage Door Canteen" and a rousing version of "God Bless America," sung by the popular Kate Smith. An interesting group of supporting players includes singer Frances Langford plus character actors George Tobias and Alan Hale. An extra added attraction is the appearance of Sergeant Joe Louis, heavyweight boxing champion of the world. (Louis was persona non grata in Germany as he had beaten German boxer Max Schmeling for the heavyweight title of the world.)

The film was a tremendous hit, with almost two million dollars of the profits going to the Army Emergency Relief Fund. Berlin also signed over to the government all existing and future royalties of "God Bless America" sung in the film, a tribute to the adopted homeland that he loved so much.

The Stage Door Canteen of the irrepressible Irving's song was located in New York City's theater district. The brainstorm of the American Theater Wing, the canteen, like its counterpart in Los Angeles, provided entertainment for servicemen stationed along our eastern coast. A percentage of the profits of the 1943 film *Stage Door Canteen* (United Artists) were donated to this very worthy institution. Amid a galaxy of star turns by such luminaries as Katharine Hepburn, Edgar Bergen and Charlie McCarthy, Ray Bolger, Katherine Cornell and Ethel Merman plus the music of Count Basie, Benny Goodman and Guy Lombardo, lies a slim story of romance between hostesses and servicemen. They are played by a group of Hollywood unknowns, only one of whom, Lon McCallister, went on to a modicum of fame in the industry.

The film was quite successful, thanks to its all-star cast. A year and a half later, the Hollywood Canteen would be immortalized on the screen by Warner Bros.

The brothers had a precursor to *Stage Door Canteen* in *Thank Your Lucky Stars* (1943). The locale of the film is Hollywood and its flimsy premise has two show business hopefuls (Dennis Morgan and Joan Leslie) trying to land spots on a benefit show. They are aided and abetted by the exuberant Eddie Cantor as the cabbie who befriends them. Cantor also appears as himself. Among those performing at the "benefit" are Errol Flynn, Olivia de Havilland, Ida Lupino, Humphrey Bogart, Ann Sheridan, John Garfield and Bette Davis, who "growls" the movie's only imaginative song, "They're Either Too Young or Too Old," spoofing the shortage of eligible men on the home front. The film did not have the impact of the studio's other extravaganza, *This Is the Army*.

Another entry in the all-star category came from MGM in the form of *Thousands Cheer*. The love story, taking place on an army base, involves Kathryn Grayson as a colonel's daughter and Gene Kelly as the soldier she loves; a variety show is staged at the base. With Mickey Rooney as emcee, the performers put through their paces include Judy Garland, June Allyson, Red Skelton, Lena Horne, Eleanor Powell, Ann Sothern, Lucille Ball, Gloria De Haven and famous piano virtuoso Jose Iturbi. (The latter was kept busy in several MGM movies of the 1940s and gave all productions in which he appeared a touch of class.)

As 1943 came to a close, all eyes in Hollywood were focused on the Academy Awards; the ceremony would be held during the early part of 1944. *Watch on the Rhine*, a Warner Bros. production, gave Hungarian-born Paul Lukas the role of his career and won him a Best Actor Oscar. The film's compelling story is about a dedicated anti–Nazi who comes to Washington during the early part of 1941 with his American-born wife and their European-born children. Seeing all around him complacency, indifference and a seeming inability to comprehend the implications for the American way of life in what is taking place abroad, the patriot returns to his native land to continue the fight for democracy.

Lukas, who had created the role on the Broadway stage, gives a performance of assurance and strength as the resistance leader, while Bette Davis is more restrained than usual in the less showy role of the understanding wife, a quiet heroine in her own right. In excellent support of the two stars are Lucile Watson playing Bette's mother and George Coulouris as a Rumanian exile out to betray Lukas for a price.

Not the least interesting aspect of the movie is that the screenplay, based upon the stage hit by Lillian Hellman, is the work of her long-time lover and companion, mystery writer Dashiell Hammett. Both the film and Lucile Watson were Oscar-nominated; the film lost to *Casablanca* and Miss Watson to Katina Paxinou (*For Whom the Bell Tolls*).*

Of course, with the attack on Pearl Harbor, complacency and indif-

---

*Casablanca, Michael Curtiz, Charles Coburn and Katina Paxinou won four of the five major Academy Awards for 1943. Newcomer Jennifer Jones won the fifth, Best Actress honors, for her moving portrayal as the visionary in *The Song of Bernadette*. Hers was the only top role that had nothing whatsoever to do with World War II.

ference were no longer problems. Even before this occurrence, Hollywood was producing a few documentaries and short subjects depicting events abroad and citing our need for preparedness; these projects had been given limited release. Once we were actually engulfed in the hostilities, however, the number of films of this type greatly increased and were government-supported. The overriding aim of the day was to spur Americans at home and those fighting abroad on to victory. Informational and propagandistic in content, the documentaries and shorts produced at the time provide a view of an era that future generations are in danger of forgetting.

In retrospect, seen from the vantage point of many decades after the fact, these films not only appear one-sided, they are highly simplistic. Nevertheless, they got the job done. Let's now take a look at some of these "fighting films."

Chapter Seven

Praise the Lord and Pass the Propaganda

As the sounds of Pearl Harbor reverberated throughout the nation, propaganda machines began to operate in earnest. The recruiting of a mighty military force was, of course, our first priority. It is one thing to raise an army, however, but quite another to give it a *raison d'etre*, a reason for being. To win a war, the battle for men's hearts and minds must first be won.

And no one knew this better than Adolf Hitler. To tell the world his evil story, he had utilized the art of documentary filmmaking to its fullest. In 1934, under his orders, perhaps one of the greatest pieces of propaganda ever conceived was filmed. Directed by Leni Riefenstahl, one of the few women directors of the era, *Triumph of the Will* is the official record of the sixth Nazi Party Congress at Nuremberg. An absorbing study of the National Socialist movement, the film also gives a visual picture of its leaders and the millions who enthusiastically greeted Hitler as their messiah. Although full of pomp and ceremony, the production did succeed in imparting the brutal doctrines of Hitler, not only to Germany, but to the world at large. That not many heeded this testament to the dictator's strength and insidious schemes would prove fatal to millions just a few years later.

A 1935 film, also made by Riefenstahl, documents the military might of Germany. Titled *Tag der Freiheit* (*Day of Freedom*), it vividly shows the country's manpower and formidable arsenal of weapons and vehicles in mock raids and drills; these would soon become a reality. The finale, filmed with squadrons of aircraft in the formation of a swastika soaring through the heavens while strains of the militant "Deutschland uber Alles" are heard, is a masterpiece.

Seven. Praise the Lord and Pass the Propaganda

Very soon after Pearl Harbor and our entrance into the war, several famous Hollywood moviemakers, realizing America's need for professionally made documentary and propaganda films, volunteered their services to the government. Among them was Frank Capra, who had come to these shores in 1903 as a six-year-old. Italian by birth, but American in both heart and mind, his films were noted for the common touch and for their embodiment of patriotism and of "melting pot" virtues. For a Depression-ridden populace, Capra mocked and chastised the rich in such screwball comedies as *It Happened One Night* and *You Can't Take It With You*, pitted good against evil in his serio-comic *Mr. Deeds Goes to Town*, and paid homage to the American form of government with *Mr. Smith Goes to Washington* and *Meet John Doe*.

At the onset of hostilities, Capra was commissioned a major (by the end of 1943, he was a lieutenant-colonel) in a Special Services Unit of the United States Army. His earliest concept of the job to be done emerged as the definitive documentary series made during the war years. Between 1942 and 1944, seven fifty-minute training films were released under the umbrella title of *Why We Fight*. Each had a different subtitle: *Prelude to War, The Nazis Strike, Divide and Conquer, The Battle of Britain, The Battle of Russia, The Battle of China* and *War Comes to America*. Originally produced for the Army, all seven were soon being requisitioned by the Navy, the Marine Corps and the Coast Guard. The recognizable voice heard doing the narration belongs to actor Walter Huston, whose son John was a member of the Special Services Film Production Unit.

Capra had seen *Triumph of the Will* and profited by the experience. In an interview for *The Men Who Made the Movies* by Richard Schickel (Atheneum Books, 1975), Capra told the author:

> Leni Riefenstahl made what I think is the powerhouse propaganda piece for all time, a film called *Triumph of the Will*, which glorified the Nazi Party and in a sense deified Hitler. There was a lot of worry before I got an idea that might work. And the idea was to just fight back with their own words. I thought if our young soldiers could just hear what the enemy had to say, they would know why we were fighting without being told. That was the premise of the *Why We Fight* films.

Utilizing captured enemy footage, newsreels and animated maps, Capra's films graphically detail the rise of the Axis powers and show how their machinations were endangering the freedom-loving peoples of the world. An interesting sidelight to this series is that President Roosevelt, upon viewing *Prelude to War*, ordered this film into general release. It won the 1942 Academy Award as Best Documentary.

Another important contribution to the war effort made by the Special Services Unit under Capra is *The Negro Soldier*. Used as a training film to counteract the very real discrimination going on at the time, its message reads that we are one people and that there are no color lines in a foxhole. It would take a while before all branches of the military were desegregated, but this was a first step in the right direction. Capra also distinguished himself in the short subject category, as will be seen later on in this chapter.

Darryl F. Zanuck, the peripatetic head of Twentieth Century–Fox, craved action and was commissioned a lieutenant-colonel in the Signal Corps just after America entered the war. Using all the influence he could muster, he finagled his way from a tame job on Long Island to becoming senior liaison officer at the London headquarters of the British Army Film Production Unit. Still unhappy after a couple of overseas assignments which did nothing to satisfy his yen for adventure, he was posted to Gibraltar with instructions to film the invasion of North Africa from the American point of view. This he did with relish, and within three months he had completed *At the Front*. For a good part of the shooting schedule, he worked with famed director John Ford, who, although a commander in the navy, had been ordered to join the Zanuck unit. Only Darryl F. received credit for the film, however.

The Fox mogul recorded his North African stay in a diary and it was published under the title *Tunis Expedition*. The book received better reviews than did the motion picture.

By 1943, as previously mentioned, another moviemaker was in the military. While his famous father was narrating the *Why We Fight* series, John Huston was doing his bit abroad. *Report from the Aleutians*, *The Battle of San Pietro* (filmed in Italy) and *Let There Be Light* were made by the young director between 1943 and 1945.

As an American Air Force officer, German-born Academy Award winner William Wyler directed two of the finest documentary features of the war. *The Memphis Belle*, released in 1943, tells the story of the B-17's part in a raid over Germany and brings to the home front the realities of aerial combat, while *The Fighting Lady*, about an aircraft carrier, details the day-to day lives of the men aboard her and the dangers they face. For his efforts, Wyler was honored by both the French and American governments. (In 1990, Catherine Wyler, daughter of the legendary director, was co-producer of a fictional re-enactment of that bombing raid over Germany by the "Belle." Featured in the cast are Sean Astin, Matthew Modine and singer Harry Connick, Jr.)

Another giant of the entertainment industry, George Stevens joined the Signal Corps as head of a combat photography unit. His men covered the American Sixth Army campaign in North Africa, then went to Europe and were cited for their work during the Normandy landings on D-Day. In 1945, the unit further distinguished itself with a documentary filmed during the liberation of the infamous Dachau concentration camp. It was a searing indictment of the Nazi regime, the ultimate example of man's inhumanity to man.

Other moviemakers, in addition to those just named, gave their all in the struggle for peace, either as civilians or in the military. By war's end, over forty thousand industry personnel had served in the armed forces; added to this, the civilian resources of the studios in both manpower and materiel. Pettiness and competition were set aside for the duration as Hollywood rolled up its collective sleeves and went to work.

Besides those named previously, many other feature-length documentaries were produced, among them *The Battle of Midway* and *Africa, Prelude to Victory*, released in 1942, *War Department Report* and *Baptism of Fire* in 1943, the interesting *Resisting Enemy Interrogation* in 1944, plus *The True Glory* and *The Stillwell Road* in 1945. The last named is narrated by Ronald Reagan. The documentaries of the era were filmed under several different banners besides those of the regular Hollywood film industry. For instance, *The Battle of Midway* is listed as being produced by the U.S. Navy and Twentieth Century–Fox while another, *Africa, Prelude to Victory*, is credited to the March of Time. Then again, *Baptism Under Fire* was filmed under the auspices of the US Navy and *The War Department Report* by the Field Photographic Branch, Office of Strategic Services. It is not too confusing when keeping in mind that a presidential appointee to the War Department coordinated all film production.

Mention should also be made of some non–Hollywood films that document the battles fought by our allies which fired up their individual peoples with a sense of pride and determination. To name just three: *September, 1939*, produced by the Canadian government, *Moscow Strikes*

Back, filmed in Russia, and *Desert Victory*, a previously mentioned British endeavor. The latter, an especially well-made look at the North African campaign, was released to all Allied countries and became an effective piece of propaganda.

No less effective and perhaps even more so in the long run were the short subjects and newsreels which emerged during the half-decade between 1941 and 1945. These "mini-films," as they might be called today, did not have the luxury of time that their longer counterparts enjoyed; they had shorter shooting schedules and needed to tell their stories in more abbreviated forms.

Almost every phase of the war was covered, from the attack on Pearl Harbor to the victorious meeting of the Allies on the banks of the Elbe River in Germany and the signing of the peace treaty which ended the war in Japan. Both live and animated, short films go a long way in telling the story of the second worldwide conflict.

A comprehensive listing is quite impossible in a book such as this, but several examples may provide a clue to the psyche of the generation that lived through that era, to their attitudes, concepts and understandings of a time when America shed her wrap of isolation and joined with other freedom-loving nations in their struggles for peace.

By 1942, as in the case of the feature-length documentaries, production of short subjects was in high gear. Among the many film operations taken over by the army was the filming of a bi-weekly newsreel for those in the military. The brainchild of the previously mentioned Frank Capra, *The Army-Navy Screen Magazine* began to appear during the early part of 1943. The series was mainly informational, detailing major battles and events, and also interviewing important military personnel. The magazine became known as a forum for GIs when it began to encourage them to write and share their thoughts with others.

Among the first shorts released after Pearl Harbor were *The Price of Victory* and *Inside Fighting China*. Narrated by Vice-President Henry Wallace, the first mentioned is similar to the *Why We Fight* series in its theme and in its use of the enemy's own words in documentary footage. The second details the rise of Japanese imperialism, from the invasion of Manchuria to the Pearl Harbor attack. (No mention is made of the infighting going on in China between the American-backed Nationalist Chiang Kai Shek and the Communist revolutionists led by Mao Tse Tung. An uneasy truce held them together until the end of hostilities.)

Seven. Praise the Lord and Pass the Propaganda

As the war progressed, short subjects provided on-the-spot coverage of battles in the faraway places with strange-sounding names which would soon become footnotes in our nation's history books. One such film, *Life Line*, produced by the Army Signal Corps and released in 1943, details the capture of an island in the Solomon chain. So close was the camera to the action that the narrator apologizes for shakiness and underexposure of the footage.

Two related Signal Corps efforts were *Cape Gloucester, 7th Marines* and *5th Air Force Report from New Guinea*, one providing grim footage of men fighting the battle for New Guinea on land and the other detailing what had gone on in the air.

Many wartime shorts contained messages to the civilian home front exhorting them to do even more than they were doing for the war effort. *A Letter from Bataan* is a mini-drama in which actor Richard Arlen appears with Susan Hayward. Its message is simple: Wasting and hoarding are inimical to the winning of the war. (Rationing was in force soon after the onset of hostilities.) This film and one called *U.S. News Review Issue #2* may have hit home for certain Americans who were involved in the black market and other illegal practices.

The Rear Gunner is another dramatic short. In the cast are lieutenants Ronald Reagan and Burgess Meredith. The film, which serves to show how the Air Force trains its men, contains some very effective combat scenes.

By the beginning of 1944, with the war going our way, people on the home front began to take a quick end to the war for granted (the Battle of the Bulge was still several months away). In order to counteract this complacency, the government produced and released several short films. *Battle Wreckage* shows bullets, cartridges and grenades, tons of used post-battle materiel, "the hammered guts of war," left behind on D-Day and at other sites of armed conflict. It then urges those who built them not to slack off, that armaments still need to be produced. *The War Speeds Up*, narrated by Jose Ferrer, also asks the home front to "keep 'em coming."

It Can't Last, a bit different from the foregoing, is a dramatized story of two Americans from the same town. The older man is at home, enjoying a peaceful autumn afternoon, while the other, a downed pilot, clings desperately to a rubber raft "somewhere in the Pacific." The civilian has the feeling that that the war cannot last much longer; the camera then pans down to his feet for a shot of the evening paper whose front page carries the story of a combat mission during which one of our planes has been shot down. Simplistic, but highly effective.

Like the civilian in the film, many people, both at home and abroad, strongly suspected an end to the war by Christmas of 1944. The Battle of the Bulge proved that this was not to be. Before the fighting in the Ardennes Forest halted with the surrender of the German forces, heavy casualties had been reported. This was documented in *The Enemy Strikes*. Close-ups of dead GIs and captured footage of German soldiers smoking cigarettes taken from American bodies gave new impetus to the war effort at home.

The old cliché that one picture is worth a thousand words was put to even better use just after the war. The excesses of the Axis powers were documented for the world to see in all their brutality. Civilized people, who had closed their ears to reports of concentration camps and "final solutions," now saw footage of atrocities committed in the name of totalitarianism. Much of this footage had been captured; combined with documentaries shot by Allied combat photo units, the barbarism of Hitler and the Japanese warlords were on view for all to see, condemn and ultimately punish. The Germans in particular had been meticulous in detailing every aspect of the war, including their crimes against humanity; the Nazi-made films were included in shorts made soon after V-E Day.

Though most animated short films were not as somber as the above, they proved to be just as effective, especially in the field of propaganda. Walt Disney was the first producer of animated films to grasp the idea that a cartoon could be political and entertaining at the same time. He led the way for other animators like Leon Schlesinger, Paul Terry, Walter Lantz and the Fleischer Brothers, Max and Dave.

The energetic Walt set a frenetic pace for them and for himself by producing training, informational, patriotic and propagandistic films, both commercially and under contract to the armed forces, as well as to various government agencies. At the same time, the Disney Corporation was also working on such features as *Bambi, Saludos Amigos* and *The Three Caballeros*, the last two salutes to our Latin-American neighbors.

Topical references were not just a wartime phenomenon for animators. With the rise of authoritarian states and dictators, some of the cartoons of the 1930s had begun to take on new meanings. American audiences, seeing *The Three Little Pigs*, could either read "Old Man

Depression" or Adolf Hitler, the twin evils of the decade, into the character of the wolf. By 1942, the allegory was even clearer: In *Blitz Wolf*, a MGM release, three pigs confront a wolf named Adolf.

Upon America's entrance into the war, animators went into the propaganda business with both barrels blazing. Since most of the live-action releases were training- and combat-related, a great many of the animated shorts produced were relegated to home front topics. Though several satirized the Axis powers, the majority were about the civilian population which had to contend with such new or little experienced phenomena as the draft, rationing and shortages; also women in factories working the "swing shift," i.e., the evening work shift. The cartoons produced during this time were cleverly in tune with these concepts and give a humorous but accurate view of the home front.

America coped with her problems.

As the daze of Pearl Harbor wore off, caricatures of the Axis dictators and parodies of spy melodramas became more popular than ever. *The Ductators* (Warner Bros.) satirizes the rise of Hitler and Mussolini; both are portrayed as ducks. Into focus, in a "cameo appearance," swims a third duck, with buck-teeth and slanted eyes, an obvious reference to the Japanese warlords.

Another cartoon on the rise of the dictators is *Song of Victory* from Columbia and Dave Fleischer. Its opening title reads, "Any similarity between the Vulture, the Gorilla and the Hyena to certain dictators, either living or dead (we hope) is purely intentional."

Destruction, Inc., released by Paramount, features the ever-popular Superman breaking up a ring of saboteurs at a Metropolis munitions plant. With the previously noted capture by the FBI of a Nazi espionage ring during the early part of the war, sabotage had proven to be a real menace to our defense.

In Warners' *Confusions of a Nutsy Spy*, (taking its name from the studio's 1939 production *Confessions of a Nazi Spy*), Porky Pig captures a spy, known as the "Missing Lynx," who is trying to blow up a bridge. In *Patriotic Pooches*, a Paul Terry cartoon, dogs are inducted into the military. A small white canine is rejected because he is too small, but he rounds up three Nazi pigs, including one named Adolf, and is rewarded. Though a satire, it is somewhat of a salute to the K-9 Corps, which trained and used dogs throughout the war.

Conditions on the home front were reprised in such shorts as *Cin-

derella Goes to a Party (Columbia) and *Swing Shift Cinderella* (MGM). Both cartoons have the original fairy tale as their basis and contain references to women in defense work. *Family Fables* (Warner Bros.) and *The Early Bird Dood It* (MGM) are about the woes of rationing. *Yankee Doodle Swing Shift* (Universal) and *All Out for "V"* (Twentieth Century–Fox) are cartoon versions of the production lines so vital to the war effort. In *Yankee Doodle Swing Shift*, a band of jive cats goes to work in a factory and in *All Out for "V,"* war comes to a peaceful woodland and the animal residents mobilize for defense.

Nothing was sacred as the animators went about their business. Even "The Battle of the Baritones," a radio program of the 1940s, came in for its share of lampooning. *Swooner Crooner* (Warner Bros.) features Porky Pig as the manager of the "Flockheed Egg (read Lockheed Aircraft) Factory." His hens, distracted by Frankie Rooster, are not producing enough eggs, but soon old Bing Rooster sets them on course again. The cartoon not only satirized the Sinatra-Crosby "rivalry," it was also a send-up of wartime factory conditions and the women who went off to work while their men went off to war.

One of the most popular American cartoons of the war years, *Any Bonds Today*, a post–Pearl Harbor release sponsored by the government, is based upon the Irving Berlin hit tune of the same name. The ubiquitous Bugs Bunny (voice supplied by actor-comedian Mel Blanc) is "starred," exhorting the audience to aid in the war effort by buying defense bonds and stamps. Bugs is seen first in the garb of Uncle Sam and then on bended knees *a la* Al Jolson at the finale. Defense bonds had been sold for several months; with the outbreak of hostilities, they became known as war bonds.

Walt Disney won an Academy Award in 1942 for the equally popular *Der Fuhrer's Face*. Donald Duck dreams that he is a citizen of the Third Reich. Upon waking up in his own bed, he hugs a miniature Statue of Liberty. This famous cartoon was greatly helped along by the title tune which had been recorded by the zany Spike Jones and his City Slickers. The record sold one million copies and became one of the band's greatest hits.

The Brits had their entry in the short subject category, Their most famous and oft-seen short of the entire war is *Schickelgruber Doing the Lambeth Walk*, released in 1944. With typical British wit and some clever editing of newsreel footage, Hitler and his goose-stepping soldiers are seen "doing their thing" to a recording of "The Lambeth Walk," a popular English tune of the day.

Documentaries, newsreels and animated films made substantial and essential contributions to the war effort. They informed the public, educated the military and, with humor, chronicled the very real problems of the home front. It was a heady time for the movie capital. Its wartime accomplishments should never be underestimated.

As previously noted, it was not only on the battlefields or behind the camera that Hollywood fought. When morale needed boosting and when money had to be raised, its citizens were called upon and, time and time again, covered themselves with glory. In our next chapter, we'll take a closer look at these "soldiers in greasepaint."

Chapter Eight

Soldiers in Greasepaint

Letters from home were the most important morale boosters of the war. Family news from parents, husbands, wives and sweethearts kept servicemen and servicewomen going during many a tough battle. Photographs, dog-eared from handling, were as precious to them as food and water. Postal workers stayed busy sorting and shipping V-Mail letters to different parts of the world.

Running a close second to "mail call" were the morale-building efforts of the film industry. Civilian Hollywood went to war in the best way it could. To quote from *The Hollywood Reporter*, an industry paper:

> Aside from the rare, purely social event, much of the forties decade was devoted to war work. There was hardly a private party that was not simultaneously a benefit for a worthy cause. Stars spent entire weekends and time in between films on bond-selling tours or visits to camps and/or hospitals. Almost every top celebrity made at least one junket overseas. Some had their bags perpetually packed. Their arms resembled pincushions from the numerous shots they needed to keep them from getting strange "native" diseases.

Coordinating all of these activities was the Hollywood Victory Committee for Stage, Screen and Radio.

Bond-selling tours and premieres helped to raise dollars for defense. A September 1942 bond drive brought several Hollywood stars to Washington where they auctioned off personal mementos in order to raise money. At the same time, a two-hour bi-coastal radio show was broadcast to publicize this "billion dollar" drive. War bond premieres were held with films supplied gratis; the price of admission was the purchase of one or more war bonds.

Short subjects asking the public to buy war bonds and stamps were filmed for release to the nation's theaters. Just before a scheduled program started, the house lights were dimmed and a popular performer was shown on the screen. Stepping out of character, the star talked about the war effort and how "each and every one of us must dig down deep in our pockets and give." Often war footage was used to demonstrate what the money was being used for. When the star had finished speaking, the lights came on and collection canisters were sent along each row.

The All-Star Bond Rally, produced by Twentieth Century–Fox for the Office of War Information, is an example of this type of short. It features master of ceremonies Bob Hope and a celebrity cast including Bing Crosby, Harpo Marx, Frank Sinatra, Harry James and wife Betty Grable plus pin-up cameo bits by Jeanne Crain, June Haver and Linda Darnell, among others.

The pin-up was a phenomenon of the war years. Sent by request to the GIs, posted above bunks, pasted on locker doors and in the cockpits of bombers, these photos brought a bit of Americana to weary and lonesome men far from home. Many a Hollywood beauty posed for pin-up pictures, but the two most famous photos feature blonde Betty Grable in a white bathing suit, peering back at us over her shoulder, while red-headed Rita Hayworth posed for a *Life* Magazine layout in a black and white satin nightgown. That was the stuff of which dreams were made, the "shots " seen around the world, from the sands of Africa to the cosmopolitan cities of Europe to the steamy jungles of the Pacific.

The previously mentioned *Army-Navy Screen Magazine* shorts were morale building as well as informational. Within a few months of its inception, the series began a feature called "By Request." Many GI wishes were complied with via film, including one fellow who wanted Carole Landis to sigh into a microphone. The blonde actress happily complied. Another serviceman wanted to hear the sound of a steak being pan-fried by Lana Turner. His wish was her command.

Under the aegis of the "Victory Committee," the United Services Organization Inc., more familiarly known as the USO, was formed to provide recreation for the men and women in the armed forces. Its camp show units produced much-needed entertainment for those in the military based stateside, while its hospital units sent the stars to visit the sick and the wounded. To the latter it mattered little whether these personalities could sing or dance. The fact that these famous people came to the hospital wards, perhaps just to shake hands or to chat for a minute or two, was sometimes better than all the medicine and therapy they were receiving.

By the time the war ended in 1945, the USO had presented almost three hundred thousand camp shows and had played to a combined audience of over one hundred sixty million servicemen and -women.

Radio also had some of its finest moments during World War II. Top stars of the era, among them Bob Hope, Jack Benny, Edgar Bergen and Charlie McCarthy, Eddie Cantor, Red Skelton and bandleader Kay Kyser, all wanting to do their bit, arranged to have their shows broadcast from a different camp each week. Kyser, with his gimmick "The Kollege of Musical Knowledge," was especially popular with the military, using GIs on the show and awarding prizes of war bonds for correct answers to the easy questions asked.

Shows sponsored by tobacco companies were also very popular. Cartons of cigarettes were donated to service personnel both at home and abroad. *Your Hit Parade*, which highlighted the top songs of the week, gave away thousands of Lucky Strike cigarettes to each branch of our fighting forces on a rotating basis.

Name bands and singers entertained at the bi-coastal canteens (Stage Door and Hollywood), in hospitals and at services bases. They also made broadcasts which were beamed overseas by the Armed Forces Radio Network. Several famous musicians volunteered or were drafted into Special Services Units and performed wherever and whenever needed. Bandleader Glenn Miller lost his life when his plane crashed over the English Channel on his way to France. There are many fascinating theories as to how the popular Miller lost his life, but this is the official version of the incident.

As the fighting troops moved to foreign shores, so did the Hollywood troops. Armed Forces Radio brought a variety of transcribed programs to our personnel overseas: comedy, drama, musical and military, but it was the in-person appearances of the stars which did the most to build up the morale of our fighting forces all over the world. Some of the widely traveled performers included Bob Hope, Al Jolson, Jack Benny, Joe E. Brown, John Wayne, Humphrey Bogart, Paulette Goddard and the "Four Jills in a Jeep," Martha Raye, Kay Francis, Mitzi Mayfair and Carole Landis. Their globe-hopping jaunts covered the world, from Goddard's trek over the Himalayas in the China-Burma-India theaters and Wayne's tour of Australia and nearby Pacific bases to those of Bogart and Marlene Dietrich (heading separate shows) in Italy and North Africa.

Eight. Soldiers in Greasepaint

Often these shows took place, not in comfortable theaters, but on a platform laid between two trucks or some other kind of makeshift stage. The performers ate GI food, slept in GI tents and wore GI fatigues when not on stage. They catered to the needs of those craving entertainment and were rewarded by the applause of men and women daily risking their lives.

If many of the non-musical or non-comedic performers were concerned about what they could do in front of an audience, these qualms were put to rest, as witness this quote from John Wayne in an interview upon his return from a three-month tour of the Pacific: "I was worried about not being able to do anything on stage, but I didn't realize just how much a familiar face means to them."

Many of the stars provided a link between those in battle and their loved ones back home by delivering personal messages from overseas to anxious families. The performers felt that this was the least they could do for those giving so much.

Joe E. Brown gave more than time and talent to the war effort. The rubber-faced comic, who had lost a son on a bombing mission, was the first "Soldier in Greasepaint" to perform in Alaska, the Aleutians and in Indo-China. His homely familiar face and wide grin were a welcome sight, spelling home to youngsters in these remote areas.

Brown's enormous popularity with the servicemen and -women was matched by that of Bob Hope. "Old Ski Nose," and his troupe, consisting of singer Frances Langford, comedian Jerry Colonna, dancer Patti Thomas and musician Tony Romano. They made several overseas trips; by war's end, they had played to over six million men and women in Europe, Africa, Asia, Alaska, the Aleutians and the Caribbean. Whether top brass or lowest dogface, it didn't matter to Hope. They were all Americans and he was trying to give them a couple of light moments while they engaged in the deadly game of war. As Hope once noted, "It was pretty rugged, but it was worth it." At some bases, the troupe played to small numbers; at others, thousands were in the audience. Their largest crowd, according to a press release at the time, was at Pearl Harbor. More than fifty thousand military personnel were assembled at the naval base where it had all begun.

For Hope and his group of entertainers, rank had no privilege. To quote from the reminiscences of a 25th US Army Division GI, a veteran of the Pacific theater of war who saw action on New Caledonia, on Guadalcanal and in the Gulf of Leyte:

Bob Hope and his gang did a show for us. When he saw that only officers were occupying the front rows, he calmly said there would be no performance unless the wounded were brought up front — the officers had to vacate their seats. Hope won my respect that day.

Another tireless performer who toured wherever and whenever possible was Al Jolson. The famed "Mammy" singer was delighted to learn that the boys remembered him and the songs he had made famous. After the war, Jolson's career was revitalized and two films were made about his life before he died in 1950.

Some Hollywood ladies were not far behind Hope, Brown and Jolson in popularity with the military. German-born Marlene Dietrich, whom Hitler had promised the sun, moon and stars if she'd return to Germany and its flagging film industry, was a tireless worker for the Hollywood Victory Committee. She later stated that one of the biggest thrills of her war work came in June of 1944 when she announced the news that the Normandy invasion had begun to an audience of GIs at a base in Italy. As she wryly noted, "They went wild, but not over me."

The actual North African tour of four Hollywood performers became the basis of a 1944 film titled *Four Jills in a Jeep* (see Chapter Nine). The group included the disparate talents of dramatic actress Kay Francis, loud-mouthed singer-comedienne Martha Raye, dancer Mitzi Mayfair and golden-haired performer Carole Landis. The mediocrity of the film, as will be seen later on in this narrative, cannot undo the contributions of this quartet who gave of their time and energy. (Landis met a soldier while on the tour and married him. This union did not last, but it was well publicized at the time.)

As mentioned previously, raven-haired Paulette Goddard toured the China-Burma-India theater of war. Hers was the first group to visit these out of-the-way bases and she was the first white woman seen in some of the areas to which it traveled. In a thirty-eight thousand-mile trek, she saw first-hand the need for entertainment in the fighting zones. Like the tours of Hope, Dietrich, and others, Goddard's war work, and that of several other entertainers, many of whom are unknown today, brought a brief respite to those who needed it most with a minimum of publicity. To quote from the 1993 Zebra Books publication *Over Here, Over There—The Andrews Sisters and the USO Stars in World War II* by Maxene Andrews of the singing trio:

Eight. Soldiers in Greasepaint

Performers of every kind did all they could — singers and dancers, musicians playing both popular and classical music, comedians, actors and actresses and athletes. There were ballet dancers too, and mimics and jugglers, and artists who sketched the faces of wounded GIs in hospitals far from home that would be sent to their families.

As reported by many performers upon their return from overseas, motion pictures ranked high on the list of GI priorities. In every theater of operations, commanding officers stressed the need for screen entertainment and the film studios kept them coming. Another quote from the 25th Division:

> It rained the night we saw *Two Girls and a Sailor*. Who cared that we were sitting in mud and soaked to the skin? Seeing Gloria De Haven and June Allyson up there and hearing Harry James play his trumpet made us forget for just a little while.

In essence then, as America went to war, so did the film capital. Its war was waged against the loneliness, homesickness and battle fatigue that many were experiencing for the very first time in their lives. The industry raised money for and donated the latest films to the war effort. But above all, Hollywoodians gave of themselves. Those not soldiers in the military became "Soldiers in Greasepaint." They gave at the Hollywood Canteen and they gave at hospitals and army camps at home and abroad. They traveled to places they had never heard of, slogged in mud up to their knees and often did shows not very far from enemy lines. But for every last one of them, as Bob Hope had remarked, any effort made was "worth it." They would to the end of their days remember the thanks and appreciation of those to whom they played.

Chapter Nine

The Longest Day

By daybreak of June 6, 1944, the most ambitious undertaking of the war had begun. From English bases across the Channel came a mighty armada, consisting of more than one hundred seventy-five thousand men, over five hundred ocean-going vessels and upwards of nine thousand war planes, preceded by airborne paratroopers, to storm the German-held French coast of Normandy. The Allies had heeded the sage advice of Churchill: "In times of war, Lady Truth is so precious that she should be surrounded by a Bodyguard of Lies."

The landings were successful; by a series of brilliant ruses, the Germans were duped into believing that the invasion would take place at Pas de Calais to the north, at the narrowest part of the Channel. But there were a tremendous number of casualties, many of them on the beaches, on that "longest day" (General Eisenhower had prepared a communiqué taking full responsibility for the failure of the operation if that should be the case). Within twelve weeks, however, the Allies had overrun Normandy, fought their way into the Brittany section of France and assisted in the liberation of that country.

At the same time, Allied units on Italian soil were in the process of taking Rome after establishing a beachhead on Anzio and enduring weeks of heavy fighting at Monte Cassino. Germans living in Berlin were being subjected to daily raids by American bombers, and on the ground, we had begun to push towards the enemy's frontier.

On July 20, the world was stunned to learn that an unsuccessful attempt to assassinate Adolf Hitler had been made. In the purge which followed, many lost their lives, including Erwin Rommel. Unlike those who were brutally tortured before being murdered, the popular field marshal was given the "option" of committing suicide. To save his wife and son from horrific reprisals, he did not resist this order. At his state funeral, it was disclosed that the Desert Fox had "died of his war wounds."

Although the main Allied threat took place on the European continent, American forces were also heavily engaged in the war against Japan. Highlights in this sector included mid-spring attacks on the Marshall Islands and the October invasion of the Philippines. By December, troops under the command of General MacArthur were twenty-five miles from the Philippine capital city of Manila. As he had promised, the general had returned.

The main focus of the war soon shifted back to the European theater of operations: The Germans launched a last ditch offensive in the Ardennes Forest of Belgium. "The Battle of the Bulge" took the Allies by surprise. Fierce fighting, which resulted in heavy casualties on both sides, continued for a couple of weeks into the new year until the Germans were routed and began their final retreat eastward.

The political news in Washington was that President Roosevelt, seeking election to an unprecedented fourth term, had sanctioned United States participation in a conference calling for the establishment of a worldwide organization dedicated to peace. The organization would henceforth be known as the United Nations.

The "political" news in Hollywood centered on one item: George Murphy had become the president of the Screen Actors Guild. By the 1960s, his billing read "United States Senator Murphy." (As is well-known, Ronald Reagan had also served as Guild president as he climbed the political stairway to the presidency.)

Though the major emphasis in Hollywood was still on the war effort, town gossips Louella Parsons and Hedda Hopper had much to tell the fans who avidly read their daily columns.

Betty Grable and Harry James became the proud parents of a baby daughter whom they named Victoria. Actress Virginia Gilmore married a foreign-born stage actor, one Yul Brynner — who later went on to great fame in the stage and screen versions of *The King and I*. Eventually, both of these marriages would end up in the divorce courts.

An interesting bit of trivia was *Look* magazine's nomination of Hedy Lamarr, Ingrid Bergman, Gene Tierney and Linda Darnell as having the most beautiful faces in Hollywood. The number of noses put out of joint as a result of this "announcement" can only be imagined.

The less happy side of the news emanating from the movie capital dealt with the several divorce suits that were filed throughout the year. Judy Garland, Deanna Durbin and Veronica Lake were among those telling their marital woes to the judge. (Durbin and Lake already had their next mates picked out.) Lucille Ball and Desi Arnaz split up, but later reconciled, as did Cary Grant and heiress Barbara Hutton. The harmony between "Cash and Cary" did not last for long, and the debonair Grant was soon a bachelor once again.

Over at Warner Bros., Howard Hawks began production on *To Have and Have Not* (1944), based upon an Ernest Hemingway novel. The film starred Humphrey Bogart as Harry Morgan, a tough skipper for hire on the island of Martinique, and a tall slim newcomer named Lauren Bacall as Marie, stranded on the island and singing in a bar that Harry frequents. The setting of the film was supposed to have been Cuba, but it was changed to Martinique so as to give no offense to the Latin American republics. Instead of Hemingway's Chinese immigrants being smuggled into the United States, it is members of the French Resistance (being pursued by Nazi agents) who are to be smuggled into Martinique. In the cast are Walter Brennan, Sheldon Leonard and songwriter-singer-actor Hoagy Carmichael. The latter and lyricist Johnny Mercer wrote the song "How Little We Know" which is sung by Carmichael and then reprised by Bacall.

The on-screen fireworks between the forty-four-year-old "Bogie" and Hawks' nineteen-year-old Bronx, New York–born discovery carried over into real life and in 1945 the two were married. This unlikely union lasted until Bogart's tragic and untimely death in 1957.

Though there was a decline in the Hollywood production of films showing actual combat, many war-related movies were still being released in 1944: spy dramas, musicals, comedies, romances and propaganda films. These, plus the productions not dealing with the war, made for a varied menu during this last full year of conflict.

We begin our 1944 journey with *Candlelight in Algeria*, which concerns the meeting of Allied leaders at a secret rendezvous on the Algerian coast in preparation for the landings in North Africa. A British agent and an American woman defeat the efforts of enemy agents to obtain a roll of film which details where the meeting is to take place. Filmed in Britain, but released by Twentieth Century–Fox, the production stars James Mason and combines fact with fiction.

Like Mason, George Sanders was a versatile English-born actor. In *Action in Arabia* (RKO), he stars as a newspaperman in Damascus investigating the demise of a colleague. With the aid of an Allied agent, he not only finds the murderer but also exposes an attempt to blow up the Suez Canal. Virginia Bruce is the lady agent. Others in the cast are Lenore Aubert, Gene Lockhart, Robert Armstrong and H. B. Warner.

In their final 1943 films. both Paul Lukas and Veronica Lake had been on the side of the Allies, he winning Academy honors for his role in *Watch on the Rhine*, she playing a doomed heroic nurse in *So Proudly We Hail!* By 1944, the two had crossed over to the other side (on celluloid only), Lukas in Columbia's *Address Unknown* and Lake in Paramount's *The Hour Before the Dawn*.

Address Unknown is the engrossing story of a German-American art dealer who espouses the Nazi cause while on a trip to his native land just before the outbreak of war. His fate is sealed, however, when he begins to receive incriminating letters from the United States; they are intercepted by the Gestapo who then brand him an enemy of the Third Reich.

In Lake's film, which is based upon a novel by Somerset Maugham and updated to World War II, she plays a German spy who poses as a refugee and marries an Englishman (Franchot Tone). As in *So Proudly We Hail!*, the blonde actress does not survive at the end of the film: Tone discovers he has married a spy and strangles her. This time, Veronica was hissed instead of applauded by American audiences.

Like Lukas and Lake, Canadian-born Alexander Knox undertook two roles that were diametrically opposed, but his occurred during the same year. He played the title role in the Twentieth Century–Fox production *Wilson*, a biography of American President Woodrow Wilson, and shortly afterward he was signed by Columbia Pictures to star in *None Shall Escape*. In this stark drama, he portrays a Nazi officer on trial for war crimes whose career, shown in flashbacks, symbolizes all that is abhorrent in Hitler's brutal regime. An embittered World War I crippled veteran, he returns to his home. Losing his fiancée because he espouses the Nazi cause, he leaves his village and joins the Nazi party. After the outbreak of war in 1939, he comes back to wreak havoc on the villagers who forced him to leave. Also in the cast are Marsha Hunt, Henry Travers and Kurt Kreuger.

An English locale and a wartime spy motif adapted from a story by famed suspense novelist Graham Greene make *Ministry of Fear* an inter-

Ministry of Fear: Ray Milland and Marjorie Reynolds star in this tale of espionage and intrigue. Carl Esmond is sprawled on the floor.

esting movie. Directed by Fritz Lang, the Paramount production is one of the better screen efforts in the spy genre, good enough to win a place on several critics "ten best movies" lists. Ray Milland stars as a man released from a mental hospital who becomes involved in a spy ring when he purchases a cake at a village fair. There has been a case of mistaken identity involved in the sale and the well-plotted tale goes on from there. All-American Marjorie Reynolds, with an improbable foreign accent, plays the woman to whom Milland turns for help; she does not know that her own brother, played by Carl Esmond, is involved in espionage. Also in the cast are Hillary Brooke and Dan Duryea.

Another Columbia contribution to the 1944 spy game genre, *Secret Command* stars Pat O'Brien as an FBI agent who learns of a plot to sabotage a West Coast shipyard. and gets a job there to find out as much as he can, complete with "wife," "children" and a house. The film ends with the plot foiled and with O'Brien marrying his "wife" (Carole Landis). Others in the cast include Ruth Warrick, Chester Morris, Barton MacLane and Tom Tully.

A drama of an entirely different nature is set in wartime England. MGM's *The White Cliffs of Dover* is the warmly sentimental story of an American woman, played by Irene Dunne, who loses her British husband in the first World War and her son in the second. In the supporting cast are veteran actor Frank Morgan and young Roddy McDowall plus rising stars Van Johnson and Peter Lawford. The popularity of the film was immeasurably aided by a hit recording of the title song by the Glenn Miller Orchestra.

Another film with an English background is *The Way Ahead*. Directed by famed British director Carol Reed and with an all–English cast including David Niven, Peter Ustinov, Trevor Howard and Stanley Holloway, the film is the story of a group of raw recruits who come together and form a cohesive fighting unit. Originally intended as a training film, it was co-scripted by Ustinov.

One of the most fascinating dramas to come out of the war years is *Lifeboat*. Directed by Alfred Hitchcock, the action of this story by John Steinbeck is confined to a small boat in the vast Atlantic. Its characters are a group of survivors from a torpedoed American freighter and the German captain of the attacking submarine which has also been sunk. The convenient sinking of the latter does not take away from the high drama of how these disparate people cope with their situation. Starred are Walter Slezak as the Nazi captain and Tallulah Bankhead as a lady journalist. William Bendix, Hume Cronyn, John Hodiak and Canada Lee lend strong support to the stars. For her performance, Bankhead received the New York Film Critics Award while Hitchcock and Steinbeck were honored with Oscar nominations. Neither man won.

From the same studio came another adventure from the world of cinematic warfare, *Tampico*. Edward G, Robinson is cast as an oil tanker captain who rescues a girl (Lynn Bari) after her ship has been sunk by an enemy sub. He marries her and as the plot thicken, his ship is sunk. Though his wife is under suspicion for the deed as she has lost her identification, the captain finds the real culprit in the person of his first mate, played by Victor McLaglen, who is a German agent. Several scenes were filmed in the Mexican port of Tampico.

In the previously mentioned *Lifeboat*, Slezak is the prototype of the

Nazi fanatic who vows to follow his leaders to the end. Paramount's *The Hitler Gang* details the rise of the group of misfits who had led their people to Armageddon. The production strove for accuracy and was well-researched; fact in this case proved more lurid than fiction. Starred is Hitler look-alike Robert Watson and he is aided by Martin Kosleck as Goebbels, Alexander Pope as Hermann Göring, Luis Van Rooten as Heinrich Himmler and Victor Varconi as Rudolf Hess. A reviewer called the film "a devastating history on the rise of National Socialism."

How much the Hitler gang had indoctrinated the people of Germany is the subject of RKO's *The Master Race*, wherein a fanatic German officer arrives in a Belgian village disguised as a Belgian patriot and tries to spread disunity wherever he can, hoping to keep the concept of the "master race" alive. Featured in the cast are George Coulouris, Osa Massen, Lloyd Bridges and Carl Esmond.

On the lighter side is the fanciful *Passport to Destiny*, a 1944 RKO entry, most of which takes place in Germany. Elsa Lanchester is an English charwoman convinced that a charm given to her by her late husband renders her impervious to harm; she therefore decides to assassinate Hitler. Although this "mission" is, of course, not accomplished — many had tried, as we shall see later on in our journey — our intrepid heroine manages to get involved in the German underground and is arrested. The conclusion of the film finds the lady on her way back to England in a German plane piloted by a member of the German underground. This was a relatively minor film, but the performance of its star raises it up a notch.

The Pacific theater of war had *its* share of war-related feature films in 1944. By this time, government reports of Japanese atrocities in dealing with prisoners of war were made public. The Twentieth Century–Fox production *The Purple Heart* is the fact-based story of eight Americans shot down during the famous 1942 Doolittle raid over Tokyo and tried by a military court. During the trial, various tortures were used to get the men to "confess" and also to pry military information from them. The prisoners did not give in to their captors and were found guilty and summarily executed. In the film, one of the judges, played by Chinese actor Richard Loo, commits suicide because he has been unsuccessful in breaking the prisoners down. The film, produced and co-written by Fox head Darryl Zanuck using a pseudonym, stars Dana Andrews, Richard Conte and Farley Granger and was, at the time, a fitting tribute to the bravery of Americans captured in the line of duty.

The Purple Heart: Prosecutor Richard Loo (center), along with three unidentified Asian actors, tries eight American airmen, who were shot down in a raid over Tokyo. Front row, from left: Dana Andrews, Sam Levene, Donald Berry, and an unidentified actor. Back row: two unidentified actors, Farley Granger, and Richard Conte.

Like *The Purple Heart*, the previously mentioned MGM production *Thirty Seconds Over Tokyo* is concerned with the bombardiers of the Doolittle raid. Unlike the somber *Purple Heart*, the theme of the second is triumphant; the success of the mission had been well-documented long before the movie's release. While the film's chief asset is Spencer Tracy's portrayal of the famed general, moviegoers also got to see three up-and-coming actors in important roles: Van Johnson, Robert Walker and Robert Mitchum.

The war against the Japanese is the subject of two films released in 1944: *The Fighting Seabees* from Republic and *Dragon Seed*, an MGM production. The first stars John Wayne as head of a construction team building fortifications in the South Pacific. As in any Wayne epic, major or minor, there is an abundance of action which does not in the least deter "Duke" in his amorous pursuit of Susan Hayward to the consternation of the film's third star Dennis O'Keefe. In the cast is William

Frawley, who would go on to television immortality as Fred Mertz on the *I Love Lucy* series and then Bub O'Casey on *My Three Sons*.

Dragon Seed, based upon the bestseller by Pearl S. Buck, takes place before and during the 1937 Japanese invasion of China. The production pays tribute to the Chinese peasantry fighting for their land and for their lives; this would continue until the defeat of Japan. More interesting than the film itself is its cast which includes Katharine Hepburn, Walter Huston, Turhan Bey, Aline MacMahon, Agnes Moorehead and J. Carrol Naish, none of whom are of Chinese descent. The movie premiered at Radio City Music Hall in New York City and drew upwards of one million customers to the world-famous theater.

Though war-related dramatic films remained popular during 1944, it was the musical movie genre that moviegoers mostly wanted to see, regardless of the fact that many were mediocre in quality.

A case in point is *Pin-Up Girl* from Twentieth Century–Fox, which stars Betty Grable, Martha Raye and Joe E. Brown. The flimsy plot revolves around a Washington secretary (with show business aspirations) who falls in love with a naval hero. He barely knows she exists until she doffs her glasses and lets her hair down. The title was a come-on, cashing on Miss Betty's popularity with the GIs. The critics felt there was too little comedy, the guys in uniform felt there was not enough leg.

In another minor war-related film musical called *Meet the People* (MGM), the action takes place in a shipyard at which a movie star, played by Lucille Ball, takes a job for reasons of publicity. When she falls for a co-worker (Dick Powell), her motives undergo a radical change. Also on hand are the orchestras of Spike Jones and Vaughn Monroe plus studio contract players Virginia O'Brien, Bert Lahr, Rags Ragland and June Allyson. The last named became Mrs. Dick Powell shortly after filming was completed.

The most incongruous teaming of 1944 had to be that of laid-back Bing Crosby and frenetic Betty Hutton in a Paramount offering titled *Here Come the Waves*. As if one Hutton is not enough, the bombastic blonde plays twins in this lightweight musical salute. The crooner-turned-gob gets the quieter sister while rival Sonny Tufts settles for the kook. The highlight of the film is Bing's rendition of the Johnny Mercer-Harold Arlen hit song, "Accentuate the Positive."

While Crosby and Tufts were in a fictitious story taking place in a naval training station, *See Here, Private Hargrove* was based upon the misadventures of real-life GI Marion Hargrove. Relating the trials and tribulations of life in an army camp, Hargrove turned out a bestseller which was promptly made into a successful film by MGM with Robert Walker starred in the title role and featuring Keenan Wynn as his conniving buddy. The love interest is supplied by Donna Reed, with the supporting cast headed by Robert Benchley and Chill Wills. Though perpetually in and out of trouble, Hargrove managed to "graduate" from boot camp and even move up in rank. A sequel, *What Next, Corporal Hargrove?* with Walker again starred and Wynn featured, was released by Metro in 1945. This time the boys are cutting up in France.

Four Jills in a Jeep and *Two Girls and a Sailor* have already been mentioned, although briefly, in these pages. The only redeeming feature in *Jills* is the morale-building intent of their actual tour. Had the trek of the four ladies (Francis, Raye, Landis and Mayfair) been produced as a documentary, it might have made for a far better film; the talents of guest performers Betty Grable, Alice Faye and Carmen Miranda, who were not even part of the tour, are poorly interpolated into the plotline and are thoroughly wasted, as is crooner Dick Haymes, who made his film debut as a singing serviceman.

On the other hand, *Two Girls and a Sailor,* enjoyed so much by the men of the 25th, is a bright, tuneful film from the sound stages of MGM. June Allyson, Gloria De Haven and Van Johnson are seen in the title roles, while the great Jimmy Durante supplies a bit of pathos and lots of laughter as a long-forgotten vaudeville comic. In the context of the plot, the girls inherit an empty old building, find Jimmy there and open a canteen for lonely servicemen (by the end of the film, each girl has found her own private serviceman — Van Johnson for June, Tom Drake for Gloria). Guest stars include Lena Horne, Jose Iturbi, Virginia O'Brien, trumpeter Harry James and Gracie Allen, who performs a riotous "One Finger Concerto" with full orchestral accompaniment.

Something for the Boys from Twentieth Century–Fox tells a similar story, but in different fashion. Three cousins (Vivian Blaine, Carmen Miranda and Michael O'Shea) inherit an old plantation and turn it into a home for wives of servicemen. In order to pay for the upkeep of the place, they devise a theatrical production, which allows Blaine and Miranda to strut their stuff. Featured in the cast is an up-and-coming young singer named Perry Como. The crooner would go on to make two films with Vivian Blaine, *Doll Face* in 1945 and *If I'm Lucky* in 1946, both for Twentieth Century–Fox. His last film was *Words and Music* for MGM in 1948. He went on to a spectacular career in the recording industry and on television.

Fox again put the theme of servicemen's wives into their production of *In the Meantime, Darling*. Jeanne Crain stars as a wealthy girl who marries an army officer (Frank Latimore) and becomes a camp follower, traveling with him as he is sent from base to base. She is soon disgruntled by having to find living accommodations in crowded conditions and wants her father (Eugene Pallette) to use his influence in getting her husband a permanent posting. This causes a rift between the young couple, but all is forgiven when the wife accepts the reality of wartime conditions.

The "reel" canteen of *Two Girls and a Sailor* brings to the fore the two real ones, established during the war; their morale-building efforts have already been discussed and mention has been made of one of the films they inspired, 1943's *Stage Door Canteen*. Also as stated previously, a salute to its West Coast counterpart followed in 1944. *Hollywood Canteen*, a Warner Bros. production, features practically every star under contract to the studio at the time, including canteen organizers Bette Davis and John Garfield. The plot concerns a soldier (Robert Hutton) who comes to the canteen and finds his dream girl in actress Joan Leslie (Miss Leslie was also under contract to the studio at the time). Among the stars contributing their talents are Jane Wyman, Jack Benny, Eddie Cantor, Jack Carson, Ida Lupino, Joan Crawford, Barbara Stanwyck and cowboy star Roy Rogers in a sequence with Trigger, his famous palomino. Roy introduces Cole Porter's "Don't Fence Me In," which became a huge hit for Rogers as well as for Bing Crosby and the Andrews Sisters. Interestingly enough, "Don't Fence Me In" was not nominated for an Oscar; a lesser-known tune, "Sweet Dreams Sweetheart," from the film was, but lost to "Swinging on a Star" from Paramount's *Going My Way*.

Universal put out their version of the all-star extravaganza with *Follow the Boys*. The plot has George Raft married to dancer Vera Zorina. They separate and Raft then devotes his time and efforts to organize a Hollywood Victory Committee. (Reel life followed real life: A Hollywood Victory Committee was organized shortly after the war had begun.) The finale has Raft and Zorina together again. Featured in the film are many of the Universal contract players including Randolph Scott, Turhan Bey, Noah Beery, Jr., Nigel "Dr. Watson" Bruce, Lon Chaney, Jr., Andy

Devine, Susannah Foster, and Thomas Gomez, but the highlights are its specialty and musical numbers: Orson Welles sawing Marlene Dietrich in half, W. C. Fields doing a pool table routine, Peggy Ryan and Donald O'Conner in a specialty dance number, "I'll Get By" sung by Dinah Shore, "I'll See You in My Dreams," sung by Jeanette MacDonald, "Beer Barrel Polka" sung by the Andrew Sisters and Chopin's "Polonaise in A Flat Major" played by Artur Rubinstein.

Just as a parallel has been drawn between the two canteen films, one can be seen when discussing *Wing and a Prayer* and *Winged Victory*, both from Twentieth Century–Fox. *Wing and a Prayer* tells the story of an aircraft carrier and her involvement in the Pacific theater of war. Before production started, director Henry Hathaway was given permission to spend some time aboard a carrier and took from the experience some actual footage that was used in the film. Don Ameche, Dana Andrews, William Eythe, Charles Bickford and Sir Cedric Hardwicke are featured in the highly realistic motion picture. A song of the era took its title from the film. Among the lyrics is the phrase, "Tho' there's one motor gone, we can still carry on." Anyone fighting an air war could relate to those words.

Winged Victory, a Twentieth Century–Fox tribute to the Army Air Corps, is essentially a story which describes the training of the pilots, navigators and bombardiers who would soon go into active duty. Produced by Darryl F. Zanuck, directed by George Cukor and adapted from the Moss Hart stage hit by the author himself, the film features several well-known actors who were actually in uniform at the time of production: Sergeant Edmond O'Brien, Corporals Lee J. Cobb, Red Buttons, and Barry Nelson and Private Lon McCallister. The off-base activities of the men are shown in romantic interludes between the training and action scenes. Two of the actresses supplying the love interest are Jeanne Crain and Judy Holliday; both went on to Hollywood stardom. The movie did well at the box office, with all proceeds going to service organizations.

For his work on three of the most important films of 1944 (*Winged Victory, The Purple Heart and Wilson*), Darryl Zanuck was chosen to receive the coveted Irving Thalberg Award at the Academy Awards ceremony for outstanding achievement in motion picture production. The presenter was Thalberg's widow, actress Norma Shearer.

Moviegoers were very interested in what was happening on the home front; Hollywood, with an eye towards both patriotism and profit, did what it could to oblige. Motion pictures about the home front released during the war years are generally patriotic in theme and deal with the way Americans coped with problems brought on by a war they had not wanted.

Tomorrow the World, from United Artists, presents a unique problem for a typical small town family (one of many represented in films during that era) — the pitting of democracy against the forces of dictatorship and demagoguery.

Throughout the 1930s, the world outside of Germany had read about Hitler's master race theory, seen propaganda pictures of the blue-eyed blonds who would populate his "New Order" and were aware of the fact that Germany's youth was being indoctrinated with the diatribes and ultimately dangerous ideas of the destructive dictator. The plotline of *Tomorrow the World* builds on this scenario: Into an average American town comes a young German refugee, nephew of one of its most beloved citizens. The boy, full of hatred and hostility, cannot make an adjustment to his new life. Only at film's end, and after almost losing his life, does he realize the true meanings of America and democracy. Fredric March, Betty Field and Agnes Moorehead are the adults in this perceptive drama, while fourteen-year-old Skip Homeier repeats his Broadway role as the troubled youngster.

Of course *Tomorrow the World* settles the problems of just one family. There were many difficulties on a much larger scope dogging the American public in 1944 and these were served up in various forms to moviegoers in the film output of the year.

The housing shortage of *The More the Merrier* had not abated. Like that classic of the year before, *The Doughgirls* from Warner Bros., a frantically paced comedy, is set in wartime Washington. The plot revolves a group of women and a much sought-after hotel suite. The film, however, lacks the charm and subtlety of the earlier one. An experienced cast, including Ann Sheridan, Jack Carson, Jane Wyman and Alexis Smith, tries their best, but it is Eve Arden who gives the production its finest moments as a Russian guerrilla fighter on leave in America.

Washington is also the setting for another comedy about the housing shortage. Paulette Goddard in *Standing Room Only* (Paramount) has a unique way of finding a place to stay in our nation's capitol: She hires herself and her boss, played by Fred MacMurray, who has important things to do in the city, as servants in a large home. After some embarrassing situations, they come clean, and secretary and boss are able to get their real business done. Taking part in these shenanigans are Edward Arnold, Roland Young, Anne Revere and Porter Hall.

During his lengthy film career, the gifted producer-director-writer Preston Sturges satirized many of the things that this country holds dear. Among his scathing works are two 1940 films, one a take-off on the political scene, *The Great McGinty* (for his original story, Sturges received an Oscar), and the other, a devastating portrait of our preoccupation with quiz shows titled *Christmas in July* (has this preoccupation changed with succeeding generations?). In 1944, Sturges brought out two films, courtesy of Paramount, which have become classics and, when seen sixty-five years later, are as funny now as they were then.

Hail the Conquering Hero pricks the bubble of hero worship, as an army reject, wrongly thought of as a decorated war hero, returns to his hometown where he is given a tumultuous welcome, complete with brass band. The local politicos are so taken with him (substitute for this the publicity he has given them) that he is asked to run for mayor. By the end of the film, the basically honest young fellow sets things right and even gets the girl. Eddie Bracken, who made a comfortable living during the 1930s and 1940s in the role of a slightly bewildered hero, is starred along with veteran character actor William Demarest and newcomer Ella Raines.

Unlike Bracken, Dan Dailey plays a real hero, cinematically speaking of course, in the Twentieth Century–Fox production *When Willie Comes Marching Home*. Though released in 1950, the film is a perfect fit for this part of our narrative. Willie is first in his hometown to enlist in the service and is eager to go overseas, but instead he becomes an instructor. Through the illness of a man scheduled to go overseas, the eager recruit is sent to France. There he meets a beautiful resistance fighter and obtains vital information about the German rocket program. With her help, he gets back to America and reports his findings to the proper authorities. He is thereupon sworn to secrecy and has to wait until the end of the war to reveal what he has accomplished. William Demarest, James Lydon, Lloyd Corrigan and French actress Corinne Calvet head the lineup of supporting players who keep the action going under the direction of John Ford.

That man Demarest is back again, this time co-starred with Eddie

Bracken and Betty Hutton in the second great Sturges film to be released in 1944, *The Miracle of Morgan's Creek*. Hutton plays the irrepressible Trudy Kockenlocker, who goes to a "kiss the boys goodbye" party. She enjoys herself so much that nine months later, she gives birth to sextuplets. The problem is that she does not know who the father is; in her hazy memory, she *thinks* that she married a certain Private Ratskiwatsky. Her father (Demarest) is irate and is tearing out what little hair he has. Her bumbling boyfriend (Bracken) tries to help save her reputation and winds up the town hero (people think that he is the father). The multiple birth knocks every headline off the front page; even Hitler cannot compete.

Sturges' one-man assault on some of the era's usually unassailable topics (heroes, wartime marriage and motherhood) is dated in light of today's moral values, but audiences of the 1940s loved it, as would anyone, even today, who admires satire. The multi-talented Sturges received Oscar nominations in the Original Screenplay category for both productions, but Lamar Trotti won for his work on *Wilson*. In those days, who could compete with a president?

The Fighting Sullivans is the story of five true heroes from a small Iowa town who went down with their ship, the *Juneau*, in the South Pacific off Guadalcanal. Tremendously appealing, even after several decades have gone by, the Twentieth Century–Fox release wisely sticks to the home life of the boys; the only war scene (the fatal one) comes towards the end of the film. Thomas Mitchell and Selena Royle are remarkably effective as the senior Sullivans, as are the relatively unknown actors playing the brothers. This casting gave the film an authentic feel and many a "gold star" mother and father agonized with the Sullivans in the poignancy of their great loss. The navy made the decision to never allow all the members of one family to serve on the same ship soon after the release of the motion picture. An interesting sidelight: When first released as *The Sullivans*, it did not do well box office–wise, but when the studio added the word *Fighting* to the title, it became a big hit.

Co-starred as the sweetheart of a Sullivan is the gifted Anne Baxter. The granddaughter of famed architect Frank Lloyd Wright, she had begun her career in 1940 and, within three years, was playing leads. Besides the Sullivan saga, the young actress made two other war-related films that year, *The Eve of St. Mark* and *Sunday Dinner for a Soldier*, both Twentieth Century–Fox releases.

Nine. The Longest Day

The Eve of St. Mark, adapted from the play by Maxwell Anderson, a well-known playwright of the era, is a story familiar to many people living through the war years: A small town boy goes off to fight and a girl waits for him. The tragic ending of the stage production is avoided in the film; the latter has the boy and his unit in the Philippines with no indication as to whether or not he or they will survive. This has weakened its impact, but a strong cast, which also includes William Eythe, Michael O'Shea and Vincent Price, is a major asset.

The setting of *Sunday Dinner for a Soldier* is the backwoods country of Florida. Baxter plays a member of a poor family, living on a houseboat, who scrapes enough money together to invite a soldier to dinner. The heartwarming story co-stars character actors Charles Winninger, Anne Revere, Chill Wills and Jane Darwell and features John Hodiak as the lonely soldier of the title who accepts the invitation, then falls in love with his hostess. Fact followed fiction: Hodiak and Baxter were married two years after the film's release, but divorced in 1953.

One of the most prestigious films of the home front made during the war years is *Since You Went Away*. The plotline of the production, which has a running time of almost three hours, revolves around a family coping with their problems while the man of the house is away in the service of his country. Producer David Selznick, who wrote the screenplay, spared no expense bringing his flag-waving bit of Americana to the nation's filmgoers. Claudette Colbert, Jennifer Jones and Shirley Temple portray the members of this "typical" family. Helping them in their trials and tribulations are Joseph Cotten, Robert Walker, Hattie McDaniel, the irascible Monty Woolley and Agnes Moorehead, the latter contributing a memorable portrait of a selfish snob who can't be bothered by something called a world war.

The most interesting aspect of the film, however, lies in Selznick's casting of Jennifer Jones and Robert Walker as lovers. The two, married in real life, were in the midst of a painful separation which ended in divorce. All of Hollywood buzzed at this juicy morsel of gossip and no one was surprised when the ex–Mrs. Walker later became the new Mrs. Selznick.

The film proved popular with the ticket-buying public, but received only mixed reviews from the critics; some considered it overly sentimental and highly unrealistic. Nevertheless, *Since You Went Away* was nominated as Best Film. Also nominated were Colbert (Actress), Jones

Since You Went Away: Shirley Temple (left), Claudette Colbert and Jennifer Jones keep the home fires burning while the man of the family is away fighting a war. There is an interesting bit of casting involved in this film.

(Supporting Actress) and Woolley (Supporting Actor). Neither the film nor the actors won. The only Oscar went to Max Steiner for Best Musical Score.

Though several of the films discussed in this chapter are of excellent quality and were quite popular at the time of release, none figured in the major categories at the 1944 Academy Awards ceremonies. It was the year of Father O'Malley: *Going My Way*, the story of a priest taking over a parish from an older one, received six Oscars, including one for Best Picture and two for Leo McCarey, who won for Original Screenplay and for his direction. It was the first Best Picture for Paramount since 1927 when *Wings* won the coveted award. (*Wings* was the first and last silent film to receive an Oscar.)

Bing Crosby as Father O'Malley and Barry Fitzgerald as the elderly Father Fitzgibbons were also honored as Best Actor and Supporting Actor. (In a curious sidelight to the voting, Fitzgerald had been nominated in both categories for the same role.) The icing on the cake occurred when tunesmiths Johnny Burke and Jimmy Van Heusen each took home a Best Song statuette for "Swinging on a Star," sung by Crosby in the film.

Completing the list of major winners for the year were Best Actress Ingrid Bergman, who plays a woman fearing for her life in *Gaslight*, and Best Supporting Actress Ethel Barrymore, honored for her role as Cary Grant's "mum" in *None But the Lonely Heart*.

The Oscars for 1944 were not handed out until March 15, 1945. That the latter year would be a momentous one for America, as well as for the rest of the world, was not as yet known when the motion picture industry gathered in celebration.

Chapter Ten

The Road to Victory

It was not "All Quiet on the Western Front" as 1945 began. The fighting at the "Bulge" raged and, although its duration was short, when the smoke of battle had cleared, it was estimated that over half a million men had sacrificed their lives in the bleak Ardennes Forest.

In another part of the world, General MacArthur's forces were engaged in the largest land campaign of the war in the Pacific, the liberation of the Philippines. By the first week in March, Manila, the capital city of the island chain, was in American hands, though Japanese General Yamashito and his men continued to fight from stronghold pockets until the very end.

The world was also reading about a battle taking place on the barren volcanic island of Iwo Jima, used by the Japanese as a radar warning station and fire interceptor. The enemy was well prepared to resist invasion, but had not counted on the hearts and bravery of American Marines as they fought inch by inch and finally raised the Stars and Stripes on Mount Suribachi. By April, Americans were landing on Okinawa, and after more than two months of heavy fighting, the island chain was in American hands.

Several conferences marked the year, the first being one at Yalta, a seaport on the Black Sea, between Roosevelt, Churchill and Stalin. This meeting has been called the most controversial of the war. Many contend that Roosevelt, by then a very sick man, honored too many of Stalin's conditions (read: demands) and that this in turn led to a Cold War which lasted almost half a century.

An important but far less controversial meeting, establishing the charter of the United Nations, took place in San Francisco. An organization dedicated to world peace, it officially came into being a year after the cessation of hostilities.

Besides these conferences, other momentous events were taking place. Within one month, the world lost three leaders: On April 12, Franklin Delano Roosevelt died of a cerebral hemorrhage in Warm Springs, Georgia; on the 25th, Italy's Benito Mussolini was hanged in a public square near Lake Como; and on the last day of April, the evil architect of the war, Adolf Hitler, along with Eva Braun, his bride of one day, committed suicide in his Berlin bunker. Almost three weeks previously, when the news of Roosevelt's death had reached Der Führer, it was regarded by the deluded dictator as a good omen, a turning point of the war, even though Allied forces were only seventy-five miles from Berlin.

The Allies continued their relentless march to the German capital. Liberating the death camps as they advanced, grown men were reduced to tears upon seeing the full depravity and excesses of Hitler's "Thousand Year Reich."

Things went from bad to worse for Germany and two days after the death of their tyrannical Führer, German forces asked for a ceasefire and on May 7, their new leaders surrendered the country unconditionally. V-E Day was officially proclaimed a day later. The European phase of the war was over.

In July, Churchill and Stalin met at Potsdam, Germany, with the new American president, Harry S Truman. This was the last and least effective of the wartime conferences. It had been convened to discuss postwar problems, territorial and monetary, but little agreement was reached.

Meanwhile, the first atomic test had been successful. Japan was given a surrender ultimatum; the nation was summarily refused. In August of 1945, two bombs heard around the world were unleashed over the Japanese cities of Hiroshima and Nagasaki. The destruction they caused was devastating. On August 14, the Japanese warlords agreed to an unconditional surrender and August 15 was proclaimed V-J Day.

World War II was over.

With the fighting overseas winding down, there was lots of news coming from the Hollywood domestic front. Marriages included Judy Garland's to director Vincente Minnelli and Donna Reed's to agent-producer Tony Owens. Paulette Goddard said "I do" to actor Burgess Meredith and ventriloquist Edgar Bergen married model Frances Westerman (from this union came a little "sister" named Candice for Bergen's alter ego, the delightful and irreverent dummy Charlie McCarthy).

The wedding events of the season, however, were those uniting child star Shirley Temple with John Agar and the previously mentioned nuptials of Humphrey Bogart and Lauren Bacall. It was the first time around for both Agars; they opted for a traditional church affair with all the trimmings. The thrice-wed Bogart and his "Baby" were married at the farmhouse of Bogie's friend, author Louis Bromfield. Not given a snowball's chance in hell to survive, the Bogart-Bacall merger did, whereas the Temple-Agar marriage did not.

The stork was very much in evidence during the year as glamour gals Betty Grable (Mrs. Harry James), Susan Hayward (Mrs. Jess Barker) and Hedy Lamarr (Mrs. John Loder) announced impending motherhood. The Barkers became the proud parents of twin boys.

The film output for this last year of actual combat again proved to be a potpourri, combining drama, music, adventure and comedy. A couple of spy melodramas, a story of the gallant PT boat crews in the Pacific, a poignant drama of wartime love and the reflections of two famous writers led the pack.

James Cagney and his brother William produced *Blood on the Sun*, which was released by United Artists. Jimmy plays a reporter in Tokyo during the early thirties. He gets hold of the Japanese premier's plan for world domination, and pressure is put on him to drop it. He meets Eurasian Sylvia Sidney, who is a Chinese agent pretending to help the Japanese. After several violent incidents, they escape to America with the vital information. In the supporting cast are John Emery as the Japanese premier, Robert Armstrong as the militaristic fanatic General Tojo and Rosemary De Camp. A trivia note: De Camp, more than a decade younger than Cagney, plays his mother in the previously mentioned *Yankee Doodle Dandy*, the production which cast the actor in the role of Broadway star George M. Cohan.

Another interesting but highly improbable film came from RKO. *First Yank into Tokyo* stars Tom Neal as an American soldier who undergoes plastic surgery so that he can pass through enemy territory. His task is to locate an imprisoned American atomic scientist and help him escape. The film is notable as the first to acknowledge the existence of the nuclear age. Co-starred are Barbara Hale, Keye Luke and Richard Loo. Hale

Ten. The Road to Victory 117

would go on to play Della Street, secretary to lawyer Perry Mason, in the successful television series *Perry Mason*.

The Pacific theater of war is our next venture into the world of film.

You did not have to be a celebrity to either have known Ernie Pyle or to have read his words. The veteran newspaperman became the GIs'

The Story of G.I. Joe: Burgess Meredith (left) was a natural to play Ernie Pyle (right). The famed journalist, who vividly brought the war home to his readers, died in April of 1945, just before the end of the war.

favorite war correspondent because they felt that he best described for posterity the day-to-day emotions in fighting a war: loneliness, humor, triumph, terror, boredom, fatigue.

Taken from his own writings, *The Story of G.I. Joe* (United Artists) is a posthumous tribute to Pyle, who died shortly before the film was released. It is also a testimonial to the bravery of the "mud, rain, frost and wind boys" of whom he wrote, the foot soldiers. Burgess Meredith, somewhat resembling Pyle in build and in facial characteristics, plays the writer and there is not one false move in his portrayal. Co-starred as one of Ernie's "boys" is Robert Mitchum who, as a result of his performance, received a Best Supporting Actor nomination.

The Story of G.I. Joe is based upon incidents which occurred during Pyle's days with the Fifth Army group in their bloody Italian campaign. As the war in Europe was ending, he opted to go to the Pacific Theater. Three weeks before V-E Day, he was mortally wounded by a sniper's bullet on the island of Ie Shima. The inscription on his grave marker reads:

> AT THIS SPOT
> THE 77TH INFANTRY DIVISION
> LOST A BUDDY
> ERNIE PYLE
> 18 April, 1945

Many other well-known writers circled the globe while describing the war to their readers. Among them was the famous novelist John Hersey who, like Pyle, wrote about the fighting in the Pacific as well as that which took place on European soil. One of the memorable battles Hersey covered so vividly was the campaign in Italy and from it came his best-selling story of postwar life in the defeated country. *A Bell for Adano* was picked up by Twentieth Century–Fox and became one of the studio's most popular releases of the war.

With the end of the war in Italy came the Allied occupation forces whose aim was to democratize the towns in which they were stationed. Adano is a small village whose church bell has been ruined in the fighting. John Hodiak stars as the American major who realizes that its replacement will do more for the morale of the townspeople than all the material goods and democratic speeches he can give them. Featured along with Hodiak are Gene Tierney as a local beauty and William Bendix as the major's adjutant.

Ten. The Road to Victory

Ie Shima, where Pyle lost his life, is a small island in the Pacific. More famous targets in Indo-China and in the Philippines were subjects for several Hollywood films of 1945, three of the most successful being *Objective, Burma!*, *They Were Expendable* and *Back to Bataan*. To be sure, a partial reason for the success of these films was that the first stars Errol Flynn, the second John Wayne and Robert Montgomery and the third, again the legendary Duke.

Objective, Burma!, from Warner Bros., has Flynn commanding a unit of paratroopers who are assigned to blow up a radar station important to the Japanese defense of Burma and then get out alive. Destroying the station is easier than getting away. The men must fight their way through miles of Japanese-infested jungle until, at the film's conclusion, they are rescued by American forces. The movie was criticized by the British, who felt that it presented a one-sided picture of what had actually happened, and did not give their forces any credit for the victory in Indo-China. The film, withdrawn from distribution throughout the British Isles one week after its London premiere, was not shown in that country until 1952.

One interesting note for the trivia buff: In the cast are young actors Stephen Richards and Hugh Beaumont. Richards changed his name to Mark Stevens and later made films with such leading ladies as Lucille Ball and June Haver, while Beaumont had the lead in several low-budget features before starring as the father on television's *Leave it to Beaver*.

Produced and directed by John Ford, himself a Navy man, MGM's *They Were Expendable*, based upon a best-selling novel by William L. White, is a factual account of those who manned PT (torpedo) boats in the Pacific during the early part of the war. Robert Montgomery, who had served in the area as a naval officer, plays the leader of the operation, John Wayne, who owed his career to Ford when the feisty director cast him as Ringo in the western *Stagecoach* (1939), is his second in command, and Donna Reed is the nurse with whom Wayne falls in love. The romance angle is discreetly handled and does not get in the way of the film's action. Under Ford's direction, the actors give the script the authenticity to which many navy men could well relate. (During the presidential election of 1960, it was disclosed that one of the candidates, John F. Kennedy, a naval lieutenant on a PT boat, had spent several days on a raft during World War II after his boat was sunk.)

In RKO's *Back to Bataan*, set in the Philippines, Wayne is a Marine.

His rank has been upped to colonel. This time, with Bataan cut off from the American lines, his mission is to organize a guerrilla resistance. In support of Wayne (who as a member of every branch of the military, cinematically speaking, almost single-handedly won the reel war) are Anthony Quinn as the leader of the native resistance and character actress Beulah Bondi as an American teacher who refuses to be evacuated. Also in the cast are some veterans of the Pacific theater of war who were held in a prison camp just outside of Manila. The liberation of this camp was dramatized in the film.

Filmed by the Motion Picture Industry War Activities Committee and released by Warner Bros., *Appointment in Tokyo* is a fifty-four-minute documentary which presents a factual account of the Pacific and the recapturing of the Philippine Islands. Involved in the production were Hollywood industry men who had joined the military.

God Is My Co-Pilot is an interesting film in that it is based upon the actual adventures of Colonel Robert Lee Scott, Jr., who fought with the Flying Tigers in China. After a mission over Hong Kong, Scott's plane was forced down over enemy territory, but he survived, hence the title. Dennis Morgan is starred as Scott and receives good support from Andrea King. Raymond Massey, Alan Hale and Dane Clark. The film did well at the box office, but many of the critics felt that Scott's best-selling book was much better than the picture. This was due to the fact that Warner Bros. had taken the title of Scott's book too literally. There are far more religious overtones than the author intended, and this takes away from the overall quality and excitement of the film. The real importance of *God Is My Co-Pilot* is that it pays tribute to General Clare Chennault and his men, a group of Americans who gave so much of themselves in the struggle for China.

The struggles in China are the basis for *China Sky* (RKO). Adapted from the novel by the famed Pearl S. Buck, the plot revolves around two doctors who help a guerrilla movement in a remote village which is under constant pressure from Japanese soldiers. Randolph Scott and Ruth Warrick are the medical team who manage to aid guerrilla leader Anthony Quinn in spite of Ellen Drew, who is co-starred in the role of Scott's selfish and jealous wife.

The use of the Japanese Air Force in China before and during World War II had done much damage to the country and Americans became even more aware of this fact with the bombing of Pearl Harbor. A motion picture detailing the use of air power in warfare is *Journey Together*. Produced by the Royal Air Force film unit, this film, now called a docudrama, is about the training of pilots in both the United States and Great Britain. It is also about the interaction of pilot to pilot and also of pilot to instructor. Featured in the cast as an instructor is Edward G. Robinson.

The war-ravaged countries of Europe provided the backdrop for several interesting films released in 1945. *Paris Underground* (United Artists), based upon a true story, stars Constance Bennett and English music hall entertainer Gracie Fields (in a rare dramatic role — it was her last appearance on the screen) as women who elect to stay on in the city as part of the resistance movement. They are instrumental in helping Allied fliers in eluding the Gestapo. After killing a German agent, the duo is arrested, spend time in a concentration camp and are set free when the city is liberated.

Counter-Attack, from Columbia, is a fictional tribute to the daring and cunning Russian guerrillas fighting their own type of war against the Nazis. Paul Muni stars as the leader of a group which lands behind enemy lines on the eastern front, holds seven German soldiers in the basement of a converted factory and tricks them into revealing information vital to the defense of the sector. In the cast are Marguerite Chapman and a newcomer named Larry Parks, who would soon become famous for playing entertainer Al Jolson.

By 1945, nearly all of the biggest stars in Hollywood had appeared in one or more war-related films and MGM's Lassie was no exception. As fans of the beloved collie know, the first Lassie was played by a male named Pal and as a saying of the time went, Pal was the only star in the movies that could play a bitch better than Bette Davis, who relished such roles.

In *Son of Lassie*, a sequel to *Lassie Come Home* (1943), the precocious pooch, as a male, follows his now grown master (played by Peter Lawford) on a mission to German-occupied Norway. The human is captured but, with his courageous canine, makes his way back to England where both man and dog are reunited with family. Featured in the cast is June Lockhart, who later starred in the *Lassie* television series.

One year after *Son of Lassie*, Pal was seen as Bill in *Courage of Lassie*, this time co-starring with old chum Elizabeth Taylor, with whom she/he had appeared in *Lassie Come Home*. War hero Bill returns to his young mistress with a psychological disorder, but is cured by her love and by the help of a man, played by Frank Morgan, who goes to court to defend him when he is condemned to die. A question is raised, why the title? The answer is that Lassie's name on a marquee meant good business at the box office in that era.

There is no questioning the title of *Hotel Berlin*, which is set during the last stages of the battle for the German capital. The Warner Bros. production is based upon the novel by Vicki Baum, who also wrote the novel which translated to the screen in 1932 as *Grand Hotel*. Using the same type of scenario as the earlier film, the story focuses on the fates of people who live and work in the hotel, Nazi and anti–Nazi alike. Featured in the cast are Raymond Massey as a defecting general, Peter Lorre as an apolitical scientist and Helmut Dantine as an underground leader fleeing for his life.

Throughout the war years, Dantine made a career of playing both pro–Nazi as well as anti–Nazi Germans. As previously noted, he had made an impact in the role of the doomed flier who finds himself in Mrs. Miniver's kitchen. In *Hotel Berlin*, he is a resistance leader, but in *Escape in the Desert*, also from Warner Bros., he is an unrepentant follower of the Führer. The locale of the latter film is the southwest American desert; Dantine is an escaped POW who takes Philip Dorn and Jean Sullivan as hostages in his escape attempt. The film's interest lies in the fact that it is a curious remake of *The Petrified Forest*, the 1936 film which made a star of Humphrey Bogart, who played the role of escaped convict Duke Mantee. In no way can *Escape in the Desert* be compared to its illustrious predecessor.

A far better film about Nazis in America is the spy melodrama *The House on 92nd Street*, a Twentieth Century–Fox release. Producer Louis de Rochemont, experienced in both documentary and newsreel filming (known for his "March of Time" series), combined his expertise with actual Federal Bureau of Investigation files and the result is an exciting and excellently crafted screenplay. What many people, seeing this popular film on television, may not know, is that the story's central character, played by William Eythe, was based upon a real person, an FBI agent working for the Nazis under instructions from the Bureau. Through the work of this largely unknown hero, several spies and saboteurs were apprehended before they could do much harm to the war effort. Lloyd Nolan as an FBI man and Signe Hasso as the chief spy, co-star. Actual FBI staffers of the era were given small roles in the production.

Ten. The Road to Victory

The House on 92nd Street: **Leo G. Carroll, Charles Wagenheim (standing) William Eythe and Signe Hasso are members of a Nazi spy ring. But all is not what it seems. Much of the content of the film was taken from the files of the FBI.**

The locale of *The House on 92nd Street* is New York City. A film of a vastly different nature also takes place in the Big Apple. In the tumult of the war years, servicemen and their wives and sweethearts had to live for the moment because, in the words of an old but timely cliché, no one knew what tomorrow would bring.

The Clock, an MGM release, stars Judy Garland and Robert Walker as a girl and a soldier who meet under the clock in Grand Central Station, fall in love and marry, all within the span of 48 hours. The slight plotline under the sensitive direction of Judy's then husband Vincente Minnelli takes on added luster through the acting of its appealing stars and a capable cast of supporting players including Keenan Wynn and James Gleason. Playing the latter's wife is Lucille Gleason, Mrs. James Gleason in real life.

The wartime theme of living for the moment is also the subject of an RKO film titled *Those Endearing Young Charms*, which stars Robert Young and Laraine Day. Young, a wealthy and cynical playboy enlisting in the army for the thrill of it, meets Day through an army buddy engagingly played by Bill Williams in his first screen role. At first thinking in terms of a brief fling, Young's character soon finds himself falling in love. Though he tries to break away, he cannot, and at the final fade-out, Miss Laraine tearfully promises to wait for him. Not a major effort, the film does mirror the emotions felt by many during the war years and benefits from the emoting of its two stars.

Throughout these years, war bond drives were part and parcel of a celebrity's life. Paramount's *You Came Along* presents a variation on that theme. Robert Cummings, Don DeFore and Charles Drake portray three war heroes who embark on a bond-selling tour. Along as their guide and public relations person is Lisabeth Scott, in her screen debut. Cummings, brash and cocky on the outside, is harboring a tragic secret: He has contracted a fatal disease. He and Scott fall in love and, in spite of their uncertain future, marry; they will share whatever time he has together.

A Medal for Benny from Paramount is another version of the war hero theme. The locale is a small town in Southern California. Benny (never seen in the film) is the no-account son of one of its residents. Killed in battle, he becomes the town's hero; hitherto hated by the townspeople, he is now the darling of the publicity-hungry local politicians. Starred are J. Carrol Naish and Dorothy Lamour, *sans* sarong. Taken from a story by John Steinbeck, who used Southern California as the setting for many of his stories, the film garnered applause from both critics and moviegoers. A trivia note: Naish, an Irish-American, plays an Italian in the film. In his long acting career, he played many roles in different dialects, and on radio starred in *Life with Luigi*, about an Italian immigrant in America.

A poignant and even more pertinent drama brought out by Warner Bros. in 1945 was a portent of things to come. *Pride of the Marines* is a portrait of an authentic war hero named Al Schmid, a Marine blinded by a grenade after killing two hundred Japanese during the battle of Guadalcanal. The beautifully crafted story is not so much concerned with the shooting war, which has ended for Schmid, as with the ongoing war within him that he (and other handicapped veterans) would forever have to fight in adjusting to a civilian life far different than the one he had left. John Garfield gives a brilliant performance as Schmid and receives excellent support from Dane Clark as an army buddy and Eleanor Parker as the girl whose love for him remains unchanged.

On a less somber note, several comedic and musical movies rounded out Hollywood's film fare for the year. Though some well-known performers are to be seen in them, in retrospect, these films are feeble attempts at humor and not as good as they could have been. But the public, increasingly tired of battleground scenes, found them quite diverting.

Over 21 is based upon the reminiscences of actress-writer Ruth Gordon, whose husband, writer-director Garson Kanin, had been in the service. Their alter egos are well played by Irene Dunne and Alexander Knox, but the acting honors go to Charles Coburn as Knox's boss who wants him back at his civilian job and "to hell with this army nonsense." The Columbia release contains some potentially funny scenes as the over-aged husband goes through officer candidate school and the wife goes through the trials of living on an army base, but the script is a weak one; the Gordon-Kanin collaboration was at its best on films which starred their friends Katharine Hepburn and Spencer Tracy.

MGM's *Keep Your Powder Dry* describes the experiences of three girls from vastly differing backgrounds who join the Woman's Army Corps. Lana Turner, Laraine Day and Susan Peters (a promising young actress later injured in a hunting accident and confined to a wheelchair) star in this film, which was lambasted by the critics and has largely been forgotten, even by today's serious movie buffs.

Over at Warner Bros., in a real departure for her, Ida Lupino starred in a comedy titled *Pillow to Post* as a young businesswoman who poses as a soldier's wife in order to get a room at a motel near an army base that caters to married couples only. In the predictable end, Lupino does become an army bride. Variations on the housing shortage had been used to better advantage in other films, and the production received unfavorable reviews from both critics and moviegoers. Lupino wisely returned to drama, later becoming a successful director.

Unlike Lupino, Barbara Stanwyck was equally adept in both comedy and drama. Warner Bros.' *Christmas in Connecticut* finds Barbara playing the role of a magazine columnist who writes about cooking and homemaking. She is asked by her boss (Sydney Greenstreet) to invite a war hero (Dennis Morgan) to spend the Christmas holidays with her and her family. She does not want to tell her rotund employer that she has no family and knows nothing about homemaking. She needs a ready-made family and thereby hangs the tale. After the usual antics inherent in this type of situation, Stanwyck and Morgan are in love and all's well with the world. The delightful supporting cast includes Reginald Gardiner as Barbara's pretend "husband" and S.Z. Sakall as her uncle, the cook who has been supplying recipes for her column.

Of all the war-related musicals released in 1945, one of the better ones is *Anchors Aweigh*. The MGM opus stars dancer Gene Kelly and crooner Frank Sinatra as sailors on leave in Hollywood who come upon an adorable youngster (Dean Stockwell) running away from home to "join" the navy. Upon meeting the boy's aunt Suzie (Kathryn Grayson), an aspiring opera singer (which gives the studio's resident classical musician, Jose Iturbi, a chance to get in on the act), both Gene and Frank fall in love with her; the dancer, not the singer, gets the girl. It is Kelly, in his landmark dance with a cartoon mouse, who stands out in the film; he was Oscar-nominated, as was the picture and the lovely ballad "I Fall in Love Too Easily."

Tonight and Every Night, from Columbia, is set in wartime London during the Blitz of 1940. The forgettable plot revolves around a troupe of performers who adhere to the old show business tradition that "the show must go on." Many moviegoers felt that the show should not have gone on. The songs are mediocre and not even a cast which includes Rita Hayworth, Janet Blair and Lee Bowman can save this bland musical. The story was inspired by London's Windmill Theater, which remained open as a morale booster during the height of the Blitz.

Bring on the Girls stars Eddie Bracken in his usual role of the schlemiel who wins out at the end. In this go-round, Eddie plays a millionaire who joins the navy to avoid the gold-digging girls who surround him, one of whom is Veronica Lake. He winds up with Marjorie Reynolds, leaving Veronica to cry on the broad shoulders of Sonny Tufts, who just happens to be her ex-boyfriend. This lightweight opus was one of several routine musicals put out by Paramount during the 1940s.

Where Do We Go from Here? is an ambitious undertaking, courtesy of Twentieth Century–Fox, combining musical numbers by foreign composer Kurt Weill and America's Ira Gershwin with comedy and fantasy. Fred MacMurray's character wants to join the army, but is rejected and classified 4-F. He meets up with a genie who takes him through periods of American history, including sessions with George Washington at Valley Forge and Columbus on the *Santa Maria*, before getting him into World War II and into the arms of Joan Leslie.

The movie's real interest lies in the fact that Fred's other leading lady, June Haver, became his wife in 1954, after the untimely death of the first Mrs. MacMurray. The MacMurray-Haver merger was said to be among the happiest in the film capital and ended only with the actor's death in 1991.

The happiest stars in Hollywood at year's end, professionally speaking, were Joan Crawford and Ray Milland. With the beginning of a new era of peace, Tinsel Town got ready to don its best bib and tucker and attend its most important event of the year, the annual Academy Awards ceremony, which would take place at Grauman's Chinese Theater in early 1946.

English-born Milland had been around since the early 1930s and was a capable leading man to many of the movies' top leading ladies. He was adept in adventure, comedy and romantic drama roles. For Milland, *The Lost Weekend* was the role of a lifetime. Milland, not the first choice for the role (Jose Ferrer was), gave a finely honed performance as an alcoholic writer and was awarded the coveted Best Actor trophy. The Paramount production and its director, Billy Wilder, were also honored.

Joan Crawford had left MGM in 1943. The consensus of opinion there had been that she was washed up. She then signed with Warner Bros., who briefly used her in their all-star vehicle lauding the wartime Hollywood Canteen. When a novel by James M. Cain caught her fancy, the old pro asked studio head Jack Warner to buy it for her. The result of this purchase made movie history. The film version of *Mildred Pierce* won for the canny star her only Academy Award. Reportedly ill on this most important night of her professional career, she was at home when her name was announced. Many people in Hollywood wondered just how sick the publicity-wise Crawford had been. *Mildred Pierce* was nominated as Best Picture. Two of its supporting players, Ann Blyth as Crawford's scheming daughter and Eve Arden as her friend and business partner, were also nominated. Neither won.

Everyone connected with *The House I Live In*, a short film on tolerance, was awarded a Special Oscar. Among the recipients was Frank Sinatra, who sang the title song and spoke to a group of boys about prejudice and bigotry. All personnel connected with the film worked without compensation. RKO donated the facilities used for shooting and the final cut was given to movie houses free of charge.

Sharing master of ceremonies chores during the festivities were Bob Hope and Jimmy Stewart. Telegrams from General Eisenhower and Navy Admiral Chester Nimitz, praising the Hollywood community for its service to the country, were read. All the excitement that had been missing during the dark days of the war was back in all its glory. The lights of Hollywood were on again.

The last scene in *Where Do We Go from Here?* shows star MacMurray, in uniform, marching in a parade with crowds cheering. This was also a scene in which many serviceman took part when the war ended. Amid all the cheers, Americans tried to catch their collective breaths. The respite was brief: Uncle Sam had to hitch up his pants and deal with the myriad of problems which the end of the war had brought.

Part II

Après la Guerre: War-Related Films

Chapter Eleven

In the Wake of War

Many important and far-reaching events took place in the wake of World War II between 1945 and 1950. The General Assembly of the United Nations met for the first time in the name of peace and the Nuremberg Trials, set up to punish those who had stood in the way of this peace, was convened. Around the world, people listened in horror as, via the testimony of its victims, the use of explicit films and grisly exhibits, the "accomplishments" of Hitler's Third Reich were laid bare for all to see, to condemn and to punish.

Germany was divided into occupation zones, each governed by one of the victorious powers. Winston Churchill foresaw problems with Russia and, in a speech given in Missouri, first used the term "Cold War" to describe the machinations of his former ally. It was a portent of things to come, but not many saw it as such at the time. Sir Winston's prophetic words went on to haunt us until the 1990s, when Communism collapsed.

The Marshall Plan, aimed at helping European recovery, was proposed and passed. Though costly, it proved successful and helped contain the spread of Communist doctrines into the western democracies, one of which was the newly proposed Federal Republic of Germany.

No sooner had the fledgling state of Israel been established than it was immediately attacked by the surrounding countries of Jordan and Egypt. The Israelis fought with amazing courage and stemmed the tide of the much larger Arab states. A tenuous ceasefire was proclaimed seven months later, in January of 1949.

In a far lighter vein, these years saw Hollywood busily engaged in putting its main industry back on a peacetime footing. As did other villages, towns and cities all over the nation, the film capital greeted its veterans with thanks and gratitude and, in the case of the returning stars, with much fanfare and hoopla.

"Gable's back and Garson's got him," trumpeted the publicity releases on MGM's production of *Adventure*. A story about a prim librarian who meets and marries a rough-hewn sailor, the film was a turkey, much to the embarrassment of everyone concerned, including Gable, Garson and co-stars Joan Blondell and Thomas Mitchell.

Some others besides Gable coming back to resume their careers were James Stewart, Henry Fonda, Cesar Romero, Robert Taylor, Tyrone Power, Robert Montgomery and Glenn Ford. Things began to take on an air of normalcy missing during the forty-five months we had been at war.

As they had done before and during the conflict, and would continue for several more years, columnists Hedda Hopper and Louella Parsons were serving up titillating bits of gossip for their readers. The ladies oohed and aahed in "literary" fashion over birth announcements given out by the stars, gushed over weddings and clucked over marital woes. Among the choice items during these years were the birth of Liza Minnelli to Judy Garland and husband Vincente Minnelli, Joan Crawford's divorce from yet another husband (actor Philip Terry, who must have tired of being called Mr. Crawford), bandleader Artie Shaw's marriage to wife number six, authoress Kathleen Windsor (there would be a few more wedding marches played for the popular clarinetist) and Van Johnson's off-again-on-again romance with Evie Wynn, wife of pal Keenan Wynn. (Van and Evie eventually married, but their state of wedded bliss did not last.)

Many good films were released during these years of recovery. and there was a potpourri to choose from. Interestingly, not many productions used battlegrounds for their settings. As has been noted previously, even before the end of the war, moviegoers had become tired of this type of motion picture.

Three fighting films, however, however, did become hits: One is aptly titled *Battleground*, the second tells of *A Walk in the Sun* and the third is *Sands of Iwo Jima*, which deals with the Pacific theater of war. A fourth, though taking place in a war zone, contends with another kind of conflict, which has never really ended.

Battleground, an MGM film released in 1949, traces a group of American soldiers through the Battle of the Bulge. Starred are Van John-

Eleven. In the Wake of War

Battleground: The Battle of the Bulge is raging in the Ardennes Forest. George Murphy (left), Van Johnson, John Hodiak, unidentified, and Don Taylor are among those involved in the fighting. The project was difficult to get off the ground, but the end result was a resounding hit.

son, George Murphy, Ricardo Montalban, John Hodiak and a French import named Denise Darcel.

Studio head Louis B. Mayer had not wanted to make this film as he felt that no one would want to see a war picture in 1949. Producer Dore Schary, Mayer's second in command, saw it differently and he prevailed. Both the production and its director, William Wellman, were Oscar-nominated. Neither won, the film losing to *All the King's Men* and Wellman to Joseph L. Mankiewicz for *A Letter to Three Wives*.

A Walk in the Sun, from Twentieth Century–Fox, was made in 1945, but premiered in the early part of 1946. Like *Battleground,* this film traces a group of men, though on a much smaller scale. The location is a few miles inland from a captured Italian beachhead. A small group of men is ordered to attack an isolated farmhouse being held by a platoon of Nazis. Starring Dana Andrews and Richard Conte with a supporting cast including John Ireland and Lloyd Bridges, the film's scope is a realistic

A Walk in the Sun: Dana Andrews (left) and Herbert Rudley are leading a column of infantrymen to their possible death. They need to capture an isolated farmhouse in Italy from a platoon of Germans. What is going through the minds of these young Americans as they march to their objective?

and unsentimental one: It focuses on each of the men and their feelings while showing what must have actually occurred in many of the smaller encounters the Allies had with the enemy.

The third film, *Sands of Iwo Jima* (1949), produced by Republic Pictures, stars John Wayne as a veteran Marine sergeant who molds raw recruits into fighting men. The actor is ably supported by John Agar (still Shirley Temple's husband — they would divorce some time later) and Forrest Tucker. A review written at the time gave the film's battle sequences good marks for realism and for the use of authentic combat footage. Three of the men who raised the flag on Mt. Suribachi have small parts in the movie. Critics and fans alike felt that Wayne's performance was one of his best. He was Oscar-nominated, but lost to Broderick Crawford in *All the King's Men*.

The Pacific is also the setting for a hard-hitting drama which deals with the insidious problem of racial discrimination in the armed forces. *Home of the Brave* (United Artists, 1949) is the story of a black soldier taunted by intolerant white members of his platoon. James Edwards, who plays the central character in the film produced by the then twenty-five-year-old Stanley Kramer, is co-starred with Frank Lovejoy and Lloyd Bridges. All performances are excellent. Though there were some instances of integration in the armed forces during World War II, it was a rare phenomenon. Only in the 1950s, during the Korean conflict, when President Truman issued a presidential order, did the military officially integrate. *Home of the Brave* was one of the first films to touch on anti-black bias in the service. An interesting sidelight is the fact that in the play upon which the movie is based, the bigotry is anti–Semitic in nature.

Twelve O'Clock High (1949), which in Air Force language means "bombs away," deals with another kind of combat problem: the stress of leadership in times of war. The Twentieth Century–Fox film stars Gregory Peck as the commander of a bomber unit stationed in England during the height of the conflict. It is his job to send men out on mission after mission, and he soon begins to crack under the strain. A caustic commentary on the differences between a wartime and a peacetime mentality, the Oscar-nominated film, which lost to *All the King's Men*, features Gary Merrill, Hugh Marlowe and Dean Jagger. Receiving nominations were Peck, who lost to veteran actor Broderick Crawford for his powerful performance in *All the King's Men*, and Jagger. The latter won the Best Supporting Actor Award.

Two of the greatest postwar productions were made in Italy, one filmed practically on the heels of the fleeing Germans. Though the concentration of this book has mainly been on Hollywood-produced films, several British-made motion pictures have been discussed previously and serve as a precedent for what will follow.

The two imports, *Open City* and *Paisan*, bear the imprint of director Roberto Rossellini, who was also co-writer on both projects. The first, starring Anna Magnani and Aldo Fabrizi, graphically describes Rome during the final stages of its occupation by the Germans and tells the story of a priest who aids the underground in routing out some hidden enemy soldiers. The production was filmed on the streets of Rome in late 1944 and early 1945, just after the Allies had captured the city.

Paisan (1946), Rossellini's next project, co-written with Frederico Fellini, gives an episodic account of life in Italy during the war, culminating in the Allied invasion. The film concentrates upon the ravages of war and the ensuing strains and tensions of the fighting as seen from the Italian viewpoint.

Both *Open City* and *Paisan* show the mercurial Rossellini at his best. This is the man to whom Ingrid Bergman wrote the fan letter which began the tumultuous love affair and subsequent marriage that stunned the world and changed her life. Never during his liaison with the incandescent Ingrid did the filmmaker reach the heights of the two motion pictures which had caught her fancy.

A Swiss-American collaboration released in this country by MGM showing the legacy of war in both material and human terms is *The Search* (1948). The plot ostensibly focuses on an American GI who finds and cares for a young boy he has met in the bombed-out streets of Germany, but the real story is about a mother's convictions and her search for a child that she will not believe is dead, As inmates of concentration camps were being freed, many began this type of odyssey, but only a few would be reunited with the loved ones they prayed had not died. The nominal lead is well-played by Oscar-nominated Montgomery Clift, but the true stars of the film are opera singer Jarmilla Novotna, in a rare dramatic role, and Ivan Jandl as mother and son. The final fade-out in which they hold onto each other for dear life will leave no viewer unaffected. Young Jandl, not German but Czechoslovakian, received a special award as outstanding juvenile performer of the year.

A film of a vastly different nature has as its locale the bombed-out streets of Berlin. *A Foreign Affair* (Paramount, 1948), written by the team of Billy Wilder and Charles Brackett and directed by the German-born Billy, is a satirical look at the problems of an American officer (John Lund) and his German girlfriend in postwar Berlin. What could possibly be wrong when the fräulein is a sultry night club singer, played with wicked abandon by Marlene Dietrich? Plenty. Things become complicated when a Congressional fact-finding commission, led by Jean Arthur, decides to investigate reports of fraternization between the occupiers and the occupied.

The officer soon realizes that he prefers the straight-talking but vulnerable Iowa-born Congresswoman to the calculating fräulein. This delightful film, full of sparkle and zest, takes a look, albeit in fun, at what was considered a problem during the late 1940s. Many of our soldiers fell in love with and married girls of countries which scant months before had been the enemy. The military soon realized that decrees issued against fraternization could not be enforced, and the powers-that-be allowed these edicts to die a natural and unlamented death.

Not so funny is a British production also set in Germany. This time, the locale is a prisoner of war camp. The central character in *The Captive Heart* (Ealing Studios, 1946) is a Czech officer who, having assumed the identity of an English officer he sees killed in battle, is subsequently captured and interned. The film is a moving account of human beings who exist through the mail they receive and dream of the day when they are free and the victory for which they have fought so bravely has arrived. Starred is Michael Redgrave as the Czech, who, through the letters she has written to him, falls in love with the wife of the man he is impersonating. Gordon Jackson plays a blinded prisoner bitter about the life to which he'll have to return. (Television fans of the British-produced *Upstairs, Downstairs* will doubtlessly remember an older Mr. Jackson in that popular series of the late 1980s.)

A forerunner of the modern-day Central Intelligence Agency was the Office of Strategic Services (OSS). Possibly because of the sensitivity of the subject matter, many of the films about the OSS were made after the war.

A physicist is recruited by the OSS to rescue a scientist from the clutches of the Gestapo and find out how far along the Germans are in nuclear research: This is the story line of *Cloak and Dagger* from Warner Bros.. The 1946 film, directed by Fritz Lang, stars Gary Cooper and is a tightly scripted suspense thriller notable for the American screen debut of Lilli Palmer, known in those days as Mrs. Rex Harrison. Also appearing in the production is Robert Alda, father of *M*A*S*H* star Alan Alda.

A Paramount 1946 entry in the espionage genre is simply titled *O.S.S.* Forties heartthrob Alan Ladd co-stars with Geraldine Fitzgerald in the film, which is about a group of American agents who parachute into occupied France in 1943 with orders to blow up a vital tunnel. Mission accomplished, but the usual happy ending does not occur. Instead there is a more realistic one: Fitzgerald is captured and tortured before being murdered by Gestapo agents.

13 Rue Madeleine (1946) is a taut, spine-tingling film, courtesy of Twentieth Century–Fox, also about a group of OSS agents. The operation they undertake entails parachuting into wartime France to deter-mine the location of a German rocket site. Only after they have undergone rigorous training and have been thoroughly briefed is it discovered that one of them is a German spy. It is up to their leader, played by the feisty James Cagney, to expose the villain. This he does in glorious Cagney style, and though his character dies in the end, he takes the Nazi with him. Featured in the cast are Annabella, Richard Conte (the nefarious one) and Frank Lattimore.

Britain's answer to *13 Rue Madeleine* is *Against the Wind* (Ealing Studios, 1948). Again there is a traitor in the midst of a group of agents sent to parachute into occupied France. A young Simone Signoret stars with Robert Beatty and Gordon Jackson. Not quite as exciting as the Cagney film, it is nevertheless better than average and its documentary-style training scenes contribute to the strength of the production.

At the end of the war, several unrepentant Nazis fled the bombed-out cities of the Germany they had helped to wreck and sought refuge in other countries. Many went to South America. There they lived like kings and plotted for the day when a Hitler-like leader would again rise and lead them to the glory they felt they had been denied.

Notorious (RKO, 1946) centers around a group of neo–Nazis in Rio de Janeiro. American agent Cary Grant uses Ingrid Bergman, the daughter of a convicted spy, to infiltrate the group and help break it up. Her assignment is to marry one of its members (played by Claude Rains), but of course the fireworks are between Ingrid and Cary. The plot of this Alfred Hitchcock film provides lots of excitement, including a shot which starts at the top of a staircase, moves down to a party on the main floor and ends with a closeup of a key clutched in Bergman's hand. (Veteran actor Rains was nominated for his role in the film, but lost to Harold Russell for his performance in the landmark film *The Best Years of Our Lives*.) *Notorious* was a tremendous hit at the box office and it is still fondly remembered many years later.

Closer to home, in a small Connecticut town, unknown to his neighbors and his new bride, is a Nazi war criminal. He has changed his name and is teaching at a nearby prep school. Thus begins the cat-and-mouse tale of *The Stranger* (1946). Directed by Orson Welles, who also stars, the film features Loretta Young and Edward G. Robinson. Welles brings a good deal of menace to the role of the villain, Loretta is properly bewildered as the hapless wife and Robinson is quietly authoritative as a War Crimes Commission investigator who finally brings his quarry to justice. The electrifying climax, in which the three principals take part, involves a church clock on which the Nazi is impaled. An interesting finale to an interesting film.

Notwithstanding these motion pictures, there are two productions, one British in origin, the other American, which many think dominated the immediate postwar era.

The first, England's *The Third Man*, again stars Orson Welles. The film revolves around the search for Harry Lime (Welles), a black marketer who, presumed dead, is alive and well and living in Vienna. The 1949 movie, however, is much more than this one sentence implies. Director Carol Reed took his lead from a novel by suspense writer Graham Green and, using the latter's premise, created a masterpiece of mood and atmosphere which has landed on many all-time greatest film lists. To best describe and sense the power of *The Third Man*, a quote from Ivan Butler's book *The War Film* (A.S. Barnes & Company, 1974) follows:

> The weary, cold aftermath of a devastating defeat permeates every scene: the battered city, itself, with its gimcrack offices and tawdry, shabby homes in the midst of ruined ornate buildings, is both a background to and a symbol of the human existence dragged out within it — of the whole grotesque muddle into which we had all allowed ourselves to fall.

The film, co-produced by David Selznick and Britain's Alexander Korda, has lost none of its greatness in the ensuing years. Highlights include the scenes in which Lime appears out of the shadows to confront his writer friend, Holly Martens; the climactic chase in the sewers of the Austrian capital; and the closing shot in which Harry's girl is seen walking down the long avenue approaching and passing Martens, who has fallen in love with her. They are all parts of a whole that is every bit as good today as it was more than half a century ago.

Starred along with Welles, who steals every scene in which he appears, are American Joseph Cotten, Italy's Alida Valli and British actor Trevor Howard. The durable Cotten, who got his start with Welles and the latter's Mercury Theater in the late 1930s, has never been better in the role of the not-too-talented pulp writer, while both Valli, as Lime's sweetheart, and Howard as an officer in the British sector of the city, doing his job, are nothing short of superb. The haunting "Third Man Theme," played throughout by Anton Karas on the zither, lends itself to the action of the story and is almost as unforgettable as the film. The Karas recording of the melody sold a million copies.

The other film which has been described as dominating the postwar era takes place thousands of miles from the Vienna of Harry Lime, in a typical American town just after the end of the war. Its theme is a powerful one, and though it contains no mystery, no murkiness and no exciting climax, it holds the audience's interest, and *will* for as long as wars are fought and men return from combat.

Chapter Twelve

The Best Years of Our Lives

Yes, World War II had ended on a euphoric note and the guns of August were quiet, but in the process of demobilization, numerous peacetime problems arose. High on America's list of priorities were her returning GIs.

At first there were parades, tearful reunions and prayers of thanksgiving. After a time, however, "It's great having you back," home cooking and mounds of mom's apple pie, faded into "What are you going to do for the rest of your life?"

For thousands of veterans, it was an almost insurmountable problem. Hollywood, with its finger on the pulse of the country, noted this and several films dealing with this sensitive topic were released during the years between 1945 and 1950.

"All Brides are Beautiful," a story about a couple of newlyweds coping with the Depression, had been purchased by RKO in 1940 and had gathered dust for six years. Updated in 1946, it emerged as *From This Day Forward*. Starring Joan Fontaine and Mark Stevens as a young couple trying to adjust to the postwar world, the production mirrored the story of many young marrieds who, parted by the exigencies of battle, had to adapt to many things after the return of the man, including differences in each other and in everyday living. (In 1942, Fontaine had made *This Above All*, another Twentieth Century–Fox war-related film, based upon the powerful novel by Eric Knight. The story, set in England, is about an embittered British army deserter, Tyrone Power, who falls in love with a girl and subsequently proves his bravery during one of the incessant air raids which plagued the nation in 1940.)

Two years before *From This Day Forward*, Columbia had released a film with the same premise: the problems of the homecoming veteran. *The Impatient Years* stars Jean Arthur and Lee Bowman as a couple who marry after a whirlwind four-day courtship and are separated by war. Upon his return, the two have to make many adjustments to the new situation and begin to think that the marriage has been a mistake. They become estranged, but at the finale, they relive their honeymoon and are back together again, stronger than ever. In the cast are Charles Coburn, Jane Darwell, Edgar Buchanan and Harry Davenport.

A problem of another sort is the theme of our next film.

Infidelity in wartime was a two-sided phenomenon. On the one hand, it involved women promising to wait, who met other men and wrote the famous (or infamous) "Dear John" letters to husbands and sweethearts expecting very different kinds of messages. Then again, there were those servicemen who met other women while overseas and fell in love with them. Though it did happen and was a problem for some military personnel and those they had left behind, it was not as widespread as many movies suggest.

Homecoming, an MGM 1948 release, teams Clark Gable with Lana Turner. Anne Baxter plays the home front wife to whom Gable should be true, but it is Lana who is on the receiving end of his ardor. In true Hollywood fashion, however, he returns to his wife. Featured in the cast is John Hodiak, who at that time, as noted previously, was married to Baxter in real life.

Homecoming was made to revive the sagging career of "The King" and though the Gable-Turner coupling had been a potent one in the early forties, it was not so in 1948. Far better material than this film was needed. Most of the postwar Gable films were fairly successful, but never did the aging actor truly regain the pre-war eminence he had known until he co-starred with Marilyn Monroe in *The Misfits*, which marked his last screen appearance.

Apartment for Peggy (Twentieth Century–Fox, 1948) treats in serio-comic fashion the struggles of returning veterans in availing themselves of the GI Bill of Rights. Through legislation enacted by the government, thousands of men and women, hitherto financially unable to further their educations, now had the funds to do so. There were, however, psychological and practical problems faced by those choosing to go back to school; they would be dealing with fellow students younger and less world-weary than themselves, and many would also have to come to grips with the realities of married life on a college campus. This is the premise of *Apartment for Peggy*. Popular stars Jeanne Crain and William Holden make an attractive couple and are ably supported by the cherubic Edmund Gwenn as an elderly professor who gets a new lease on life when he takes a fatherly interest in them.

Marlon Brando made an auspicious debut in a postwar film simply titled *The Men* (1950). The production proved to be a big winner both with critics and the public (but not the hit that his second film, *A Streetcar Named Desire*, became). It also set Hollywood and the world at large to talking about its intense young star. At the time of its release, the adjectives used to describe the film were "potent," "thought-provoking" and above all, "honest." Produced by Stanley Kramer and directed by Fred Zinnemann, the United Artists release, with a script by Carl Foreman, centers on the plight of the paraplegic and his adjustment to a life he has never envisioned. A forerunner of the equally shattering anti–Vietnam statement *Coming Home* in its treatment of the paralyzed, *The Men* powerfully portrays the agony and scope of the horrors of war and its aftermath. Brando receives some superb support from co-star Kim Hunter as the fiancée whom he believes is only staying with him out of pity and from a young, slightly known actor by the name of Jack Webb, as his hospital buddy. Webb, of course, went on to make his mark in radio and television as Sergeant Joe Friday, hero of *Dragnet*.

Based upon a best-selling novel titled *They Dream of Home* by Niven Busch, *Till the End of Time* (RKO, 1946) is the story of three ex-servicemen who find the adjustment to civilian life both stressful and difficult. Robert Mitchum, Bill Williams and Guy Madison play the trio of veterans, each with problems; Williams and Mitchum's are the physical kind, while Madison experiences emotional difficulties. In trying to find himself, the latter meets and falls in love with Dorothy McGuire, the widow of a flyer, outwardly a calm and collected woman, inwardly a mass of instability.

What is wrong with this film is that, although the problems it pinpoints are some of the issues faced by returning vets, it soon takes on the characteristics of a soap opera. Madison and McGuire take turns straightening each other out and still have time to play around with the lives of Mitchum and Williams. It's a wonder that they can even do this.

Another serious flaw lies in the performance of Madison as Cliff Harper. A very good-looking young man, first seen in *Since You Went*

Away, Madison is given the brunt of the storyline and he staggers under this burden. A more experienced actor would have made the film more convincing. There is, however, one very good performance and it is by Robert Mitchum as the vet with a steel plate in his head. His character is also much more interesting than those of the others and he makes the most of his role. The production's haunting title song is based upon Chopin's "Polonaise in A Flat Major." The lovely melody became a hit via a recording by popular singer Perry Como.

Till the End of Time is a variation on the theme of a landmark production released the same year, the amalgam of all World War II screen stories about those who had served their country and come back to find it (and themselves) radically changed. *The Best Years of Our Lives* was the pinnacle of Samuel Goldwyn's lengthy and distinguished career.

Goldwyn, nee Goldfish, was a Hollywood pioneer during the early years of the twentieth century. Along with the Jesse Laskys, the Adolph Zukors, the Cecil B. DeMilles and others of that peculiar breed, he shaped the film industry with untutored but intuitive vision. However calculating, vulgar, coarse and uneducated the movie moguls are reputed to have been, one thing is certain: Unlike the conglomerates which today run the movie industry purely for profit, they loved their vocation with every fiber of their being and worked tirelessly in the creation of their product.

By 1918, Sam Goldfish was Samuel Goldwyn and had begun a career as one of the film capital's most famous independent producers. Though supposedly he tended to fracture the English language, and supposedly was a master of the malaprop which would send his employees into paroxysms of laughter, he was known for the tasteful productions made under his banner, such prestigious pictures as *Street Scene, Dead End, Wuthering Heights* and *The Little Foxes* plus both silent and sound versions of *Stella Dallas*.

It was Goldwyn who put into focus the feelings and emotions of a postwar people, of those who had served and of those who had waited. The veteran producer had seen a photograph in *Time* magazine showing a group of Marines coming home. The story accompanying the photo hinted at some of the problems returning servicemen might soon be facing. Goldwyn asked novelist McKinley Kantor to write a screenplay based upon this theme. Kantor turned the producer down, but did write a novel which he titled *Glory for Me*. Goldwyn bought the film rights, and the production emerged as *The Best Years of Our Lives*.

Twelve. The Best Years of Our Lives

The Best Years of Our Lives: **Servicemen in uniform (from left) Harold Russell, Dana Andrews and Fredric March mirror the problems that returning vets have faced from time immemorial. Teresa Wright, Myrna Loy and Hoagy Carmichael look on sympathetically.**

The distinguished film tells the story of three ex-servicemen returning to civilian life who meet on a transport plane. They are headed for the same town. Each, in different stages of life, is trying to resume an existence broken up by World War II. The eldest of the trio is Al Stephenson (Fredric March), an ex-infantry sergeant who seemingly has it all: a wife (Myrna Loy), a family and his old job as vice-president of a bank.

Then there is Fred Derry (Dana Andrews, in probably the best role of his career). A soda jerk before donning his uniform, Derry has returned home from the war both a highly decorated Air Force captain and a married man.

The third man in the group is Homer Parish, a machinist's mate who lost his hands in battle. Harold Russell, a veteran who had lost both hands during the war, was signed to play the pivotal role of Homer. It was Russell's first attempt at acting and the sincerity and awkwardness he exhibits in the part was exactly the quality director William Wyler wanted. (Not until 1980 did Russell make another film, one titled *Inside Moves*.)

Upon taking the first tentative steps into civilian life, the three find the going rough. Yes, Johnny had come marching home, but what awaited him?

And, like those populating the town in the film, did the people on the home front really understand the changes that seeing so much death and destruction had wrought in their returning servicemen? Did they realize that nothing is forever?

The stories of the three men are intertwined. Several poignant and telling scenes stand out as the scenario unfolds:

- A newly reunited Al and his wife Milly, trying to engage in small talk, but soon realizing that, although they have been married for many years and are still in love, they are uncomfortable with each other.
- Their daughter, Peggy, glowingly performed by Teresa Wright, who meets and falls in love with Fred Derry.
- The latter, confronting his hard-as-nails wife (Virginia Mayo on leave from her musical comedy roles with Danny Kaye) with the current man in her life and suddenly realizing that he doesn't care.
- Fred again, as he sits at the controls of a bomber that is soon to be junked. A war hero who has returned from his day in the sun to an unfaithful wife and to bleak prospects for the future, he feels obsolete and useless. Outside the aircraft's window, the viewer sees several junked planes. This panorama reveals the similarity between the unwanted pilot and what was once the source of his glory (the symbolism of this scene is quite evident). And finally:
- Homer Parish, as he painstakingly and uncompromisingly shows his girl Wilma (Cathy O'Donnell) what life will be like should they marry.

In spite of a myriad of problems, the film ends on a hopeful note. Al has begun to find inner peace as he and Milly rekindle their love, Fred and Peggy are at the beginning of a bittersweet romance, and Homer marries his Wilma.

Goldwyn premiered the film in New York. The reviews were uniformly ecstatic. *The New York Times* called it superlative, "catching the drama of the returning veterans, a legacy of the war, as no other film has." It and director Wyler won the accolades of the prestigious New York Film Critics group. The public responded in kind in theaters all over the country.

But for Samuel Goldwyn, who had seen the film through from its inception to the finished product, March 13, 1947, was the night when it all came together, the night of the Academy Awards ceremony.

The festivities took place at the Shrine Auditorium in downtown Los Angeles. The auditorium had over six thousand seats and to fill them, for the first time in history, the Academy sold tickets to the general public.

The Best Years of Our Lives was voted the Oscar as Best Picture of 1946. Goldwyn also received the prestigious Irving Thalberg Memorial Award as outstanding producer of the year.

Returning veteran William Wyler was honored for his tasteful and incisive direction and Fredric March received a second Oscar (the first had come fourteen years before, for *Dr. Jekyll and Mr. Hyde*) for his towering performance as Al Stephenson, inwardly ravaged by the war of which he had wanted no part.

Robert Sherwood took home an Oscar for his screenplay, but it was Harold Russell who brought the house down as he stepped forward to receive two Oscars. The amputee war vet, who had never appeared in a movie, was first honored as Best Actor in a Supporting Role for his performance as Homer Parish, but it had been no mere job of acting. Never had an actor "lived" his lines as had Russell. A second statuette was given him as a symbol bringing "life and courage to his fellow veterans" and for demonstrating that the loss of a body part does not take away from the whole of a man.

The Best Years of Our Lives treated only one aspect of what Archie Bunker has lovingly called "W W Two." Since the end of hostilities, the making of war films has continued even up to this present day.

Chapter Thirteen

The End of the Forties: A Time of Darkness

The period between the end of the war and the beginning of the new decade was a time of darkness and strife for the Hollywood community. A vigorous Communist "purge," led by Representative J. Parnell Thomas, chairman of the House Un-American Activities Committee (HUAC), and Senator Joseph McCarthy, devastated Hollywood and affected the lives and careers of over three hundred film personnel who were blacklisted by this witch hunt.* Those listed who had been Communists or Communist sympathizers during an earlier stage of their lives were denied their livelihoods for several years. Included in this infamous round-up were the so-called "Hollywood Ten" who refused to testify before the committee. Some went to prison after lengthy appeals. And who was their fellow inmate? None other than J. Parnell, serving time for padding his Congressional payroll and his pocketbook. (In 1976, Woody Allen starred in a Columbia film titled *The Front*, a comical twist on this serious theme. Allen's character is asked to "front" for a group of blacklisted writers by putting his name to their work. This was an actual occurrence during the McCarthy Era. Several of the cast members, including Zero Mostel, Herschel Bernardi and Lloyd Gough, could give credence to this premise as they had been victims of the "list.")

Added to Hollywood's woes was the advent of television. Film

---

*Lucille Ball's grandfather had been a Socialist and for him, when Lucy was quite young, the entire family had joined the Communist Party. The actress had forgotten about this, but during the first year of the I Love Lucy TV show, this fact was brought out. Before one of the tapings, husband Desi Arnaz addressed the audience, saying that his wife had never been a Communist. He concluded by saying there is nothing red about Lucy except her hair and even that is not her natural color.

moguls, living in terror that the infant medium would be detrimental to their industry, barred their contract players from appearing on the small screen. Several stars not under contract did take the plunge and became more popular than ever. It would take some years before the movie and television industries would see the advantages of mutual cooperation.

Besides those listed in Chapter Eleven, other war-related films were produced during these turbulent times. Action, comedy, drama and fantasy were the themes.

Set on an airbase in England, *Command Decision*, a 1948 MGM release, is one of the better postwar pictures made by Clark Gable. The star plays a flight commander agonizing about sending his men on a suicide mission over Germany (this was the plight of many an officer during combat). The realistic production was enhanced by a cast of well-known actors, including Walter Pidgeon, Van Johnson, Brian Donlevy, John Hodiak and Edward Arnold.

That same year, another film paying homage to the Air Force was released by Warner Bros. *Fighter Squadron*, starring Edmond O'Brien as a dedicated pilot, was filmed in Technicolor, which is an asset to the production. The script is of "B" quality, but the battle scenes are quite good. Taking part in the proceedings are Robert Stack and a young unknown named Rock Hudson.

Far from the airfields of Great Britain and the United States are the streets of Paris, just before the invasion of France. That beautiful city is the setting for *Arch of Triumph*. This 1948 United Artists film stars Charles Boyer as a surgeon who has escaped from his occupied native land. He helps down-on-her-luck Ingrid Bergman find a job as a singer. Boyer meets a Nazi from his home town, played menacingly by Charles Laughton, and kills him on a quiet road. Meanwhile, Boyer and Bergman have fallen in love, but a jealous admirer of hers fatally shoots her. The film's finale finds Boyer, because of his own actions, and with the coming of the occupation forces, leaving Paris to find refuge somewhere else. The film was adapted from a novel by Erich Maria Remarque and features Ruth Warrick, J. Edward Bromberg and William Conrad.

Another 1948 film, RKO's *Berlin Express*, was partially filmed in Germany. It stressed the need for cooperation among the war-torn countries of Europe. The plotline revolves around a group of unrepentant Nazis trying to prevent the unification of their "Fatherland" while a trio of "good guys" band together to save the life of a German statesman who may have a feasible unification plan. Starred are Robert Ryan, Merle Oberon and Robert Coote as the heroes of the piece and Paul Lukas as the statesman.

Still on the theme of Nazis, but with a change of locale, is *Rogues Regiment* from Universal-International.* The 1948 film takes place in Saigon, Indo-China, with Dick Powell cast as an Army Intelligence agent who is sent there to capture an escaped Nazi war criminal. Marta Toren plays Powell's romantic interest, Vincent Price is a gun runner and Stephen McNally, who ably played both good guys and heavies on screen, is the villain.

Changing locales and the mood, we meet those three zanies, The Marx Brothers. *A Night in Casablanca,* from United Artists, bears no resemblance whatsoever to the legendary Warner Bros. masterpiece. In this 1946 offering, Groucho is the manager of a hotel; he is the owners' last resort, as those before him have been murdered. Chico is his self-appointed bodyguard and Harpo plays the silent manservant of an escaped Nazi (Sig Rumann) and his entourage. While Groucho is being vamped by a beautiful girl, the Nazis are trying to steal a cache of money which is hidden under the hotel. In spite of themselves, Groucho, Chico and Harpo manage to thwart the plans of the nasties. The film brought the trio back to the screen after a five-year absence, but it could not match the caliber of their previous offerings.

MGM had scored a hit in 1945 with *The Clock* (see Chapter Ten), about a soldier on leave and the girl he meets. Two years later, Warner Brother did a variation on this theme. *The Voice of the Turtle* is the tale of a lonely soldier on furlough who woos and wins an actress on the rebound from a broken romance. The film, adapted from a Broadway hit, opened in New York while the play was still running. Even so, the film did well at the box office. Ronald Reagan and Eleanor Parker are the couple who find each other and they are ably supported by Wayne Morris, Kent Smith and wisecracking Eve Arden.

Also in the comedy vein is *Buck Privates Come Home* (Universal-International). Bud Abbott and Lou Costello (how did we win the war, even cinematically, with those two on our side?) are the returning GIs of the title in this 1947 opus. One of the boys' more endearing films, it

---

*In November 1946, Universal had merged with an independent company called International Pictures.

was a sequel to *Buck Privates*, released six years before. This time, the duo tries to smuggle a six-year-old French refugee (Beverly Simmons) into this country. This they accomplish, but not without the usual A&C shenanigans, topped off by a hilarious car chase finale.

I have saved two of the most interesting and original film of the group discussed in this chapter for last.

Stairway to Heaven, a 1946 production made in England, meshes reality with fantasy and stars David Niven, Kim Hunter, Raymond Massey and Marius Goring (the latter stealing the show as the Heavenly Messenger). Niven plays a downed pilot who insists that he has accidentally been chosen to die and he has to plead his case before a heavenly court. With the help of his doctor and the girl who loves him, he is brought back to reality. The British title of the film is *A Matter of Life and Death*.

Another improbable yet entertaining film is *Golden Earrings*, a 1947 release from Paramount. Set in Germany, the film stars Marlene Dietrich in the role of a lusty gypsy who gives aid and refuge to a British agent, played by Ray Milland. He is on a mission to buy a poison gas formula. Finding the inventor of the formula at a party given by the Germans, he gets the formula. Mission accomplished, he returns to England, but cannot forget the gypsy and goes back to her. Also in the cast is stage star Murvyn Vye as the caravan leader. It is he who sings the title song which became very popular via a recording by singing star Peggy Lee.

The Nazis had been defeated, and we were saying goodbye to the 1940s. However, World War II–related films were still being made in spite of the changing scene and a changing society.

Chapter Fourteen

A Changing Scene, a Changing Society: The Fifties and Sixties

The decades of the 1950s and 1960s saw American involvement in both Korea and Vietnam, the launching of our first atomic submarine, the *Nautilus*, and the testing of a deadly hydrogen bomb which was the equivalent of ten million tons of TNT. During the early fifties, the junior senator from Wisconsin, Joseph McCarthy, was still finding Communists everywhere he looked (including the film industry), continuing the period of witch-hunting and smear campaigns he had begun.

Desegregation of public schools became a fact of life, along with the assassinations of three prominent Americans: John F. Kennedy, his brother Robert and the Reverend Martin Luther King, Jr., in the 1960s.

Events abroad saw a new English monarch, Queen Elizabeth, the death of one dictator, Joseph Stalin, and the rise of another, Fidel Castro. The Berlin Wall, separating the eastern part of the German capital from the western, was erected and would not come down until the 1980s, under the watch of former screen star, now president, Ronald Reagan ("Mr. Gorbachev, tear down that wall!").

The Russians further tested American resolve in the early 1960s when they decided to build missile bases in Cuba. Kennedy, president at the time, took a firm stand and the Russians stood down.

It was also a period of radical social and cultural changes for America and indeed for the rest of the world at large. An unknown boy from Tupelo, Mississippi, named Elvis, and four English lads from Liverpool who answered to John, Paul, George and Ringo stormed the musical world, changing it for all time. Rock 'n' roll was here to stay.

It was the era of the drug scene and of the sexual revolution, the

Fourteen. A Changing Scene, a Changing Society

end of a puritanical America, and the beginning of a modern age in which we "let it all hang out."

Though most of the films produced during the 1950s and 1960s reflected these changes, World War II films were still fairly popular with a large segment of the moviegoing public.

To discuss or even list all the films of this genre made within a twenty-year span is a difficult, well-nigh impossible task. Again, as in previous chapters, I have tried to write about those which I consider to be the most interesting and those which best give a feeling for the times, places and incidents they portray, and I hope the reader will agree as to their importance in a narrative such as this.

The World War II films released during the 1950s and 1960s run the gamut of movie genres. Comedies, musicals, mysteries, dramas of love and courage and melodramas of espionage and spy-catching — they all play a part in Hollywood's version of the war. Many moviegoers of the era were once again seeing some of those faraway places for which they had fought and their comrades had died. One of the films produced showed anew the early brutality of the regimes they had given so much of themselves to defeat.

I Am a Camera, a 1955 film shot in England, is set in the pre-war Berlin of the of the 1930s. Based upon the diaries of writer Christopher Isherwood, the film's plotline centers on his relationship with the amoral and reckless Sally Bowles, but also touches upon the insidious rise of the Nazis to power and the hold they would soon have over their fellow countrymen. The cast includes Julie Harris as Sally and Laurence Harvey as the writer. Shelley Winters and Ron Randell play another couple caught up in the times. *I Am a Camera* was the forerunner of the brilliant stage and screen success *Cabaret*, which will be discussed in the next chapter.

From Here to Eternity also has a pre-war setting: Hawaii, just before the attack on Pearl Harbor. The 1953 Academy Award–winning drama of life and lust, army style, was adapted from the hard-hitting novel by James Joyce and features an all-star cast including Burt Lancaster, Deborah Kerr, Frank Sinatra, Montgomery Clift, and Donna Reed. Not a war drama in the usual sense, the film is about people whose lives are intertwined through their service in the military.

As interesting as the film is, the behind-the-scenes story is even more so. Columbia head Harry Cohn had paid for the screen rights to the Joyce novel and demanded a say in its casting. Cohn wanted either John Derek or Aldo Ray, who were both under contract to the studio at the time, in the part that eventually was played by Montgomery Clift; Fred Zinnemann, who would go on to win an Oscar as Best Director, held out for Clift, standing up to Cohn and telling him that that it was either Clift or they could hire another director. Joan Crawford, Edmond O'Brien and Julie Harris were the original choices for the roles which went to Kerr, Lancaster and Reed (who went on to win the year's Best Supporting Actress Oscar). The beach pyrotechnics between Lancaster and Kerr makes for one of the screen most famous love scenes.

And then there was the part of a character named Maggio. Cohn had wanted Eli Wallach for the role, but when the latter opted for Broadway, Frank Sinatra, at the lowest point of his career, told Cohn that he would do the role for nothing and even test for it. Not until Ava Gardner, then married to the singer, made a personal plea to the mogul did the latter allow the test. Director Zinnemann was impressed with Sinatra's performance. Frank played Maggio, got eight thousand dollars for his effort, won a Best Supporting Actor Oscar and the rest, as they say, is history. (The singer also had a hit recording of the title tune.)

Others in the cast include Ernest Borgnine as the vicious bully Fatso Judson, Jack Wardon and Harry Bellaver. The production was honored with eight Oscar nominations; one went to Burt Lancaster, another to Deborah Kerr and one to writer Daniel Taradash for his screenplay of the Joyce novel.

Relationships in *From Here to Eternity* are an important element of the story. Such is also the case with *Between Heaven and Hell* (Twentieth Century–Fox, 1956). Robert Wagner is a thoughtless Southern landowner who has mistreated those who work for him. He sees the error of his ways when, as a soldier in the Pacific, his sadistic commanding officer almost breaks him. He refuses to knuckle under and becomes a hero when he saves a fellow GI. Appearing with Wagner are Broderick Crawford as the commanding officer and Buddy Ebsen as the fellow he saves. Others in the cast are Terry Moore, Skip Homeier, Robert Keith and Brad Dexter.

England had been at war for two years before the American involvement. In 1939, amid the bombings and the loss of lives in the embattled country, came the news that a famous German pocket battleship had been trapped off the coast of Uruguay in Montevideo Harbor. The *Graf*

Fourteen. A Changing Scene, a Changing Society

***The Pursuit of the Graf Spee*:** The German pocket battle ship the *Graf Spee* was personally commissioned by Adolf Hitler. The scuttling of the ship by its captain off the coast of Uruguay was a huge blow to the dictator's psyche.

Spee, a ship personally commissioned by Hitler, had been responsible for several British ships being sunk. The British avidly followed the daily happenings until the ship was scuttled by its captain. This incident is celebrated in the 1956 film *The Pursuit of the Graf Spee* (English title: *The Battle of the River Plate*). Starred are Anthony Quayle, Peter Finch and Ian Hunter.

A year later, while the Battle of Britain was raging, an amazing occurrence again gave the English people something for which they could cheer and it was immortalized on film ten years later. Shot in England, the production was released in the United States by MGM in 1958. *Dunkirk* is a dramatic retelling of the rescue of over thirty-five thousand men on the French beach by both members of the Royal Navy and civilians manning small crafts across the English Channel. Starred in the film are John Mills, Richard Attenborough and Bernard Lee. Interesting is the fact that Hitler, still thinking that England would come over to his side to battle the Communists, forbade the bombing of the beach by the Luftwaffe.

Intrigue was high on the list of cinematic priorities during the 1950s; all the better if true stories of derring-do were involved. This was the case of three interesting films released within the decade.

I Was Monty's Double, a 1958 British production, proved quite popular in its American showings. The film is based upon the actual wartime experiences of music hall entertainer M. E. Clifton James, who bore an uncanny resemblance to General Bernard Montgomery and was asked to impersonate the famed "Monty" in order to confuse German Intelligence during the African campaign early in the war. Although the melodramatic finale, wherein a group of German commandos attempts to capture the "general" in a seaside villa is contrived, the movie was made with the usual British competence and contains several exciting moments. In the cast are several well-known British actors including John Mills and Cecil Parker. Clifton-James went back to the music halls, secure in the knowledge that he had been a part of British history.

Confusion is also the order of the day in *The Man Who Never Was*. The 1956 Twentieth Century–Fox entry is an account of a triumph of Allied ingenuity which took place in 1943: Along the coast of a small fishing village in neutral Spain, a dead man having on his person some documents marked "Top Secret," is found washed ashore. German agents in the area, cautious until everything is meticulously checked out, are ecstatic with their discovery.

Only after the Allied invasion of Sicily does the enemy find out that "Operation Mincemeat" has been a set-up from beginning to end in order to divert attention from the actual objective. The documents, along with the personal letters from a "fiancée" found on the body, have done their job. Adapted from Sir Ewen Montague's book of the same name, the film stars Clifton Webb as Montague, the man who devised the scheme, Gloria Grahame as the girl "engaged" to a dead man and Stephen Boyd as an Irishman, working for the Germans, who travels to England to check out the plans and believes them to be genuine.

Five Fingers (1952), from the same studio, is the third in the group of true espionage stories filmed during the fifties; it was based upon the book *Operation Cicero*. The production's central character is the valet of the British Ambassador to Turkey. For reasons both personal and financial, the servant, code-named "Cicero," is selling military secrets to the

Fourteen. A Changing Scene, a Changing Society

Nazis. The suspicious Germans buy the information (the timing and location of the invasion of Europe) but, in one those quirks of fate that sometimes can decide the destiny of a nation, do not use it. The ending of the film is cynical and unexpected, but factual: Arriving in South America to spend his ill-gotten gains, "Cicero" discovers that the money given him by the Germans is counterfeit. James Mason stars as the valet-cum-spy along with Danielle Darrieux as the femme fatale who betrays him and Michael Rennie as a British agent hot on his trail.

Mason, one of the more versatile actors in the profession, was seen as Field Marshall Erwin Rommel on two occasions in the fifties. A Twentieth Century–Fox 1951 production titled *The Desert Fox* is based upon events that took

The Man Who Never Was: **Clifton Webb plays the mastermind of a brilliant plot to fool the Germans as the Allies prepare to invade Sicily. That the Germans were caught off guard is an understatement. The film is based on fact.**

place during the last years of Rommel's life. Defeated in both North Africa and on the beaches of Normandy, Rommel returns to Germany and, although he considers himself to be apolitical, he sees the madness of Hitler's policies and lends his name to the July 1944 plot to assassinate Hitler. The film ends with the death of the field marshal by poison (his "choice") in order to prevent reprisals against his family and the crocodile tears shed at his state funeral by the Nazi hierarchy for the benefit of a largely unknowing public (see Chapter Nine). Only after the war were these facts revealed. Jessica Tandy as Frau Rommel and Cedric Hardwicke as a family friend offer fine support in this well-made movie. However, it is Mason as Rommel, struggling as a soldier, disciplined to obey unquestioningly, but beginning to have doubts, who gives the best performance.

The Desert Rats, a 1953 Twentieth Century–Fox film, is the fictional account of an English captain during the siege of Tobruk who survives an encounter with Rommel. Along with Mason again as the field marshal, the cast includes a pre–Elizabeth Taylor Richard Burton as the captain and Robert Newton as his former teacher, disillusioned by the facts of war. Battle scenes are well done and concentrate on the part played by the Australian contingent of the British Eighth Army in the captured desert fortress.

Burton makes a second appearance in the African campaign, this time as one of the stars of a 1957 British-French production released by Columbia Pictures titled *Bitter Victory*. He and Curt Jurgens are Allied officers on a dangerous mission against Rommel's headquarters. The turgid screenplay has both in love with Ruth Roman, who happens to be the wife of Jurgens.

Another fictional drama, again from Columbia, this time with an absolutely unbelievable premise, is introduced by the noted journalist and war correspondent William L. Shirer. *The Magic Face*, a 1951 production filmed in Austria, stars Luther Adler as a small-time German vaudevillian whose wife (Patricia Knight, then Mrs. Cornel Wilde) becomes attracted to Hitler. The man is thrown into jail, escapes and kills the Nazi leader, then takes his place and deliberately leads his country into defeat. An interesting theory it is, but one must wonder how and why the highly respected Shirer, author of *Berlin Diary* and *The Rise and Fall of the Third Reich*, became involved in this project.

In my research for this book I came across a 1943 film from Universal titled *The Strange Death of Adolf Hitler* with the same premise (the murder of Hitler) but with a different ending. Ludwig Donath stars as a Viennese stage impressionist who kills the Nazi leader with the same aim as in the other film, only in this one, the impersonator is killed by his wife (Gale Sondergaard) who thinks he really is the dictator.

A more true-to-life and poignant war drama is the Austro-Yugoslav production *The Last Bridge*, which had its American showing in 1954. The gifted Maria Schell, sister of actor Maximilian, stars as an apolitical German nurse, captured by Yugoslav partisans, whose compassion and dedication to the art of healing transcends national boundaries and politics. A compelling film, it is also a statement on the horrors of war and what it can do to mankind.

All Quiet on the Western Front, released by Universal in 1930, had been adapted from the anti-war novel by Erich Maria Remarque. showing the horrors of war in a simple story of a group of young German soldiers who, one by one, are killed or maimed in action. In 1958, Universal-International released *A Time to Love and a Time to Die*, another story by Remarque, again showing the German side of war and driving home the message that war is hell, whichever side you are on. John Gavin stars as a soldier who, while home on leave, meets and marries a girl, played by Lilo Pulver. In a scene reminiscent of the closing moments of *All Quiet on the Western Front*, in which the World War I soldier dies while reaching out to touch a butterfly, this soldier is killed while clutching a letter from his wife telling him that he will soon be a father. The young, apolitical youngster has been torn from life by a group of fanatics.

Also apolitical is the hero of *Decision Before Dawn*, (Twentieth Century–Fox, 1951), a film version of what actually occurred during the final phases of the war. Oskar Werner is seen as a sensitive German prisoner of war recruited to work with the Americans; he feels that this can help hasten the end of the war and lessen the destruction of his homeland. Trained in espionage, he completes his mission, but sacrifices his life rescuing an American officer. Co-starred are Gary Merrill and Richard Basehart.

The 1957 production *The Enemy Below* (Twentieth Century-Fox) stars Robert Mitchum and Curt Jurgens. Directed by Dick Powell, the film is the story of two men pitted against each other and is, as most war films are, another statement on the horrors of war and its effect on mankind. Mitchum portrays the captain of a U.S. destroyer matching wits with the commander of a German submarine (Jurgens). The conflict finds the two vessels fighting it out on the surface. Both sink, but the men are rescued. The two officers meet, have a cigarette and salute each other.

Two superstars, both Academy Award winners (Clark Gable in 1934 for *It Happened One Night* and Burt Lancaster in 1960 for *Elmer Gantry*) appear in another film depicting underwater warfare. *Run Silent Run Deep* (1958) from the production company of Hecht-Hill-Lancaster and released by United Artists, stars Gable as a submarine commander who is thinking only of revenge upon the Japanese ship which had sunk his former ship. Second in command is Lancaster, who is worried about his superior, but at film's end, Gable redeems himself, thinking more about the needs of his men than of his own. In support of the two stars are

Don Rickles and Jack Warden. Rickles went on to become more famous as a stand-up comedian, appearing on television and in nightclubs.

On the other side of the globe, as the British import *The Sea Shall Not Have Us* (1954) begins, a bomber is shot down in the Atlantic Ocean. Michael Redgrave and Dirk Bogarde star as part of a group of survivors awaiting rescue.

Next, we come to a film which must have surprised many a moviegoer.

Cary Grant, the epitome of sophistication, as a unshaven reprobate? Better believe it. *Father Goose*, a 1965 Universal comedy-drama, casts Cary as an inebriated, unkempt bum who spends his days spotting enemy planes for the Australian government on a deserted island in the South Seas. His life is changed when a schoolteacher, played by French actress Leslie Caron, and her seven charges are marooned on "his island."

He is nonplussed at this turn of events, but at film's finale, the island is besieged and they are forced to evacuate. By this time, Grant and Caron are in love and are married via telephone and all are rescued. Co-starred is Trevor Howard as the Australian commander to whom Grant reports his findings.

Also taking place in the Pacific theater of operations are two submarine adventure stories, *Up Periscope*, a 1959 vehicle from Warner Bros., and *Torpedo Run*, an MGM 1958 production. The first stars Edmond O'Brien as a sub commander who goes by the book, thereby alienating several members of his crew, and James Garner as a demolition expert whose dangerous assignment is to capture a Japanese code book which is to be found on an enemy-held island. Though the relationship between the two officers is strained, the job is done. The cast includes Carleton Carpenter and Alan Hale, Jr.

Torpedo Run has an even more interesting premise. It involves the tracking of a Japanese aircraft carrier and sinking it in Tokyo Bay. The action scenes are exceptionally well done and quite realistic in scope. Starred are Glenn Ford and Ernest Borgnine.

John Wayne as a German? Never, you say? Check out *The Sea Chase*. The 1955 production, courtesy of Warner Brother, stars Wayne as an outspoken anti–Nazi sea captain of a German freighter caught in Australian waters at the beginning of the war. Though apolitical, he nevertheless decides to return to Germany. Among his passengers is a blonde in the person of Miss Lana Turner. At first dedicated to the Nazi cause, she

Fourteen. A Changing Scene, a Changing Society

switches allegiance to help Wayne, with whom she has fallen in love. At the conclusion of the film, the ship is attacked and is sinking. The crew, with the exception of the lovers, abandons the ship. The audience is left to ponder as to whether the captain and his lady have at the last moment gotten off the ship.

Wayne and Turner are totally miscast in this film. With other stars, this unusual story might have had somewhat of a fighting chance. A trivia note: In the cast are Tab Hunter, idol of the teenagers in the 1950s and 1960s, and also James Arness, who would go on to achieve lasting fame as television's Marshall Dillon in *Gunsmoke*. That series can still be seen over the TV Land network.

In an earlier film, RKO's *Flying Leathernecks*, Duke is more conventionally cast, this time as an American Marine fighting the Japanese on Guadalcanal. Co-starred with him in this 1951 production is Robert Ryan. The two clash as to how to run their outfit: Wayne is exceedingly tough while Ryan feels he needs to be a bit more lenient. When confronted with the actual fighting, however, Ryan sees that his superior was right all along. Battle scenes and aerial views are well-delineated if a bit on the violent side. A typical Wayne opus, it is far different from *The Sea Chase*. and far more predictable.

Also somewhat on the violent side, but far tamer than the book by Norman Mailer, is *The Naked and the Dead*, a 1958 drama from Warners. It details the lives of a platoon of soldiers holed up on an island in the Pacific. Aldo Ray, Cliff Robertson and Raymond Massey star, with Ray giving a good performance as a sadistic soldier. (Note: In this, the twenty-first century, the language and brutality of the book would be an essential part of the film.)

Of lesser magnitude is *In Love and War*, a 1958 Twentieth Century–Fox production which, like the Mailer film, traces the effects of war on three disparate Marines. Starred are Jeffrey Hunter, Robert Wagner and Bradford Dillman. Hunter marries and dies a hero's death in the South Pacific, Wagner learns the meaning of true courage and Dillman finds love with a Hawaiian nurse. The ladies involved are Hope Lange, Dana Wynter and France Nuyen.

From Columbia Pictures came a vehicle of epic proportions which was honored with seven Academy Awards. *The Bridge on the River Kwai* (1957), with an international cast including William Holden, Alec Guinness, Jack Hawkins, and former silent star Sessue Hayakawa, takes place in a Japanese prisoner of war camp. It is essentially the story of a clash of wills between a proud British colonel (Guinness) and the camp commandant (Hayakawa). The latter orders the prisoners to construct a massive bridge over the river so that troop trains can go from one vital area to another. The project becomes all-consuming to the colonel, who cracks under the strain. Unknown to him, a sabotage unit under Holden is being readied to blow up the bridge.

Among the Oscar winners were Guinness, director David Lean and the picture itself. An interesting sidelight to Oscar night took place when the winner for Best Screenplay was announced. The scriptwriters were Carl Foreman and Michael Wilson — both of whom had been blacklisted. The award was accepted by Pierre Boulle. the author of the book upon which the film was based.

The Marine Corps was paid a tribute by Twentieth Century–Fox in 1951: *Halls of Montezuma*, starring Richard Widmark, Karl Malden, Reginald Gardiner and Jack Webb, focuses on the capture of an island in the South Pacific upon which rocket sites have been set up. An advance patrol is sent out to capture and interrogate prisoners as to the location of the sites. The objective is achieved, but at a tremendous cost. An interesting aspect of the film is that it was directed by Lewis Milestone, who was at the helm of the 1930 anti-war classic *All Quiet on the Western Front*.

Marines, this time with the help of the Navy, are the heroes of *China Venture* (Columbia, 1953). Edmond O'Brien and Barry Sullivan star as a Marine captain and a naval officer; their mission is to capture a Japanese admiral from the coast of China and deliver him to top intelligence officers for questioning. The mission is accomplished in spite of a conflict between O'Brien and Sullivan. Also seen in the production are Leo Gorcey, Richard Loo and, as the Japanese admiral, Philip Ahn.

Battle Cry, based on a novel by Leon Uris, who also wrote the screenplay, focuses on the lives of a group of Marines: their training, their romances and their battle assignments. A cast of well-known players including Van Heflin, Aldo Ray, James Whitmore, Fess Parker and Tab Hunter added to the popularity of the film. The ladies in love are Mona Freeman, Nancy Olson, Dorothy Malone and Anne Francis.

The Japanese depicted in *Go for Broke!*, a 1951 MGM entry, are Nisei (Japanese-Americans), members of the 442nd Regimental Combat Unit which fought heroically both in Italy and in France. It is an

Fourteen. A Changing Scene, a Changing Society

important film if only to remember the tragedy of many Japanese-Americans who were interned in relocation camps as a result of a misguided post–Pearl Harbor governmental action. Van Johnson stars as the commander of the regiment; at first antagonistic towards the men, he soon comes to admire and respect them.

As a musical, *South Pacific*, a 1958 film from Twentieth Century–Fox, lacks the star quality of the stage hit, but the story of an American navy nurse in love with a French planter who becomes a war hero, has become timeless. Mitzi Gaynor and Rossano Brazzi are a road company version of Broadway's Mary Martin and opera star Ezio Pinza; the photography, however, is lush and in perfect harmony with the incomparable Rodgers and Hammerstein musical score. John Kerr and France Nuyen play a pair of lovers doomed from the start by racial differences, Juanita Hall is Bloody Mary, the enterprising mother of Nuyen, and Ray Walston is the seabee who thinks "there is nothing like a dame." Taken from the novel *Tales of the South Pacific* by James Michener, and with Joshua Logan directing as he did on Broadway, the film version of the play was a solid hit at the box office.

For many, both the stage and screen versions of *Mister Roberts* are usually remembered as Henry Fonda vehicles, although misguided studio boss Jack Warner had wanted either William Holden or Marlon Brando for the screen role. Fonda got to play it and, in subsequent interviews, said that he considered the role his favorite in a long and distinguished career. Much more than that, the story, taken from a novel by Thomas Heggen, is a look at the humorous aspects of life aboard a cargo ship. The 1955 production was the introduction to the screen of a major talent, a stage and television actor named Jack Lemmon, who plays the role of an opportunistic ensign named Pulver. He received a Best Supporting Actor nomination, and the film was nominated for Best Picture; he won, the film did not. Along with Fonda and Lemmon, the cast boasts two old pros, James Cagney as the irascible captain of the ship and William Powell as its philosophical medic. It was Cagney's last film for the studio that had signed him to a contract fresh from his Broadway success in 1930.

On a ramshackle submarine sailing from the Philippines to Australia in the early days of World War II is Ensign Pulver's alter ego, a scheming junior officer played by Tony Curtis. Both he and his commanding officer Cary Grant are determined to make their sub seaworthy again, the latter by fair means, the former by any way he can. This is the plotline of Universal-International's 1959 release *Operation Petticoat*. To complicate matters, the ship takes on a compliment of nurses, adding to the hilarity. The Grant-Curtis team is a delightful one, with the ageless Cary giving one and all a lesson in the art of making the ridiculous sublime. The cast includes Arthur O'Connell and Gene Evans plus Dina Merrill and Joan O'Brien as two of the nurses. In the 1977 television version of *Operation Petticoat*, Jamie Lee Curtis, daughter of Curtis and his then-wife Janet Leigh, was featured as one of the nurses.

By 1958, Curtis had come a long way. Far removed from his earlier "pretty boy" status, he had become an actor of some versatility. adept at both comedy and drama. His more serious side comes to the fore in *Kings Go Forth*, a United Artist 1958 production in which he co-stars with Frank Sinatra. Southern France in 1944 is the setting, as both Sinatra and Curtis, as his radio operator, are attracted to the same French girl (Natalie Wood). They are shocked to learn that the girl's dead father was black, but both men overcome their prejudice. On a dangerous mission, Curtis is killed by the Germans and Sinatra is wounded, but survives minus an arm. The final scenes take place after D-Day and have Sinatra again seeing the girl, who is now teaching war orphans.

A serious film, albeit with many comedic overtones, is Paramount's *Stalag 17* (1953). Based upon a successful stage hit and no doubt the forerunner of television's *Hogan's Heroes*, the story concerns the day-to-day existence of some Americans in a German prisoner of war camp. The production is a mixture of hi-jinx, violence and mystery as the men discover that there is a Nazi spy in their midst. William Holden, as the loner they suspect of being the traitor, was honored as Best Actor of 1953 for his performance. He receives superb support from Robert Strauss who, repeating his stage role as "Animal," gives the movie its funniest moments, Don Taylor, Neville Brand, Richard Erdman and future television star Peter Graves.

The Colditz Story, an interesting British production released in 1954, is another POW film. More serious than *Stalag 17*, it revolves around the escape attempts of the men who are interned in Colditz Castle, a maximum security prison in the German province of Saxony. Starred in the film are John Mills, Eric Portman, Lionel Jeffries and folk singer Theodore Bikel, who has appeared throughout the years in several non-singing roles.

Fourteen. A Changing Scene, a Changing Society   165

Three Came Home (Twentieth Century–Fox, 1950) is based on a true story. It stars Claudette Colbert as an American woman captured by the Japanese on the island of Borneo and Japanese actor Sessue Hayakawa as the commandant of the prison camp in which she and her child have been interned. The movie depicts with startling realism the harsh conditions under which the prisoners are forced to live.

Sealed Cargo (RKO, 1951) pits Dana Andrews against Claude Rains in a taut melodrama of an American seaman who rescues the captain of a "Danish" ship, only to discover that the vessel is of German origin and the captain is a rabid Nazi.

The Last Blitzkrieg (Columbia 1959) is interesting as it stars all–American, redheaded Van Johnson as a German spy who infiltrates the American lines. Too late he realizes that he has been on the wrong side when he sees the American friends he has made shot in cold blood. Also in the cast are Dick York and Larry Storch.

To Hell and Back (Universal-International, 1955), in which Congressional Medal of Honor winner Audie Murphy appears as himself, is the retelling of his infantry heroics. Murphy, a poor Texas farm boy, enlisted in the army in 1942 at the age of eighteen. He served in North Africa, Italy, France, Germany and Austria. Twenty-four medals attest to his bravery in battle and thus far, he has been the most decorated soldier in United States history.

Red Ball Express (Universal-International, 1952) stars Jeff Chandler in a fictionalized account of an actual part of the armed forces — the United States Army Transport Unit, whose job it is to see that those at the front get the gas and ammunition they need. Sidney Poitier co-stars as a soldier in the unit and others in the cast include Charles Drake, Hugh O'Brian and Jack Kelly.

Hellcats of the Navy (Columbia, 1957), a submarine drama, is notable as the only film in which Nancy Davis, already Mrs. Ronald Reagan, and her husband appear together. The future president plays a sub commander in the Pacific theater of war who is at loggerheads with his next in command (Arthur Franz). Eventually this situation is cleared up. Nancy, of course, supplies the romance.

The next two are from MGM. *Until They Sail* (1957) is about four sisters, Joan Fontaine, Jean Simmons, Piper Laurie and Sandra Dee, who find love and murder in wartime New Zealand. Simmons gets Paul Newman. *Never So Few* (1959) has Americans fighting in Burma and boasts

Hellcats of the Navy: Ronald and Nancy Reagan were husband and wife while making this film about a submarine commander at odds with his second in command. This is the only film starring the couple. Other actors are unidentified.

a cast which includes Frank Sinatra, Peter Lawford, Steve McQueen, Brian Donlevy, Charles Bronson and Philip Ahn.

The last film to be noted in our meanderings through the decade of the 1950s is *The Young Lions* (Twentieth Century–Fox, 1958), based upon the novel by Irwin Shaw, starring Marlon Brando as a German ski instructor who is anti-war (with so many anti–Nazis and apolitical Germans populating the films of the 1950s, it's a wonder there even *was* a war), but nevertheless becomes a soldier. Dean Martin and Montgomery Clift co-star as his American counterparts. The lives of Martin and Clift become intertwined as they serve in the same unit. At the end of the film, now in Europe, the two Americans shoot and kill the German. Hope Lange and Barbara Rush are the women in the lives of the Americans, Mai Britt is in Brando's love and Maximilian Schell is seen as his friend.

Fourteen. A Changing Scene, a Changing Society

Seven years later, also for Twentieth Century–Fox, Brando would again play a German who does not espouse the cause of National Socialism. In *Saboteur: Code Name Morituri*, he is a spy employed by the British, sailing on a cargo vessel bound from Japan to Germany. His mission is to turn the ship over to the Allies. Co-starred is Yul Brynner as the captain who, at the end of the movie, sides with the spy. The interesting supporting cast includes comedian Wally Cox, Trevor Howard, Martin Kosleck and Bing Crosby's son Gary.

The 1960s dawned with a new kind of Hollywood on the horizon. The movie capital was a town in transition as the studio system lost ground to several independent companies. Contract players were a thing of the past, as were the outputs of twenty to thirty films a year by one company. The Mayers, the Cohns and the Warners were all gone by mid-decade. The Hollywood that they had once known and loved was ended, to be replaced by one of big business and corporate finance. Under the old system, stars used to make three, four and even five films a year (and even more in the heyday of such studio as Warner Bros., where young contract players like Bette Davis, Joan Blondell and Jimmy Cagney made at least ten programmers per annum). Now they were lucky to appear in one or two independently financed productions.

The decade can also be thought of as a period of greater flexibility. By the end of the 1950s, a new Production Code for monitoring films had come into being; it was an improvement on the unrealistic Hays Office. Because there were many infractions of the new rules, however, by 1968 the code was scrapped in favor of a rating system which is still in effect today.

The 1960s were also thought of as the years of the "epic"— the larger-than-life stories which swept across the screen in larger-than-life proportions. World War II was the subject of many such films including *The Battle of Britain*. Shot in England and released by United Artists in 1969, the movie relies on special effects, stunt flyers, Technicolor and a cast of familiar faces to recall the time when the British were subject to daily and nightly raids by the Luftwaffe, but were cheered by the heroic retaliatory deeds of the RAF. Among the well-known actors in the cast are Michael Caine, Robert Shaw, Trevor Howard, Ralph Richardson, Michael Redgrave and Christopher Plummer.

Across the Channel, a group of gutsy POWs are busy planning *The Great Escape* (United Artists, 1963). Based on fact and shot on location in Germany, the movie details the plans which a group of Allied prisoners have made to escape from a German prison camp. This is to be done through three tunnels. One tunnel is discovered and several men are caught; however, a large group of men manage to elude capture, and the film follows their attempts to get out of Germany. Starred in the film are Steve McQueen, James Garner, Richard Attenborough, David McCallum, Gordon Jackson, Donald Pleasence and Charles Bronson.

And speaking of escapes, a film based upon fact, *The Password Is Courage*, an MGM 1962 production filmed in England, tells of the exploits of a British sergeant-major who made a "career" of escapes from German POW camps. Inappropriately, his name was Charles Coward.

A hero of another type is the subject of *Triple Cross*, a 1967 Warner Bros. production. Also based upon fact, it is the fascinating story of Eddie Chapman, a double agent. A British safecracker, Chapman was in German-occupied Jersey (one of the islands in the English Channel off the coast of Normandy) when he volunteered to work for the Nazis; in reality, he was reporting to the British. Hailed as a hero in England, he also received the Iron Cross in Germany. Christopher Plummer plays the double agent and is supported by Yul Brynner, Trevor Howard and German actor Gert Frobe.

Another type of hero is the subject of *Hell Is for Heroes* (Paramount, 1962). Steve McQueen is the leader of a group of GIs who must attack a German pillbox (a structure of reinforced concrete in which there are machine guns). The defenders are made to think that the group of attacking Americans is larger in number than it actually is. Mission accomplished with the help of supporting players James Coburn, Nick Adams, Fess Parker and Harry Guardino. Also in the cast, playing it straight, are comedian Bob Newhart and singer Bobby Darin (McQueen and Darin would die at the peak of their careers).

Sometimes hell can be located under the water when opposing forces release torpedoes or depth charges against each other. *Submarine X-1* (United Artists, 1968) tells the story of a naval group that is trained on the north coast of Scotland for an attack on a German warship based in a Norwegian fjord. The commander of the team, played by James Caan, having had his sub sunk in a fierce battle with the enemy, is given a chance to use a midget sub in a raid to sink the warship. This time — mission accomplished.

Screen epics of the 1960s were huge and lumbering, with several

Fourteen. A Changing Scene, a Changing Society 169

multi-lingual and multi-national in production. Though not always critically acclaimed, these films were nevertheless enjoyed by the public and occasionally can still be seen on TV and DVDs.

Gregory Peck, Anthony Quinn, David Niven and Anthony Quayle are the principal players in the 1961 adventure-thriller *The Guns of Navarone*. The plot of this Columbia film, shot on location on Rhodes, centers on a group of Allied soldiers who team up with some guerrilla fighters; their assignment is to infiltrate a Nazi-held Greek island and blow up a pair of radar-controlled guns that are wreaking havoc on Allied shipping. Audiences are treated to a bloody hand-to-hand skirmish between the good guys and the bad guys, a tidal wave of epic proportions and our heroes scaling a treacherous cliff before "The End" is flashed on the screen. Peck is the leader of the mission, Quinn is a Greek resistance fighter and Niven is a British demolition expert. Also in the cast are James Robertson Justice, Richard Harris, Italy's Gia Scala and Greek actress Irene Papas. The film received a Best Picture nomination, as did Carl Foreman, who wrote the screenplay based on the best-selling novel by Alistair MacLean. It had been four years since Foreman's Oscar for *The Bridge on the River Kwai*.

A British-made sequel, *Force 10 from Navarone*, was released in 1978. This time, the group's mission is to blow up a bridge vital to the Nazis in Yugoslavia. Though hampered by a traitor, the job is done. It was again taken from a story by Alistair MacLean; the cast includes Harrison Ford, Robert Shaw and Franco Nero, the latter being the bad guy. Though full of action, this film is not the classic its predecessor is.

The Longest Day, a 1962 epic from Twentieth Century–Fox, is studio head Darryl Zanuck's three-hour account of the June 1944 landings on the Normandy coast of France. Besides the cast of regular actors which includes John Wayne, Henry Fonda, Robert Ryan, Curt Jurgens, Peter Lawford, Richard Burton and Robert Mitchum, Zanuck hired three directors, used over four hundred veterans as extras and gave singer Paul Anka a role in the film. Anka also composed its stirring title song.

One of the first multilingual motion pictures, it is a sprawling version of the best-selling book by Cornelius Ryan. Zanuck used actual locations in the production: command posts occupied by the Germans and the French underground, the beaches on which the Allies fought so bravely and the small villages whose names have become immortalized to those who survived the carnage on that "Longest Day." The film received four Oscar nominations, one of which was Best Picture. It lost to *Lawrence of Arabia*. Though we know the outcome, getting there is still history in the making, a lesson for future generations and a thrill to watch.

Six years before, Twentieth Century–Fox made another film about this tumultuous day in the history of the world, titled *D-Day, the Sixth of June*. It contains more romance than action; the central characters are two men, a married American captain and a British colonel (Robert Taylor and Richard Todd), who are in love with the same woman, played by Dana Wynter. By the end of the film, Todd is dead, but Taylor, wounded in the same action and unaware of this turn of events, is on his way back to America and his wife. Although some fine fighting scenes highlight this screenplay, it does not have the scope of *The Longest Day*.

As the victorious Allies marched through France, liberating its towns and villages, Hitler gave the order to destroy Paris. By another one of those destiny-deciding quirks of fate, the German commandant of the French capital had too much respect for its history and traditions. He refused to do so and surrendered it intact. An all-star French-American vehicle released in 1966 under the Paramount banner, *Is Paris Burning?* recalls this famous World War II incident. Featured in the cast are such international favorites as Kirk Douglas, Charles Boyer, Glenn Ford, Leslie Caron, Anthony Perkins, Yves Montand, Simone Signoret, Robert Stack and Orson Welles. The screenplay was written by Francis Ford Coppola, who would go on to direct the blockbuster *Godfather* series.

Five months after D-Day, France was liberated and, to quote a popular song of the day, we were "marching to Berlin." The rumor was that the troops would be home for Christmas. Hitler, however, had other ideas and launched a last major offensive in the Ardennes Forest. Over one million men took part in the fighting and the toll of dead and wounded on both sides was staggering. This is the theme of *Battle of the Bulge*, a 1965 epic from Warner Bros.. The cast includes Henry Fonda, Robert Ryan, Telly Savalas, Dana Andrews, George Montgomery and James MacArthur.

Robert Shaw gives a chilling performance as an obsessed German tank commander who eats, sleeps and breathes war. His aide, played by Hans Christian Blech, at first an admirer of his superior, now sees the latter for what he has become, someone who wants the war to go on and on. Several actual events are covered in the film, among them the massacre of American soldiers at Malmedy and the use of English-speaking German soldiers to confuse the oncoming American troops.

The last scene in the film is really a summation of the battle and also of the war years: A lone German is shown throwing down his arms and slowly making his way eastward. He knows that the war is over. And a little while later, all of Germany knew this.

By early 1945, the American army was at the frontiers of Germany. *The Bridge at Remagen* is the fact-based effort of a platoon of Allied soldiers to commandeer the last bridge standing over the Rhine before it is destroyed. Starring in this 1965 United Artists release are George Segal as the American platoon leader, E. G. Marshall as the commanding general and Robert Vaughn as the German major whose mission it is to blow up the bridge before the Americans can get to it. Other Americans in the cast include Ben Gazzara and Bradford Dillman; on the other side, there are Hans Christian Blech and Peter Van Eyck.

A mission of another kind is the focus of *Foxhole in Cairo*. A British-made 1960 production, it is the story of counter-intelligence work in North Africa during the early days of the war wherein a German agent is allowed to get back to German lines carrying false information to Field Marshal Rommel. Featured in the cast are James Robertson Justice, Michael Caine and Peter Van Eyck.

Also taking place during the North African campaign is *Tobruk*, a 1967 Universal film. Rock Hudson and George Peppard are featured as American soldiers whose unit, in tandem with the British, must destroy a vital enemy fuel depot located in the desert fortress. This feat is accomplished before the theater lights go on again. Featured are Nigel Green as the head of the British unit and Guy Stockwell.

The actual story of Tobruk is much more interesting than the film. At the beginning of 1942, in the seesaw battles taking place in North Africa, the Afrika Korps under Rommel held the Libyan port and also possessed fuel, the not-so-secret weapon so necessary to achieve his aim of pushing on to the vital Suez Canal. Meanwhile, the British were regrouping in Egypt, getting shipments of men and materiel, and by June had recaptured Tobruk. The German forces, now low on fuel, but continuing to push westward, met the superior British forces under their daring new commander, General Bernard Montgomery, at El Alamein. An Allied victory there turned the tide in North Africa.

An interesting and offbeat film is *The Counterfeit Traitor* (Paramount, 1962), based on the true story of a Swedish businessman who is induced by a British official to pose as a Nazi sympathizer. Only at the finale, after several harrowing incidents, does his heroism become known to his family and friends. It was shot on location in Berlin, Hamburg, Copenhagen and Stockholm; William Holden stars in the title role and is ably supported by Lilli Palmer as an Allied agent (she does not survive) and Hugh Griffith as the Britisher.

Von Ryan's Express, a Twentieth Century–Fox 1965 film, stars Frank Sinatra as Ryan, senior officer of a group in an Italian POW camp. He has devised a plan to escape from the camp and reach Allied lines. The men steal German uniforms, seize a German train and start on their way to Switzerland. All survive except Ryan, who is gunned down in the final scene. Featured in a prominent role as a British officer who eventually learns to respect Ryan as an officer and as a man is Trevor Howard.

The Dirty Dozen is a 1967 MGM thriller in which a colonel (Lee Marvin) leads twelve convicts, either condemned to die or serving life sentences for committing crimes of violence, on a suicide mission — to infiltrate a Nazi generals' hideout. Those surviving will be freed. They are given sabotage training and go on the attack. The more well-known of the actors playing the dozen are Donald Sutherland, Charles Bronson, John Cassavetes, Telly Savalas, football great Jim Brown and singer Trini Lopez. Prominently featured as "good guys" are Robert Ryan and Ernest Borgnine.

Criminals of a far worse kind are the subject of *Judgment at Nuremberg*. Produced in 1961 by Stanley Kramer in conjunction with United Artists, it is a fictionalized but accurate account of the searing war crimes trials. This one deals with the trial of four generals accused of crimes against humanity. An all-star cast includes Spencer Tracy, Marlene Dietrich, Burt Lancaster, Judy Garland, Richard Widmark, Montgomery Clift and Maximillian Schell, the latter winning Best Actor honors for his role as a defense counsel. Tracy, Clift, Garland and director Kramer were Oscar-nominated.

That same year, another European took home a major award: Italian Sophia Loren won an Oscar for her performance in *Two Women*, a 1961 Italian-French collaboration, playing a woman who, along with her daughter, encounters attacking airplanes and is raped by Moroccan soldiers, yet manages to survive under the worst of conditions. At the time of the awards, Loren was quoted as saying, "I started out as a sex symbol,

Fourteen. A Changing Scene, a Changing Society 173

but it was as a symbol of mother love that I won my Oscar. And that gives me great satisfaction."

Night of the Generals, a curious 1967 drama from Columbia, has an interesting premise: A German military intelligence officer is ordered to find a psychopathic Nazi general who murders prostitutes. The stars are Peter O'Toole, who may be that general, and Omar Sharif as the intelligence officer. The cat-and-mouse game ends with Sharif homing in on O'Toole as the psychopath. Taking part in the proceedings are Donald Pleasence, Tom Courtenay and Christopher Plummer as Field Marshal Rommel.

The Enemy General, a 1960 film from Columbia, stars Van Johnson as an American posing as a French resistance fighter who is assigned to aid a Nazi general to defect even though he is responsible for the death of several innocent Frenchmen. The general supposedly has some vital information for the Allied cause. When the American finds that this is not the case, he disposes of this heinous criminal.

MGM's 1969 production *Where Eagles Dare* turned a huge profit for the studio. Richard Burton and Clint Eastwood star as Allied officers landing in the Bavarian Alps, posing as Germans in order to rescue a fellow officer imprisoned in a virtually impregnable castle.

Other films of the decade include *Battle at Bloody Beach* (Twentieth Century–Fox, 1961), which stars Audie Murphy as a civilian in the Philippines working with the guerrillas and trying to find his new bride, from whom he was separated when the Japanese attacked Manila. *The Thin Red Line* (1964), adapted from the novel by James Joyce, features Jack Warden, Keir Dullea and Kieron Moore. Raw recruits are sent to fight on the island of Guadalcanal where many of them lose their lives. *Hell to Eternity* (Allied Artists, 1960) is based on the true story of Gary Gabaldon, a war hero who had been raised by Japanese parents and his need to choose between the two cultures.

Last but not least in this grouping is *Hell in the Pacific* (1969), whose interesting plot revolves around the meeting of an American soldier (Lee Marvin) and a Japanese soldier (Toshiro Mifune) on a small deserted Pacific island and the interaction between them.

In closing out the 1960s, mention needs to made of the only World War II–related film of the decade to win Best Picture honors. *The Sound of Music*, released in 1965 by Twentieth Century–Fox, tells the romanticized story of the singing Von Trapp family who left their homeland with the coming of the Nazis. Julie Andrews stars as Maria (Mary Martin had starred on Broadway), the young girl who becomes governess to the Von Trapp children and falls in love with their widower father, played by Christopher Plummer. This version of the Broadway stage hit benefits from being shot in the lovely Austrian mountains and from the wonderful music of Richard Rodgers and Oscar Hammerstein which has been left intact.

The Sound of Music is somewhat similar to the 1972 musical remake of the film which began this chapter. Both take place in pre-war Europe and each give a portent of things to come.

Chapter Fifteen

Time Marches On: The Seventies and Eighties

Cabaret stars Liza Minnelli as the divinely amoral Sally Bowles, Joel Grey reprising his Broadway role as the sinister, decadent emcee of the Kit Kat Klub in pre-war Berlin and Michael York as the alter ego of Christopher Isherwood, upon whose writings the film and its predecessor are based. The memories of those years, brought out in living color, are certainly not a sentimental journey. Director Bob Fosse's staging of the musical numbers is brilliant, as is his handling of the political situation of the era. Though much of the story details a perverse sort of love affair between Sally and the writer, also seen is the equally perverse atmosphere which hung over the German nation and its capital when the Nazis came to power. Chilling scenes of people being dragged off by Hitler's "Brown Shirts" and a blond fresh-faced member of the "Hitler Youth" singing of the "New Order," give a vivid picture of what is in store for Germany and, indeed, for the world.

Fosse, Minnelli, and Grey were honored at the Academy Awards ceremony as Best Director, Actress and Supporting Actor of 1972. The film itself, though nominated, lost to *The Godfather*.

As in *Cabaret*, Fascism and its rise is everpresent in *The Garden of the Finzi-Continis*, a collaborative effort from Italy and West Germany. The locale of this Vittorio De Sica film is Mussolini's Italy during the 1930s. The plot centers on a wealthy Jewish family living an unchanged life in a rapidly changing world. Its deluded members are secure in the belief that they will survive the political events that are engulfing the rest of their nation. They do not see that their next stop is a concentration camp. This haunting film was named Best Foreign Film of 1971.

Cabaret: Liza Minnelli and Joel Grey won Oscars for their performances in this film which was a portent of things that came to pass in the Germany of the 1930s and then in all of Europe.

Fifteen. Time Marches On

Several other World War II–related films were made in the 1970s and 1980s. Though the war on the minds of most Americans during those years was the one escalating in a far-off country called Vietnam, the memories of the battles which had engulfed the world thirty years before were still fresh for many.

Politics and ethics were also on the mind of the American public. In 1973, Vice-President Spiro Agnew resigned, pleading "no contest" to income tax evasion while governor of Maryland, and a year later, America was shaken to her roots when, as a result of the Watergate break-in, during which a few Republicans had illegally entered the Democratic National Headquarters, Richard Nixon, to avoid impeachment, was forced to hand the presidency over to Gerald Ford.

On July the fourth, 1976, we celebrated a birthday — we were two hundred years old. In spite of all the calamities, the fiber of the nation was still intact and we had much to be proud of.

World War II–related films were still being produced both by the big studios and, in the 1980s, by independent film companies. *Raid on Rommel* (Universal, 1970) stars Richard Burton in yet another foray into North Africa. The time is 1942 and he is a commando leading a unit through enemy lines in the heavily fortified fortress of Tobruk, then held by units of the German Afrika Korps. The film makes this very dangerous assignment seem a lot easier than it really was. Similar in content to the 1960s television series *The Rat Patrol*, the movie salvaged much footage from *Tobruk*, a film from the same studio mentioned earlier in these pages.

Massacre in Rome, a based-on-fact 1973 film produced by Carlo Ponti, should be mentioned at this point if only because it again stars Burton. This time, he is on the other side, playing a Nazi officer in 1944 who must order the slaughter of innocent Italian civilians to avenge the killing of thirty-three German soldiers by Italian partisans who blew up a detachment of troops in a Rome street. He tries to resist this order, but his attempt is ineffectual. Italy's Marcello Mastrioiani co-stars in the role of a priest who tries to save the lives of his countrymen.

"Lili Marleen" was a soulful barracks ballad sung and marched to by the Afrika Korps under Rommel. As noted previously, the song was picked up by British and American troops who put English lyrics to the melody and called it "Lili Marlene." Many recordings of the song have been made throughout the years, including one sung in German by German-born actress Marlene Dietrich. *Lili Marleen*, a minor 1981 release from Germany, is a fictitious story about a cabaret singer whose recording of the song becomes a big hit.

England is the setting for two 1979 films, *Yanks* and *Hanover Street*, and also for the 1976 production *The Eagle Has Landed*.

Hanover Street, from Columbia Pictures, is a love story involving an American GI and a British woman, something which was a fact of life during the war years. But this time, there is a twist: The lady is married and has a child. Harrison Ford, Leslie-Anne Down and Christopher Plummer make up the triangle and in the contrived plot of this film, both lover (Ford) and husband (Plummer) wind up on the same mission.

Yanks is a British production about World War II GIs stationed in an English town and the women with whom they fall in love. Heading the cast are Vanessa Redgrave, Richard Gere and William Devane. Hundreds of Englishwomen became war brides and came to America after the war.

The Eagle Has Landed, adapted from the novel by the best-selling author Jack Higgins and co-produced by David Niven's son, takes place in a small English village on the Norfolk coast where Churchill is supposedly spending a weekend. Enter a group of spies whose mission is to kill the prime minister. Needless to say, the attempt is foiled. Starred are Michael Caine, Donald Sutherland, Robert Duvall and Jean Marsh.

Continuing along in the cycle of war epics are four of the more exciting films of the 1970s: *Patton* and *Tora! Tora! Tora!*, both produced at Twentieth Century–Fox in 1970; *Midway* from Universal, filmed on location in 1976; and *The Final Countdown*, a 1979 United Artists production.

Patton is the sweeping saga of the larger-than-life General George S. Patton, a gutsy, factual portrait of a man of unquestioned bravery, whose love for war was enduring, whose temper often got him into trouble, whose unorthodox methods of warfare were often questioned and whose demands upon those he commanded were uncompromising. It was named Best Picture of the year and George C. Scott's mesmerizing performance in the title role won him the year's Best Actor Academy Award. (Scott had not been the first choice for the plum part. Turning it down were Burt Lancaster, Robert Mitchum, Lee Marvin and Rod Steiger.) Co-starred with Scott is Karl Malden as General Omar Bradley,

Fifteen. Time Marches On

Patton's superior. The battle sequences tracing Patton's exploits in North Africa, Sicily and Germany are excitingly and faithfully recreated. The film remains one of the most popular ever made.

The bombing of Pearl Harbor is the subject of *Tora! Tora! Tora!* The sprawling production stars Jason Robards, Jr., Joseph Cotten and James Whitmore and depicts Japanese and American actions in the weeks and months before the attack. Admiral Isoroku Yamamoto,* Japanese commander-in-chief of the Combined Fleet, is ordered to plan an air strike over Pearl Harbor, although he believes that a war with the United States at this time would be disastrous for his country. As the planning is taking place, the Japanese begin sending 14 radio messages to their embassy in Washington which will conclude with a declaration of war. The fourteenth message is to be delivered to the embassy thirty minutes *before*

***Tora! Tora! Tora!*:** Carefully made plans would lead to the Japanese aerial attack at Pearl Harbor on what President Roosevelt, in his declaration of war speech, would call a day of "infamy," December 7, 1941. Both Japanese and American directors worked on the film.

*Yamamoto died in 1943 when his plane was shot down by American P-38s.

the attack is to begin, but the Japanese typist is slow and does not decode it quickly enough.

At film's end, Yamamoto, having learned that the attack has preceded the declaration of war, is said to have uttered the prophetic line "I fear that all we have done is to awaken a sleeping giant and fill him with a terrible resolve."

The battle sequences taking place at Pearl take up a good part of the film's last half, and although they are quite familiar, there is still a quickening of the heartbeat, and it is again exciting to watch as the controversial raid unfolds and to ponder just how much America knew of the impending tragedy. Many historical personalities of the era are portrayed in the film and actual locations have been used wherever possible.

What would have happened had the Japanese fleet been destroyed before it reached Pearl Harbor? This interesting premise is the plotline of *The Final Countdown*. Kirk Douglas, whose production company (Bryna, named for his mother) did the filming, stars as the commander of a modern-day aircraft carrier, circa 1980, who, caught in a time warp, must decide whether or not to prevent the bombing of Pearl Harbor. The premise is a fascinating one and, combined with action scenes of Japanese Zeros of the 1940s doing battle against American bombers of the 1970s, it makes for some unusual viewing. Also in the cast are Martin Sheen, James Farentino and Katharine Ross. Sheen went on to star as the president in the hit television series *West Wing*.

Midway details the decisive sea and air battle fought just off the strategic island in the Pacific. Newsreel footage and carefully staged battle scenes have been combined to recreate the event, won by the Americans, which turned the tide in the war against Japan. Among the performers are Charlton Heston, Glenn Ford, James Coburn, Henry Fonda as Admiral Chester Nimitz and Robert Mitchum as Admiral William Halsey. (The feisty "Bull" Halsey was previously played by James Cagney in the 1960 United Artists production *The Gallant Hours*. Co-starring Robert Montgomery, the film was produced by the two actors and directed by Montgomery.)

Another colorful character of World War II is the subject of a 1977 film from Universal. *MacArthur* stars Gregory Peck as the controversial general and is played out against the panorama of the war in the Pacific. In this case, the man is more interesting than the film, which omits more than it tells.

Fifteen. Time Marches On

Douglas MacArthur's military career began at West Point and ended in the halls of Congress with his emotionally charged "Old soldiers never die, they just fade away" speech. In between came military service in the first World War, the brilliance of his strategy in the second, his presence at the signing of Japan's unconditional surrender document which ended the war and finally, the arrogance of Korea. Ed Flanders is seen as in a cameo role as President Harry Truman, who although recognizing the general's larger-than-life legend, nevertheless felt it necessary to remove him from his command for the good of the nation. The subject of many books and much controversy, MacArthur, who had told the Philippine nation that he would return, came back to America to live out his life in splendid isolation.

Too Late the Hero, a Palomar–Robert Aldrich 1970 film, stars Cliff Robertson and Michael Caine as two reluctant soldiers who are sent on a suicide mission to a small island in the Pacific which is held on one side by the Japanese and the other side by the British and the Americans. They must match wits with a Japanese officer and come out on top. Others in the cast include Henry Fonda and Denholm Elliott.

Reminiscences of life in a small Japanese town just after the end of the war is the subject of a 1985 Japanese film titled *MacArthur's Children*. Shown are the reactions of the townspeople to the social and cultural changes which occurred during the American occupation and which led to the democratization of this Far Eastern country.

Fifteen years after the success of *The Longest Day*, another book by Cornelius Ryan was brought to the screen in a vivid, almost three-hour production. *A Bridge Too Far*, a 1977 United Artists release, recreates the disastrous September 1944 Allied parachute landing behind German lines at Arnheim in the Netherlands. The mission's objective was to capture and secure several bridges held by the Germans. Richard Attenbrough directed an all-star cast which included Robert Redford, Ryan O'Neal, Dirk Bogarde, James Caan, Michael Caine, Sean Connery, Gene Hackman, Anthony Hopkins and Laurence Olivier.

A different kind of film with an even wider scope, *The Sorrow and the Pity was* shot in 1970 by French, Swiss and West German motion picture units under the direction of Max Ophuls. A documentary using newsreel footage and interviews, the film focuses upon one city in France during World War II; in reality, however, it is the story of the entire French nation and takes a searing look at one of the darkest periods in its history. By 1940, the country was virtually split in two, one part occupied by the enemy, the other governed by the collaborationist Vichy regime headed by Marshal Henri Pétain, the aging hero of the first World War, and Pierre Laval, his right hand man. (The latter was executed in 1945 for treason.) The distinguished film also documents the concurrent rise of anti–Semitism and the effect this malignancy had on an otherwise respectable nation.

Unlike *The Sorrow and the Pity*, *The Hiding Place* (1975) is a story showing humanity at its best. Produced by Billy Graham's Evangelical Association, the film is about a group of Dutch Christians who aid many Jews during the German occupation of their homeland. The cast includes Julie Harris and Arthur O'Connell.

The Sorrow and the Pity should not be construed as castigating all of France and *The Hiding Place* should not be construed as celebrating the Dutch as a whole. There were many heroic deeds performed in both countries by unknown people but there were also those in both countries who collaborated with the enemy.

Three other World War II–related films seen during the 1970s were *The McKenzie Break*, *Bedknobs and Broomsticks* and *Murphy's War*.

The first named, a United Artists 1970 film, is another POW story, this time with a new slant. It takes place at a camp in Scotland. A young German Luftwaffe pilot has been murdered and an officer is ordered to investigate. He discovers an ingenious escape plan plotted by a group of unrepentant prisoners. Brian Keith portrays the irascible Irishman successfully matching wits with a bunch of crafty Germans led by Helmut Griem.

In *Bedknobs and Broomsticks*, a 1971 fantasy from Walt Disney, Angela Lansbury stars as an apprentice witch who, with three displaced children and a magical broomstick, foils a 1940 enemy invasion off the coast of England. Interestingly enough, Lansbury came to America from England during the war years and, at nineteen years of age, began a career that is still going strong.

Murphy's War, a 1971 British production, stars Peter O'Toole as a torpedoed British merchant seaman seeking revenge after his ship has been sunk by a German sub. It is a gripping and exciting film, with well-staged action scenes and a good performance by its star.

During the late 1940s, studio heads were resentful of television's impact upon moviegoers and forbade their contract players to appear in the new medium. By the mid–1950s, however, the moguls realized that the dreaded "enemy" could be the source of a potential fortune and began to negotiate the sale of their old films to what they privately called the "upstart." By the late 1960s, "the upstart" was producing its own films. TV-movie (Movies Made for Television) have become a fact of life. Two of the best produced during the late 1970s have World War II settings and are part of a breed based on actual occurrences; they are now called "docudramas."

Farewell to Manzanar, telecast in 1976, is the retelling of a sorry chapter in the history of one nation — our own. The action takes place in California, just after Pearl Harbor. A jumpy government, fearing possible enemy action on its West Coast, gives the go-ahead for all Japanese-Americans to be interned for the duration of the war. The storyline follows a family as its members pack their belongings and begin their new lives in a detention camp at Manzanar.

A detention of a far more insidious kind is the setting for *Kitty: Return to Auschwitz* (1979). The story is of a woman who survived two years of imprisonment in the infamous Nazi-run concentration camp. Returning to her native Poland with her son, she takes him on a tour of the camp in an attempt to make him and others of his generation understand what the Holocaust was about.

The 1980s saw an actor in the White House, Ronald Reagan, and the first woman Supreme Court Justice, Sandra Day O'Connor, installed. We were also witness to the marriage of Lady Di to Prince Charles and the deaths of Grace Kelly and Beatle John Lennon. World War II continued to be an interesting topic for both moviemakers and moviegoers during the decade; several new war related films were made, and a couple of old ones remade.

And a new phenomenon came into being — the video store. Studios put their films, old and new, onto video cassettes, and business boomed. In an age of instant gratification, the public was able to see popular versions of the great battles of the war and learn about the legendary personalities who shaped victory for one side and defeat for another, right in their own homes. (Now, with the new technology, more and more of these films can be seen on DVDs.)

Since the beginning of the 1980s, films released for viewing in theaters and those made for watching at home have become almost interchangeable — the lines of demarcation are quite blurry. In fact, not much time elapses these days before theatrically shown films can be seen in the comfort of one's own living room or bedroom. The war-related movies discussed in the next several pages are a combination of those produced during the decade. To avoid the constant usage of the phrase "made-for-TV-movie," TV-movie will appear in the text which follows.

Eye of the Needle and *Key to Rebecca*, the first a 1981 theatrically released United Artists film and the second a 1985 TV-movie, come from the prolific pen of best-selling author Ken Follett. Both are fast-paced, old-fashioned spy thrillers.

Eye of the Needle stars Donald Sutherland as a Nazi spy who has stolen plans for the D-Day invasion. Upon leaving England by boat after having killed his nosy landlady, he experiences a blinding storm and is washed up onto the shore of a remote island occupied by Kate Nelligan and her paraplegic husband. Sutherland and Nelligan have a brief affair; the film's finale, when she discovers his true identity and shoots him, is an exciting one, mostly due to Sutherland's quietly menacing performance.

In the TV-movie *Key to Rebecca*, David Soul portrays a Nazi spy in Cairo, circa 1942, who is furnishing Rommel with needed information and Cliff Robertson is the Allied officer out to capture him. The cat-and mouse game is played to a thrilling climax as Robertson races against time to rescue his young son, kidnapped by the Nazi. Robert Culp, who co-starred with Bill Cosby in the hit television series *I Spy*, is seen in the small but pivotal role of Rommel.

Code Name: Emerald, also a 1985 TV-movie, stars Ed Harris as an American working for the British Secret Service. The Nazis think that he is one of theirs and, when they capture a young American Army officer possessing information about "Overlord," i.e., the invasion of Europe, they assign "Emerald" to obtain it. Of course, the super-spy has something else in mind and organizes a daring rescue operation.

Rescue is the subject of *The Last Escape*, a 1970 United Artists production. Stuart Whitman stars as an American heading a group whose mission is bring various military and scientific personnel out of enemy-occupied territory. Pursued by the SS, they eventually succeed in their mission.

A rescue on a much larger scale is the subject of *Wallenberg: A Hero's Story*, a 1985 TV-movie. Richard Chamberlain (Dr. Kildare in the small-screen version of the old MGM movie series) plays Swedish aristocrat

Raoul Wallenberg, who was responsible for saving many Hungarian Jews from extermination during the last years of the war. His disappearance after the Nazis were driven from Hungary is a mystery which has defied solution for over six decades.

Another film played out to a stirring conclusion is the 1981 Lorimar production *Victory*. In a POW camp, the German commandant has scheduled an inmate-guard soccer game in order to prove Nazi superiority. The soldiers agree to play and somewhere along the line, an escape plan is hatched. Any connection between this film and the actual war is purely coincidental, but Sylvester Stallone, Michael Caine and Max von Sydow, with an assist from soccer great Pele, make the picture worth watching.

A rousing and very popular film of the 1980s is *Raiders of the Lost Ark* (1981), the first collaboration of filmmakers Steven Spielberg and George Lucas. The Paramount release is the far-out tale of an archaeologist (Harrison Ford) trying to track down the fabled Ark of the Covenant before the Nazis do. In a loving salute to the cliffhanger serials of the 1930s and the 1940s and the Saturday matinees at the Bijou (or the Strand or the Rialto), there are races and chases and a finale which utilizes some fantastic special effects to display the Ark's mystical powers. Both the film and its director (Spielberg) were nominated, but lost to *Chariots of Fire* and Warren Beatty (for *Reds*) respectively.

An interesting but vastly different film is the riveting and disquieting *Das Boot*. The West German–made 1980 production, released by Columbia Pictures, describes the day-to-day existence of the men on a German submarine circa 1941, the halcyon days of Hitler's navy, when the U-boat was a menace to Allied shipping and almost owned the North Atlantic. The film is one which could never have been made during the war years, as it portrays the enemy in humanistic rather than propagandistic terms, as characters of flesh and blood, and depicts the grime, the closeness and harrowing thoughts of being underwater when depth charges begin coming too near a target. Increased sophistication of Allied planning, involving the use of convoys under heavy air cover, began to lessen the effectiveness of these undersea raiders, and by 1943 they ceased to be the threat that they had been heretofore.

Just as there has been an ongoing fascination with the battles of World War II, filmmakers and fans alike have also been intrigued by the life and motivation of the Austrian paper hanger who was at the root of the evil taking place during this period. *Hitler: The Last Ten Days*, a 1973 British-Italian collaboration, stars Alec Guinness and tells the story of this megalomaniac who, in his last will and testament, blamed the German people for the havoc he had brought upon them as well as upon the rest of the world.

In the beginning, not many realized that the dictator had laid out his plans for domination of Europe and then the world in *Mein Kampf* ("My Struggle"), his autobiography. Charlie Chaplin had been on the mark in *The Great Dictator*, as in the role of Adenoid Hynkel he uses a globe as a balloon in a ballet scene. But by then, it was too late.

Two TV-movies also focus upon the maniacal dictator. Like the film just discussed, one documents his rise to power, the other the story of his ignominious end.

Inside the Third Reich, which was filmed in 1982, is based upon the best-selling book by Albert Speer, the architect who became Hitler's wartime head of armaments. Starring Dutch actor Rutger Hauer as Speer and featuring such distinguished performers as Derek Jacobi and John Gielgud, the film traces the ascendancy of the intellectual Speer in the Nazi hierarchy. It is also another insight into the hypnotic hold that Hitler had on the German nation, a hold which led that country to chaos and destruction.

A 1981 forerunner to this look at Hitler's Third Reich is *The Bunker*. British actor Anthony Hopkins won an Emmy for his fine portrayal of Hitler as he descends into his underground home, the last he will ever know. Susan Blakely plays Eva Braun, the woman who was his mistress until they married the day before their double suicide, and Richard Johnson is Albert Speer. Movie veteran Piper Laurie won an Emmy nomination for her performance as Magda Goebbels, wife of propaganda minister Joseph Goebbels. This rabid Nazi husband and wife murdered their six young children in the bunker before taking their own lives.

Two vintage motion pictures, one a satire, the other the recreation of a life snuffed out too soon, were filmed once more in the early 1980s.

To Be or Not to Be is the Mel Brooks version of the Jack Benny–Carole Lombard smash hit. Although the 1983 Twentieth Century–Fox release lacks the subtlety and the sophistication of its earlier counterpart, and although Brooks and his wife Anne Bancroft are no Benny and Lombard, the plot is unchanged, and remains a funny take-off on a not-so-funny time in Polish history. As a tribute to Jack Benny, Brooks uses the comedian's real name, Kubelsky, as a street designation in his film.

The Diary of Anne Frank, a 1980 TV-movie starring Melissa Gilbert, Maximilian Schell and Joan Plowright, had its genesis in a Broadway play and then in a 1959 film starring Millie Perkins. The setting of the story is a factory attic in Amsterdam, Holland, in which a Jewish family and their friends are hiding. Anne Frank, found and executed by those to whom she had done no wrong, has lived on through her writings and will continue to do so as long as the Holocaust is remembered.

The first version of the film was Oscar-nominated, as were director George Stevens and Ed Wynn and Shelley Winters as Best Supporting Actor and Actress. Only Winters won; at the end of her acceptance speech, she thanked the young girl who had written with such sincerity and simplicity.

Another young life snuffed out before its time was that of Hanna Senesh, a Hungarian freedom fighter. Her story, based upon her diaries, is told in the 1988 Cannon Films production *Hanna's War*. Working as a British agent, she was parachuted into Yugoslavia, caught and executed. Appearing as the brave heroine is Maruschka Detmers. Other names in the cast are more familiar: Ellen Burstyn, Donald Pleasence and Denholm Elliott.

One of the most searing films involving a loss of childhood to come out of the 1980s is the French-language production *Au revoir, les enfants*, director Louis Malle's factual story of his Catholic school days in German-occupied France. The school headmaster had been hiding several Jewish boys from the Germans. One day a Gestapo official marched into the classroom and arrested three boys along with the heroic teacher. "Au revoir, les infants, à bientôt" ("So long children, see you soon") were the latter's last words. This was not to be. The four, betrayed by an embittered kitchen helper, were taken to Auschwitz and murdered. Remembering this incident, Malle fashioned his film as a poignant reminder of both man's highest nobility and also his inhumanity to his fellow man. Nominated for an Oscar as Best Foreign Film of 1987, it lost to *Babette's Feast*.

The Last Metro, a 1980 film from France, concerns the hiding of a Jew, this time an adult. His wife is trying to keep their theater open during the German occupation of Paris. Thought to have fled the country, the man is being hidden inside the theater. Catherine Deneuve and Gerard Depardieu, two actors well-known in America, star. The "final solution" had not yet been put into practice.

The infamous 1942 meeting of Nazi leaders to discuss the "final solution," which led to the Holocaust, is recreated in a 1984 Austro-German production simply titled *The Wannsee Conference*. It is a quietly chilling account of how the fate of millions of Jews was settled in a Berlin suburb. Among the participants at that infamous meeting were Reinhard Heydrich and Adolph Eichmann. Both would die violently, the former by an assassin's bullet in Czechoslovakia, the latter by a hangman's noose in Israel.

Final solutions began in concentration camps where Jews and other political prisoners were interned and then brutally murdered. *Escape from Sobibor*, a 1987 TV-movie, is the story of how a few hundred Jews defied the fate that had been decreed them at Wannsee and escaped from the death camp at Sobibor in Poland. Alan Arkin stars, giving a gripping and heartfelt performance as the leader of the revolt.

An earlier TV-movie drama of the concentration camps is of 1980 vintage. The setting this time is Auschwitz. *Playing for Time* stars Vanessa Redgrave as Fania Fenelon, who survived the infamous "structure of death" by performing in an orchestra as others met their doom. Both the movie, and the book upon which it is based, vividly portray the urgency of daily living under the threat of death. As adapted for television by the noted author and playwright Arthur Miller, and enacted by a fine company of actors headed by Redgrave (you may not be enamored of her political stands, but she can act) and Jane Alexander, it is a shattering drama, one not so easily forgotten. Miller, Redgrave, Alexander and the film itself all won Emmys.

The year 1982 saw yet another drama of heroism played against insurmountable odds. *The Wall* was adapted from John Hersey's novel of the same name. Featuring Tom Conti and Eli Wallach, this TV-movie is the story of the infamous Warsaw ghetto and the Jewish uprising which took place there in 1943. The Jews held out for several days, and not until the razing of the sector did they surrender. Not many of those courageous people lived to bear witness to these heinous crimes against humanity.

Crimes against humanity were also committed by lesser-known Nazis. It was not only the Eichmanns, the Himmlers and the Heydrichs who accounted for the millions of deaths in the twelve-year reign of

Hitler. Many others bore the guilt. One of these men is the subject of a 1987 documentary.

Max Ophuls' *Hotel Terminus: The Life and Times of Claus Barbie* chronicles the life of the sadistic "Butcher of Lyons." Years after the end of the war, Barbie was caught in Bolivia and returned to France for trial. The four-and-a-half-hour documentary was edited by Ophuls from over one hundred twenty hours of footage.

Films of the 1980s did not have to be based on fact to be war-related. Fictional feats of daring were still being made as we approached the 1990s and looked forward to the dawning of a new century.

Sylvester Stallone has proven true the adage that nothing succeeds like success itself in his series of *Rocky* films. Others have heeded this fact of life. A 1985 TV-movie, *The Dirty Dozen: The Next Mission*, wherein the men are out to foil an assassination plot, is a sequel to the popular hit of the late 1960s. Lee Marvin, Telly Savalas and Ernest Borgnine reprise their original roles in this second go-round, Marvin as the leader of the renegade group, Borgnine as his commanding officer and Savalas as one of the "non-com dirties."

In a typical Hollywood move, a third go-round in 1987. *The Dirty Dozen: The Deadly Mission*, was brought to the small screen. This time, the mission is to rescue a group of scientists. In its fourth and last incarnation, *The Dirty Dozen: The Fatal Mission*, a 1988 TV-movie, the men must outwit the Nazis on the Orient Express. *The Dirty Dozen* also inspired a short-lived teleseries of the same name.

Another flight of fancy, *The Sea Wolves*, stars Gregory Peck, David Niven, Roger Moore and Trevor Howard, all old hands at the movie game and the war genre. A United States-Great Britain 1980 collaborative venture, the adventure story takes place in 1943 and has the four heading a group of retirees whose mission it is to knock a Nazi radio transmitter, set up on a ship just off an Indian seaport, out of commission. With lesser stars, the film could have been an also-ran, but with the four pros working it, a good time is had by all.

By the 1980s, more and more women had become involved in all facets of film production. In searching for vehicles with which to both express themselves and show the influences of women upon the history of our nation, several chose stories demonstrating the important roles played by "the fair sex" during World War II.

One of the more enlightening of these is *Rosie the Riveter,* a 1980

TV-movie directed by Connie Fields; the production was two years in the making. Combining interviews with women who worked at factory jobs during the war years and newsreel footage, this documentary gives an accurate picture of the working class female and her very real contribution to that era. The footage seen at the end of the film depicts many of the "Rosies" leaving their jobs once the war was over. At the time, this was presumed to be the patriotic thing to do now that the men were coming home. It was left to the 1960s generation and the feminist movement to prove that not every woman's place is in the home.

Back in the late 1930s, MGM had begun a series about Maisie Revere, a showgirl with a heart of gold, who kept getting in and out of various predicaments. Ann Sothern played the irreverent blonde in ten films from 1937 to 1947. In 1943, the studio released *Swing Shift Maisie* in which the sassy showgirl shows her patriotism by putting her career on hold while she takes a job in an aircraft factory. While there, she is accused of sabotage by a jealous co-worker and must use all of her ingenuity to clear herself of the mess that someone else has made.

Back to the 1980s.

Warners' *Swing Shift*, a 1980 film, is a fictional and more popular evocation of the "woman at war" theme. Much of the credit is due to Goldie Hawn, who produced and starred as a lonely war wife who has an affair with a factory co-worker. At film's end, adhering to the prevailing morality, she elects to stay with her serviceman husband. Featured in the cast are Kurt Russell and Holly Hunter. Many films have in some fashion portrayed the roles of women during the war years, but none as accurately as the above two titles. Fields and Hawn are to be commended for their attention to detail and for capturing the atmosphere and the spirit of the "Rosie the Riveters" who played backup to the military on the home front assembly lines.

Two war-related films of the 1980s deal with love between Jews and non–Jews. *Every Time We Say Goodbye*, a 1986 Tri-Star release made in Israel, features Tom Hanks as an American World War II pilot stationed in Jerusalem who, upon falling in love with a Jewish girl, meets opposition from her traditional Orthodox family. *Forbidden* stars Jaqueline Bisset as a Catholic in wartime Berlin who falls in love with a Jewish writer, played by Jürgen Prochnow (of *Das Boot* fame) and joins an underground movement involved in smuggling Jews out of the country. This 1985 TV-movie was adapted from a book titled *The Last Jews in Berlin*.

Fifteen. Time Marches On

Escape from the Nazis is also the subject matter of *The Scarlet and the Black,* a 1983 TV-movie, and *The Assisi Underground,* a 1985 theatrically shown film made in Italy.

Both based on fact, the first has Gregory Peck, in his first starring role on television, playing a monsignor of the Catholic Church who harbors Allied prisoners of war in occupied Rome. The Nazi officer trying to thwart these efforts is chillingly personified by Christopher Plummer. John Gielgud portrays Pope Pius XII.

The second is the story of an "underground railroad" type of rescue operation involving Jews who are hidden in monasteries in and around the Assisi area of Italy. Featured in the cast are James Mason, Ben Cross and Maximilian Schell.

It must be remembered that not only the Jews of a country were the victims of World War II. In an era during which the decent values of civilization were trod upon by the Nazi jackboot, millions of non–Jews were also murdered in the name of "The Master Race." It was a time of slavish devotion by the German people to a twelve-year regime which defied the laws of God and of all humanity.

Recalling this is a 1980 film produced under the banner of Cannon Films. *The Assault* is a provocative drama about the killing of a Dutch family by the Nazis just before war's end and of its lifelong effect upon its sole surviving member. It was filmed in the Netherlands forty years after the event; the excellent production values and attention to detail evoke the black days of the occupation. The film was honored with an Oscar as Best Foreign Film of 1986.

An event of the 1980s was the primetime network television appearance of Herman Wouk's testament to what was at once a proud and yet a terrible time in the history of the world. Set against the sweeping panorama of World War II, *The Winds of War* and its sequel, *War and Remembrance,* tell the story of an American naval commander and his family caught up in the maelstrom of the conflict. As the narrative unfolds, other characters take center stage: the younger woman with whom the commander falls in love, the Jewish family into which his son has married and the men who were the movers and shakers in the world of the 1930s and 1940s — Hitler, Stalin, Churchill and Roosevelt.

The Winds of War, shown in 1983, details the events leading up to Pearl Harbor while *War and Remembrance,* viewed in 1988, continues the saga to its conclusion at Hiroshima. Using the enforced journey of the

Jewish family as the focal point, Wouk weaves into his story the insidious machinations which led to one of the most devastating crimes of our civilization: The Holocaust. The all-star cast includes Robert Mitchum, Polly Bergen, Jane Seymour (replacing Ali McGraw, who plays the role in the first film) and John Gielgud.

We end this chapter with the retelling of the final confrontation of World War II which took place in 1945. A 1985 TV-movie titled *The Enola Gay: The Men, the Mission, the Atomic Bomb* recreates those August days when President Harry S Truman had to make one of the hardest decisions of his life, that of launching atomic attacks upon the Japanese cities of Hiroshima and Nagasaki. The film stars Patrick Duffy, Billy Crystal and Gregory Harrison and is an account of the secrecy surrounding the possible mission, the training of its men and the resoluteness of Truman in giving the go-ahead. The latter was to write in his memoirs that he regarded the bomb as a military weapon and that there had never been any doubt in his mind that it should be used to shorten the war and save thousands of American lives.

The crew of the *Enola Gay* was led by its pilot, Colonel Paul W. Tibbets, Jr., and he was to write of the mission over Hiroshima:

> There was this mushroom cloud growing and we watched it blossom. And down below it the thing reminded me more of a boiling pot of tar than any other description I can give it. It was black and boiling underneath with a steam haze on top of it. And, of course, we had seen the city when we went in and there was nothing to see when we came back. It was covered by this boiling black-looking mass.

A second person aboard the *Enola Gay*, Navy Captain William Parsons, put it even more succinctly: "The crew said 'My God,' and couldn't believe what had happened."

Chapter Sixteen

The End of a Century

There's an anti-war folk song about a dream in which the world agrees to put an end to war. The decade of the 1990s showed us that the "dream" of the song was one that did not come to pass. Under the watch of George Bush, Sr., America once more went to war, this time to protect the small, oil-rich nation of Kuwait against the machinations of Saadam Hussein, the dictator of Iraq. In a lightning strike, U.S. forces defeated the Iraqis, but their brutal leader maintained his power over the country. His time would come. As did that of Adolf Hitler.

Fifty years after the cessation of hostilities, films about World War II and Hitler's Third Reich were still being made. This would continue into the new century.

Bette Midler's contribution to this "phenomenon" is *For the Boys* (Twentieth Century–Fox, 1991). The "Divine Miss M" plays a singer who teams up with a comic (James Caan). The film shows their up-and-down relationship throughout the years beginning with a USO tour. Also in the cast are George Segal and Patrick O'Neal. Midler co-produced the film and sings songs evocative of the period.

Paradise Road, a 1997 collaboration between the U.S. and Australia, tells the true story of a group of women held prisoner by the Japanese in Sumatra during World War II who become united and form a chorus to help alleviate their misery. Starred are Glenn Close, Cate Blanchett, Frances McDormand and Julianna Margulies.

Some productions, filmed in other countries, featured American actors and did well in the United States. One such film is *Tea with Mussolini*, a 1999 British-Italian collaboration. The plotline involves a boy in pre-war Italy whose mother has died and whose father is no longer around; the lad is being raised by a group of expatriates. The women refuse to leave the country with the coming of the war and are triumphant when their "boy" joins the Allies and returns a hero. There are many familiar faces in the cast including a non-singing Cher, Judi Dench, Joan Plowright, Maggie Smith and Lily Tomlin.

The very interesting *The Nasty Girl* (1990) is the true story of a young woman from a small town in Bavaria who enters an essay contest. The subject is "My hometown during the Third Reich." Despite the hostility this theme engenders, she obstinately researches the events and comes up with several shameful details. She becomes *persona non grata* in the town and has to move elsewhere. The film received an Oscar nomination as Best Foreign Film. The director, Michael Verhoeven, and its star, Lena Stolze, had been involved in an earlier motion picture titled *The White Rose*. The 1983 film is also based upon fact: A group of students in the Munich of the war years launch an unsuccessful anti–Nazi uprising. It is quite probable that the leaders of this revolt landed in a concentration camp.

The horrors of the World War II concentration camps are brought out in a fascinating motion picture made in Italy, *Life Is Beautiful*. This 1997 production, which celebrates the human spirit, stars Roberto Benigni (who also directed) as a man who refuses to give up even when he and his family are sent to a concentration camp. He tries in many ways to shield his son from what is taking place around them. Co-starred as his wife is his real wife Nicoletta Braschi. There are some comedy bits in the pre-war scenes, which many moviegoers did not appreciate, but the film did well at the box office and also on the night of the Academy Awards. It was chosen Best Foreign Film of the year and the exuberant Benigni leaped up to receive the Oscar as Best Actor.

Steven Spielberg had been a Hollywood success story for over twenty years with such hits as *Raiders of the Lost Ark, Jaws, Jurassic Park*, and *E.T.: The Extra-Terrestrial* to his credit, when in 1993 he began filming a project very close to his heart. *Schindler's List* (Universal–Amblin Entertainment) is the story of Oscar Schindler, a German war profiteer who was instrumental in saving the lives of eleven hundred Jews in war-torn Poland. An unlikely candidate for sainthood at face value, Schindler was a rogue, philanderer, drunkard, black marketer and Nazi Party member, who suddenly experienced an epiphany and saw the horrors of the regime, which he had supported, for what they were. He is now revered — it is to him that many today owe their survival and the lives of the generations which have come after them.

When a Beverly Hills shop owner, himself a "Schindler Jew," first broached the idea to Thomas Keneally of writing an account of this act of heroism, the author demurred, saying, "But I'm a Gentile." The elderly shopkeeper's comment was, "So much the better. You've no axe to grind." Subsequent research led to the writing of *Schindler's List*, which provided the basis for the acclaimed film.

In 1982, a friend of Spielberg's came across the book and thought it would make a great vehicle for the director. Spielberg would later admit that he hadn't been ready to make this film; he felt he was not mature enough. At different times, two other top directors with great credentials were set to direct the film, Martin Scorsese and Sydney Pollack. But then Spielberg decided that he would make the film himself. He was quoted as saying he didn't want to "give away a chance to do something for my children and family about the Holocaust."

Shot in black and white, almost entirely on location in Poland, the film stars Liam Neeson as Schindler, Ben Kingsley as his Jewish accountant and often his conscience and Ralph Fiennes as a sadistic Nazi commandant. Both Neeson and Fiennes were honored by the Academy, receiving nominations as Best Actor and Supporting Actor respectively.

The stark melodrama dominated the 1993 Academy Awards ceremony. Nominated for twelve Oscars, the production won seven, including Picture, Editing and Cinematography. It also won the New York Film Critics' Award as well as the Hollywood Foreign Press Association's Golden Globe.

For Spielberg, it was a night of nights as he made his way up to the stage to receive two statuettes, one for the picture and the other as Best Director, an honor which had previously eluded him on three occasions. In an emotionally charged acceptance speech, he implored educators to make sure that the story of the Holocaust is shown all over the world for generations to come, and concluded with the poignant phrase, "Lest we forget." Spielberg has put his money where his mouth is and funded Shoah, a foundation dedicated to preserve the memories of the Holocaust.

Les Misérables (1995) is a French retelling of the Victor Hugo novel, bringing it into the 20th century. Jean-Paul Belmondo stars as a man in the style of Hugo's hero, Jean Valjean, who aids a Jewish family in the

France of 1942 in their attempts to escape from the Nazis. In support of Belmondo are Annie Girardot, Micheline Presle and Jean Marais. We often talk of man's inhumanity towards man. Like the true story of Oskar Schindler, this work of fiction celebrates one man's humanity towards his fellow man and the difference one person can make in the lives of many.

Other American-made films of the early 1990s include *Shining Through*, a 1992 adventure story, released through Twentieth Century–Fox, starring Michael Douglas, Melanie Griffith, John Gielgud and Liam Neeson (this time playing an unrepentant Nazi) in which an author relates her wartime exploits in Berlin as a spy and *The Rocketeer*, a 1991 fantasy from Disney Studios, about a 1930s racing pilot (Bill Campbell) who finds an air pack that turns him into a "rocket-man," and the Nazi spy (Timothy Dalton) who, masquerading as a Hollywood movie star, is out to get both it and its wearer.

Besides those discussed earlier, some interesting foreign films were also made in the 1990s, most of them shown in specialty movie theaters. *Eleyna*, a 1992 English film with flashbacks to 1940, is about an old lady who recalls her efforts to care for a wounded pilot she finds in the woods, while *Europa, Europa* is a French-German 1991 collaboration in which a Polish Jew, captured by the Germans, pretends to be a loyal Nazi. It is based upon a book by Salomon Perel, to whom the events actually happened.

The plotline of *Rhapsody in August*, a 1991 film from Japan, directed by Akira Kurosawa, involves an old woman who, prompted by the visit of her Japanese-American nephew, played by Richard Gere (the only non–Japanese in the cast), recalls the death of her husband during the atomic bombing of Nagasaki.

It is Steven Spielberg who we come back to for the final films in this chapter. In 1994, the filmmaker, with two partners, founded Dreamworks, a motion picture, television and music studio. From Dreamworks, in cooperation with Paramount Pictures, came *Saving Private Ryan*. A second Spielberg film, *The Last Days*, was a Shoah Foundation production.

The first, released in 1998, stars Tom Hanks as an Army captain who is assigned to take his squad of seven men to France in order to find the private of the title (whose three brothers have been killed) and tell him that he has been given a discharge. Since there are many Ryans in

Sixteen. The End of a Century 197

the Army, the search is long and maddening, but the goal is achieved. Though the story is fictional, the battle scenes are all too real and harrowing. Hanks and Spielberg would work on another World War II project as will be seen in the next chapter.

The Last Days is a 1999 documentary in which five Hungarian survivors of the Holocaust are interviewed, reliving the days of Hitler's "Final Solution" which had been the subject of the infamous Wannsee Conference. Actual footage of the era alternate with the reminiscences to present a powerful picture of brutality and man's inhumanity to man.

And as we move through the twenty-first century, we are still being haunted by "man's inhumanity to man."

When will we ever learn?

Chapter Seventeen

The Dawning of a New Century

The new century is upon us and films about World War II are still being made. Even with the horrific event of September 11, 2001, and the neverending war in which we are, at this writing, currently engaged, it is interesting to note that we Americans have an ongoing fascination for this earlier period of history, aided and abetted by obliging Hollywood and foreign film companies. If the pattern holds, students in the twenty-first century will be learning as much about those war years from a body of films as they would from their textbooks.

The events of the early 1940s are repeatedly brought back to us in movie theaters and on television. Through public television and The History Channel, events and personalities of the war years are brought back to us in living color as well as in black and white while we are comfortably seated in our living rooms.

Also, for World War II veterans and students of history, there is the National World War II Museum, envisioned by the late writer-historian Stephen Ambrose, located in New Orleans, which gives its visitors a panoramic view of the war via films and exhibits. This generation and those of the future will be able to have a feeling for those foot soldiers who fought their way through the steamy jungles and waters of the Pacific theater of war, the cold waters in the battle of the Atlantic and finally the triumphant march on the road to Berlin.

Some very interesting viewing has been part of this first decade of the twenty-first century, and not only at your neighborhood theater.

A fascinating TV-movie from Italy is *Mussolini and I* (2003). Produced by Film Alpha Productions, the film traces the complex relationship between Il Duce and his son-in law, Count Galeazzo Ciano, and his equally complex relationships with his daughter, Countess Ciano and with Hitler, in war-torn Italy in the years before its surrender.

Powerful performances are given by Sir Anthony Hopkins as Ciano, Susan Sarandon as Edda Ciano and Bob Hopkins as Il Duce, torn between his love for his daughter and son-in law and his fear and admiration of Adolf Hitler.

Band of Brothers was a project co-produced by Steven Spielberg and actor Tom Hanks for Home Box Office. The ten-part mini-series premiered in September of 2000 and is still being aired on other television channels. Based upon the book *Band of Brothers: E Company, 506th Regiment, 101st Airborne, from Normandy to Hitler's Eagle's Nest* by the aforementioned Stephen Ambrose, the series depicts the men of Easy Company, a group of paratroopers, from their training site to the invasion of Normandy, to their involvement in the Battle of the Bulge.

The events portrayed in the series are based upon interviews by Professor Ambrose with actual Easy Company veterans. Both Hanks and Spielberg placed a strong emphasis on accurately depicting the conditions under which these men lived and died. The series was nominated for nineteen Emmys, winning six, the most important of which was Outstanding Mini-Series. It also won a Golden Globe and an American Film Institute Award.

Band of Brothers is the story of the heroic men who fought in combat with guns and bullets. They were Ike's boys — General Dwight Eisenhower, who headed the European theater of war. *Ike: Countdown to D-Day*, a 2004 TV-movie, stars Tom Selleck as the general who needed to make the momentous 1944 decision to invade the European continent. As previously noted, not until that "Longest Day" turned out to be one of triumph, did Ike destroy the communiqué he had written had the operation failed.

Ultra was the name used by the British for obtaining intelligence which came from the decoding of coded German radio communications in World War II. The few people with clearance for Ultra information were given the code name "bigots." Those with this clearance could, without humor, ask the question, "Are you a bigot?"

Ultra intelligence was derived from the Germans sending out secret messages ("cipher traffic") mainly generated on an electro-mechanical machine called Enigma. The Polish government had been given one of these machines by an anti–Nazi. It was reconstructed and given to the French and British governments in 1939.

Outside of London was a little-known compound known as Bletchley Park. It was there that hundreds of personnel, mainly cryptographers, worked day and night to decode the German Enigma traffic. Bletchley Park remained top secret throughout the war and even beyond.

The film *Enigma* (2001) is a collaborative effort of the United States, Great Britain and Germany. People in Bletchley Park discover that the German navy has changed the code used to communicate with their subs at sea. Those in charge enlist the help of a brilliant young man to aid in the breaking of the code. Featured in the cast are Dougray Scott and Kate Winslet as two of the people living and working at Bletchley. General Dwight Eisenhower, then Supreme Allied Commander, was quoted at war's end as saying that Ultra had been decisive to the Allied victory.

Christian Bauer, in 2006, chronicled in a documentary the not well-known but true story of *The Ritchie Boys*. In the 1930s, seeing the future of Jews in Europe, many German Jews fled the land of their birth and made their way to the United States. With the advent of World War II, many such refugees volunteered for the armed services. Several were sent to the little-known Camp Ritchie in Maryland. Thus was born a unique intelligence unit made of German-speaking recruits. Their fighting was not with guns and bullets, but with their knowledge of the language and culture of the country from which they had emigrated. They were used to interrogate German POWs and much useful information was gained as a result.

Over in the Pacific, momentous events had occurred. Bloody battles had ensued with the cost of many lives. Okinawa, Midway, Tarawa, New Guinea, the Philippines, Guadalcanal — these were only some of the names Americans had heard for the first time. One of the bloodiest took place on the volcanic island of Iwo Jima. It was, as many believe, the pivotal battle of the Pacific war. Actor-director Clint Eastwood's *Flags of Our Fathers* (2006) retells the story of the ultimate capture of the island and the raising of the American flag over Mount Suribachi.

The snapshot of the flag-raising by six American soldiers is arguably the most famous wartime photo of World War II, though the fighting continued for a little over a month after the taking of the strategic hill with many more lives being lost on both sides. The event was photographed twice to maximize its impact.

The film follows the account by the son of one of the soldiers as to what happened after the photo was seen around the nation and the effect it had upon the three soldiers who survived the battle. The trio is flown back to the States and sent around the country to sell war bonds. This disquiets them. They do not think of themselves as heroes and in the case of one, an American Indian Ira Hayes, these feelings are certainly instrumental in his subsequent suicide. The film is an honest recreation of the times, of the adulation given to our returning veterans and, as seen in the 1946 film *The Best Years of Our Lives*, the pondering of their futures once the adulation had faded away.

Months after the release of *Flags of Our Fathers* came Eastwood's *Letters from Iwo Jima* (2007). *Letters* looks at the events that took place on the island from the Japanese side of the conflict. Unlike the earlier films of World War II which painted the Japanese soldiers as fanatical barbarians, here they are portrayed as individuals who, like their American counterparts, have families back home. The focus of the film is on General Kuribayashi, sent to command the island in preparation for the invasion they know is coming. Eastwood learned about a book of letters written by the general, some written before Iwo and some from the island before his death. With his knowledge of the United States, having lived there while completing his education, Kuribayashi realized that the Japanese warlords had awakened a "sleeping giant."

Both this film and *Flags of Our Fathers* are a credit to Eastwood, who has emerged as one of the finest filmmakers of recent times.

A film released in 2005 shows the barbaric side of the Japanese military during World War II. Benjamin Bratt (a former actor on the *Law and Order* television series) and Joseph Fiennes star in *The Raid*, which is based on fact. In the early years of the war, after the Americans have been defeated in the Philippines, stories get out about the harsh and inhuman treatment given the prisoners by their Japanese captors. The American command sends Bratt and his group of Rangers on a daring mission to free these captives. With the help of Filipino guerrillas, the Americans are successful.

The year 2006 brought to the screen a powerful film from the Netherlands. *Black Book*, a Paul Verhoeven vehicle, follows the struggles of a young Jewish woman (excellently portrayed by Carice van Houten) trying to survive in Nazi-occupied Holland towards the end of the war. She joins the Dutch underground, meets a German officer, gets a job in his office and obtains important information for her Resistance group. An ill-fated love affair ensues between the woman and the German. He dies and she goes to Israel. The world premiere of the film took place at the Venice Film Festival on September 1, 2006, sixty-seven years to the day after Hitler's march into Poland — the day which began World War II.

Other World War II–related films released during the first decade of this new century include *Enemy at the Gates,* a German-British-American 2001 collaborative effort, which stars Ed Harris, Jude Law and Bob Hoskins. Stalingrad is the setting for this story of a Russian sharpshooter pitted against his German counterpart. *The Grey Zone*, a 2002 Tim Blake Nelson film, takes place in Auschwitz where a Jewish doctor is forced to help a Nazi doctor in order to save his own life. The Nazi medical man was the infamous Joseph Mengele, who, under the guise of "science," performed monstrous experiments on camp inmates. *Hart's War* is a Gregory Hoblit 2002 film starring Bruce Willis and Colin Farrell, wherein an American POW matches wits with the German commandant of the camp. *Safe Conduct* (French, 2000) documents the true story of two men who struggle to continue working in the French film industry under German supervision. The obvious question is, did they have the chance to emigrate to another country as did others who saw the writing on the wall and fled? Many of the latter came to the United States before Pearl Harbor and had illustrious careers in Hollywood.

Before we end our journey through the years with the event that began it all for America, four films released in 2008 need to be added to this last chapter. Very different in scope, two are factual; the others, though works of fiction, are based upon events that took place during and just after the war.

Several abortive attempts upon Adolf Hitler's life had been made, beginning in the late 1930s. Always, sometimes by sheer luck, Der Führer managed to elude his fate. After the war began, many who were beginning to see the Nazis in their true light became involved in plots to destroy a regime that had dehumanized their beloved Fatherland. The most famous came on July 20, 1944, led by Count Klaus von Stauffenberg. Code-named Valkyrie, this last attempt on Hitler's life is the basis of a Brian Singer film aptly titled *Valkyrie*.

Tom Cruise stars as the brilliant but doomed Stauffenberg, who places a bomb under Hitler's conference table. Thinking that he has succeeded, he flies to Berlin only to find out that the Führer is still alive. The bomb had detonated, but had been pushed away from where the

Nazi leader was seated. Stauffenberg and his co-conspirators are killed, he and some others executed by firing squad, others hung on meat hooks. Defiant in death, the real Stauffenberg was reviled by fanatics who followed Hitler unto death, and honored by realists who looked around them.

Heroism of a different kind is the theme of Edward Zwick's *Defiance* (2008). Starring Daniel Craig and Liev Schreiber, it tells the true and amazing story of the Bielski brothers, partisans who, through cunning, courage and resilience, were able to survive, living and moving from day to day in the forests of Belarussia, while rescuing hundreds of Jews and fighting the Germans whenever possible.

The real Bielski brigade was born when the parents (and also the wife and the daughter of one of the brothers) were slaughtered by the Nazis. Throughout the war, the brothers and some three hundred others employed non-stop guerrilla tactics against the enemy, ambushing enemy patrols, derailing troop trains and blowing up bridges and electric stations. Most of this is detailed in the film. Many of the people involved lived to see the end of the war; some are still with us. It is a triumph of the will that this band of disparate people formed a community based on the need to survive under insurmountable odds.

Enemies of the state were either shot or sent to concentration camps — this included Jews like the Bielski brothers, Gypsies and all others who didn't conform to the dictates of "The Thousand Year Reich."

At the Nuremberg War Crimes Trials held in 1946, the accused tried to justify their actions by saying that they were "just following orders." This, in part, is the premise of *The Reader*. The 2008 Steven Daldry film stars Kate Winslet, David Cross and Ralph Fiennes. The centerpiece of the screenplay is Winslet's performance as a former guard in a death camp, on trial for crimes against humanity.

She is seen by a law student, observing the trial, who, as a teenager, had a brief but passionate affair with her. She always wanted him to read to her. He now knows her secret: She is illiterate. She goes to prison and laboriously learns to read, aided by the tapes her former lover has sent her. Shamed by his reluctance to see her, she commits suicide, leaving money she has earned to a former inmate of the camp. Winslet received an Academy Award for her searing performance as this ignorant and amoral woman who was "only following orders."

It is estimated that the Nazis established over fifteen hundred concentration camps in Germany and in its occupied countries during their deadly reign of terror. The setting of *The Boy in the Striped Pyjamas*, a 2008 film by Mark Herman, is a concentration camp. Although the name is not mentioned, we know that it is the infamous Auschwitz. A young German child, the son of the commandant of the death camp, befriends a Jewish boy of his age, a prisoner on the other side of an electrified fence. The German boy wants a pair of striped pajamas which the other boy gets for him. Wearing the pajamas, the German child digs a trench in order to be able to play with his friend, is caught and is killed along with him.

The film suggests that the family of the commandant did not know or did not want to know about the "ethnic cleansing" that was going on in the camp, just as in real life the townspeople of Auschwitz denied knowledge of what was taking place only a few miles away from them until General Eisenhower forced them to go to the camp to see what they had "known nothing" about.

We end our journey through the years with the event that began it all for America. *Pearl Harbor* (2001), a Michael Bay film, recounts the bombing of the naval base. With a cast of familiar faces including Ben Affleck, Cuba Gooding, Jr., Jon Voight, Dan Aykroyd and Alec Baldwin, the film is a sweeping saga telling the story of individuals stationed at Pearl and ending with the recreation of the battle scenes that made "December 7th, 1941, a date which will live in infamy."

Epilogue

Films produced during the years of fighting were propagandistic in tenor, simplistic in plot and have little shading — there are only good guys and villains. Each year that passes, however, has offered another view and another interpretation of what we considered the war to end all wars. That we were wrong in this assumption does not negate the fact that it was a glorious time in our nation's history, and who can blame us if we step back and savor it once more.

Perhaps because World War II was the last clear-cut conflict and we knew what we were fighting for, or perhaps because America had covered herself with distinction and gained the respect and admiration of the world — whatever the reasons, more films about this epic period in our history are still to be made. Events which led to the war, the battles fought and the atomic blast which ended the conflict — these are the stories that need to continue to be told.

The National World War II Museum is visited by thousands of people each year — those who participated in the conflict and those who want to learn about it. Exhibits, discussion groups and guest lecturers carry on the mission of the retelling of this historic era.

Libraries and book stores also give the readers a sense of what went on during this period in America.

But it is your television set, your video cassette player and your DVD player which give the most vivid pictures of those terrible and yet glorious days.

You are also able to see, in black and white or in color, the army and marine foot soldiers who fought on both sides of the world, the air battles which devastated both Allied and Axis cities, the naval battles during the days when the U-boats of the German navy ruled the Atlantic, the Japanese sending lots of tonnage into the depths of the Pacific and the sea battles that ensued until the Allies had control of both oceans.

Go to your neighborhood video store and check out the available films. You will find a veritable treasure trove of war films on its shelves. Then pull up your favorite chair and watch as World War II explodes into your living room in black and white or in living color.

Ladies and Gentlemen, World War II.
The war that will not go away.

Selected Bibliography

Andrews, Maxene, and Bill Gilbert. *Over Here, Over There: The Andrews Sisters and the USO in World War II*. New York: Kensington, 1993.
Bergan, Ronald. *The United Artists Story*. New York: Crown, 1986.
Blum, Daniel. *A Pictorial History of the Talkies*. New York: Penguin, 1958.
Butler, Ivan. *The War Film*. New York: A.S. Barnes, 1974.
Capra, Frank. *The Name above the Title*. New York: Macmillan, 1971.
Connors, Martin, and Julia Furtaw, editors. *Video Hounds Golden Movie Retriever*. Canton, MI: Visible Ink Press, 1994.
DeCarlo, Yvonne, with Doug Warren. *Yvonne, An Autobiography*. New York: St. Martin's Press, 1987.
Eames, John Douglas. *The MGM Story*. New York: Crown, 1982.
_____. *The Paramount Story*. New York: Crown, 1985.
Hirschhorn, Clive. *The Columbia Story*. New York: Crown, 1990.
_____. *The Universal Story*. New York: Crown, 1983.
_____. *The Warner Brothers Story*. New York: Crown, 1979.
Jewell, Richard, and Vernon Harbin. *The RKO Story*. New York: Arlington House, 1982.
Jones, Ken D., and Arthur F. McClure. *Hollywood at War: The American Motion Picture and World War II*. New York: A.S. Barnes, 1973.
Krull, Irving S., and M. Nell. *A Chronological Encyclopedia of American History*. Washington, D.C.: Eagle Books, 1952.
Maltin, Leonard. *Movies and Video Guide 2009*. New York: Penguin, 2009.
Morella, Joseph, Edward Z. Epstein, and John Griggs. *The Films of World War II*. Secaucus, NJ: Citadel Press, 1973.
Mosely, Leonard. *Zanuck: The Rise and Fall of Hollywood's Last Tycoon*. New York: Little, Brown, 1984.
Norman, Barry. *The Story of Hollywood*. New York: New American Library, 1987.
Schickel, Richard. *The Men Who Made Movies*. New York: Atheneum Books, 1975.
Shirer, William L. *Berlin Diary*. New York: Alfred A. Knopf, 1941.
Shull, Michael S., and David E. Wilt. *Doing Their Bit: Wartime American Animated Short Films, 1939–1945*. Jefferson, NC: McFarland, 1987.
Thomas, Tony, and Aubrey Solomon. *The Films of Twentieth Century–Fox*. Secaucus, NJ: Citadel Press, 1985.
Walker, John, editor. *Halliwell's Film Guide 1994*. New York: HarperCollins, 1993.
Wiley, Mason, and Damien Bona. *Inside Oscar: The Unofficial History of the Academy Awards*. New York: Ballantine Books, 1986.
Wilkerson, Tichi, and Marcia Boyle. *The Hollywood Reporter*. Los Angeles: Coward, McCann, 1984.

Index

Abbott and Costello 34–35, 150, 151
Above Suspicion 61
Across the Pacific 43
Action in Arabia 99
Action in the North Atlantic 64
Address Unknown 99
Adventure 132
Adventures of Tartu 62
Affleck, Ben 204
Africa, Prelude to Victory 83
Against the Wind 138
Agnew, Spiro 177
Air Force 64
Alexander Nevsky 10
All Out for "V" 88
All Quiet on the Western Front 12, 158–159, 162
All-Star Bond Rally 91
All the King's Men 133–135
All Through the Night 44
Allen, Woody 148
Ameche, Don 11, 24, 73, 107
American Film Institute 199
American Theater Wing 77
Anchors Aweigh 126
Andrews, Dana 16, 48, 60, 63, 72, 102–103, 107, 133–134, 145, 165, 170
Andrews, Julie 174
Andrews Sisters 35, 96, 106–107
Any Bonds Today 88
Apartment for Peggy 142–143
Appointment in Berlin 60
Appointment in Tokyo 120
Arch of Triumph 149
Arise My Love 22
Armed Forces Radio Network 92
Army-Navy Screen Magazine 84, 91
Army Signal Corps 85
Arnaz, Desi 29, 51, 65, 98, 148
Arness, James 161

The Assault 181
The Assissi Underground 191
Astaire, Fred 7, 41, 75
At the Front 82
Au revoir, les enfants 187

Babette's Feast 187
Bacall, Lauren 98, 116
Back to Bataan 119
Baldwin, Alec 204
Ball, Lucille 29, 79, 98, 104, 148
Bambi 86
Band of Brothers 199
Baptism Under Fire 83
Bataan 65–66, 68
Battle at Bloody Beach 173
Battle Cry 162
The Battle of Britain (British) 167
The Battle of Midway 83
The Battle of San Pietro 82
The Battle of the Bulge 170
Battle Wreckage 85
Battleground 132–133
Baxter, Anne 48, 61, 63, 72, 110–111, 142
Bedknobs and Broomsticks 182
A Bell for Adano 118
Benny, Jack 38–39, 92, 106, 186
Bergman, Ingrid 56–57, 59, 97, 113, 136, 138, 149
Berlin, Irving 76–77, 88
Berlin Correspondent 48, 60
Berlin Express 149
The Best Years of Our Lives 74, 144–145, 147, 201
Between Heaven and Hell 154
Bitter Victory 158
Black Book 201
Blanchett, Cate 193
Blitz Wolf 87
*Blockad*e 11

209

Blood on the Sun 116
Bogart, Humphrey 7, 42, 44, 56–57, 64, 77, 92, 98, 116, 172
Bombadier 64
Bomber's Moon 62
Das Boot (The Boat) 185, 190
The Boy in the Striped Pajamas 204
Brando, Marlon 143, 163, 166–167
The Bridge at Remagen 171
The Bridge on the River Kwai 161, 169
A Bridge Too Far 181
Bring on the Girls 126
British Army Film Productions Unit 82
Buck, Pearl S. 104, 120
Buck Privates 35, 150
Buck Privates Come Home 150
The Bunker 186
Burton, Richard 158, 169, 173, 177
Bush, George, Sr. 193
Busman's Holiday 17

Caan, James 168, 181, 193
Cabaret 153, 175–176
Cagney, James 41, 48, 116, 138, 163, 167, 180
Candlelight in Algeria 98
Cape Gloucester, 7th Marines 85
Capra, Frank 2, 81–82, 84
The Captive Heart 137
Casablanca 56–57, 78
Castro, Fidel 152
Caught in the Draft 35–36
Cavalcade 7
Chamberlain, Neville 10, 15, 21
Chaplin, Charles 8–9, 26–27, 58, 186
Chariots of Fire 185
Chennault, Gen. Clare 49, 120
Chiang Kai Shek 84
China 67
China Girl 434
China Sky 120
China Venture 162
Christmas in Connecticut 125
Christmas in July 109
Churchill, Winston 2, 15, 21, 28, 52, 55, 57–58, 96, 114–115, 131, 178, 191
Cinderella Goes to a Party 87–88
Citizen Kane 36
Clift, Montgomery 136, 153–154, 166, 172
Cloak and Dagger 137
The Clock 123, 150
Close, Glenn 193
Code Name: Emerald 184
Colbert, Claudette 22, 67, 111–112, 165
The Colditz Story 164
Collingwood, Charles 20
Coming Home 143
Command Decision 149
Commandos Strike at Dawn 47

Como, Perry 105, 144
Conan Doyle, Arthur 45
Confessions of a Nazi Spy 13, 18, 26, 42, 87
Confessions of a Nutsy Spy 87
Connery, Sean 181
The Conspirators 57
Convoy 34
Cooper, Gary 36–37, 41, 59, 137
Coppola, Francis Ford 170
Corvette K-225 41
Counter-Attack 121
The Counterfeit Traitor 171
Courage of Lassie 121
Coward, Noël 54–55
Crash Dive 63
Crawford, Joan 22, 29, 47, 61, 106, 127, 132, 154
Crosby, Bing 38, 41, 76, 88, 106, 112–113, 167
The Cross of Lorraine 69
Cruise, Tom 202
Cry "Havoc" 68
Cummings, Robert 11, 26, 45, 124

Dangerous Moonlight 33
Davis, Bette 16, 29, 41, 77–78, 106, 121, 167
Days of Glory 58
D-Day, the Sixth of June 170
Dead End 144
Decision Before Dawn 159
Defiance 203
The Desert Fox 157
The Desert Rats 157
The Desert Song (1929) 61
The Desert Song (1943) 61
The Desert Song (1953) 61
Desert Victory 64
Desperate Journey 49
Destination Tokyo 68
Destroyer 63
Destruction, Inc. 87
The Diary of Anne Frank (1959) 187
The Diary of Anne Frank (1980) 187
Dietrich, Marlene 92, 94, 107, 136, 151, 172, 178
The Dirty Dozen 172, 189
The Dirty Dozen: The Deadly Mission 189
The Dirty Dozen: The Fatal Mission 189
The Dirty Dozen: The Final Mission 189
Disney, Walt 49, 86, 88, 196
Dive Bomber 34
Dr. Jekyll and Mr. Hyde 147
Doll Face 105
Doolittle, Gen. James 40, 48
The Doughgirls 108
Douglas, Kirk 170, 180
Douglas, Michael 196
Dragon Seed 103–104

The Ductators 87
Dunkirk 155

The Eagle Has Landed 178
Eagle Squadron 49
The Early Bird Dood It 88
Eastwood, Clint 173, 200–201
Edge of Darkness 71–72
Edward VIII 8
Eichmann, Adolph 188
Eisenhower, Gen. Dwight D. 96, 128, 199–200, 204
Eisenstein, Serge 10
Elenya 196
Elmer Gantry 169
Enemy Agent 18
Enemy at the Gate 202
The Enemy Below 159
The Enemy General 173
The Enemy Strikes 86
Enigma 200
The Enola Gay: The Men, the Mission, the Atomic Bomb 192
Escape 24
Escape from Sobibor 188
Escape in the Desert 122
Escape to Glory 23
Espionage Agent 18
E.T.: The Extra-Terrestrial 194
Europa, Europa 196
The Eve of St. Mark 110–111
Every Time We Say Goodbye 190
Everything Happens at Night 26
Eye of the Needle 184

Fairbanks, Douglas, Sr. 7, 19, 26
Fallen Angel 76
The Fallen Sparrow 59
Family Fables 88
Farewell to Manzanar 183
Father Goose 160
The Federal Bureau of Investigation (FBI) 13, 87, 122–123
Fiennes, Ralph 195
5th Air Force Report from New Guinea 85
Fighter Squadron 149
The Fighting Lady 82
The Fighting Seabees 103
The Fighting Sullivans 110
The Final Countdown 178, 180
Fingers at the Window 52
First Comes Courage 72
First Yank into Tokyo 116
Fitzgerald, F. Scott 12
Five Fingers 156
Five Graves to Cairo 60–61
Flags of Our Fathers 200–201
Flight Command 24

Flying Leathernecks 161
Flying Tigers 49
Flynn, Errol 7, 29, 34, 49, 72, 77, 119
Follow the Boys 106
Fonda, Henry 11, 41, 58, 64, 132, 63, 169–170, 180–181
For the Boys 193
For Whom the Bell Tolls 59, 78
Forbidden 190
Force 10 from Navarone 169
Ford, Gerald 177
Ford, Harrison 169, 178, 185
Ford, John 36, 82, 109, 119
A Foreign Affair 136
Foreign Correspondent 18, 24–25, 42
The 49th Parallel 31
42nd Street 76
Fosse, Bob 175
Four Jills in a Jeep 94, 105
Four Sons 24
Foxhole in Cairo 171
Franco, Francisco 8, 10
From Here to Eternity 153, 194
From This Day Forward 141
The Front 148
Der Fuhrer's Face 88

Gable, Clark 7, 16–19, 35, 39, 41, 132, 142, 149, 159
The Gallant Hours 180
The Gang's All Here 76
Gangway for Tomorrow 74
The Garden of the Finzi-Continis 175
Garfield, John 41, 59, 65, 68, 77, 106, 125
Garland, Judy 22, 59, 73, 98, 115, 123, 132, 172, 178
Garson, Greer 53–54, 132
Gaslight 113
Gere, Richard 178, 196
Gleason, Jackie 44
Go for Broke 162
God Is My Co-Pilot 120
Goddard, Paulette 17, 30, 46, 67, 74, 76, 92, 94, 108, 115
The Godfather 178
Goebbels, Joseph 8, 25, 31, 102, 186
Going My Way 112
Golden Earrings 151
Goldwyn, Samuel 62, 71, 74, 144, 146–147
Gone with the Wind 16, 19, 164
The Good Earth 70
Göring, Hermann 102
Government Girl 75
Grable, Betty 16, 33, 58, 91, 97, 104–105, 116
Grand Hotel 122
Grant, Cary 22, 29, 41, 48, 68–69, 98, 113, 138, 160, 163–164

Grauman's Chinese Theater 127
The Great Dictator 167
The Great Escape 167
The Great Lie 37
The Great McGinty 109
The Great Ziegfeld 70
The Grey Zone 202
Guadalcanal Diary 68
Guinness, Alec 161–162
Gung Ho 51
The Guns of Navarone 162
A Guy Named Joe 69

Hail the Conquering Hero 109
The Halls of Montezuma 162
Hammerstein, Oscar, II 37
Hangmen Also Die 70–71
Hanks, Tom 190, 196–197, 199
Hanna's War 187
Hanover Street 178
Happy Land 73
Harrison, Rex 18, 25
Hart's War 202
Hawn, Goldie 190
The Hays Office 167
Hayworth, Rita 16, 58, 91, 126
Hearst, William Randolph 36
Hell in the Pacific 173
Hell Is for Heroes 168
Hell to Eternity 173
Hellcats of the Navy 165–166
Hello Frisco, Hello 76
Hemingway, Ernest 59, 98
Henreid, Paul 25, 47, 56–57
Hepburn, Katharine 17, 77, 104, 125
Here Come the Waves 104
Hess, Rudolf 54, 102
Heston, Charlton 180
Heydrich, Reinhard 40, 70, 188
The Hiding Place 182
Himmler, Heinrich 102, 188
The History Channel 198
Hitchcock, Alfred 13, 25, 27, 32, 45, 101, 138
Hitler, Adolf 2, 7–8, 10–11, 15, 17, 19, 21, 23, 26, 28, 58, 62, 70, 80, 87, 94, 96, 102, 108, 115, 131, 138, 155, 157–158, 170, 180, 186, 189, 191, 193, 199, 202
The Hitler Gang 102
Hitler: The Last Ten Days 186
Hitler's Children 71
Hitler's Madman 70–71
Hold Back the Dawn 30
Holden, William 16, 34, 41, 143, 161–164, 172
The Hollywood Canteen 2, 41, 77, 92, 95, 127
Hollywood Canteen (film) 106

The Hollywood Foreign Press Association 195
"The Hollywood Reporter" 90
The Hollywood Victory Committee 90, 94, 106
Home of the Brave 135
Homecoming 1423
Hoover, J. Edgar 13
Hope, Bob 35, 46, 62, 76, 91–95, 128
Hopkins, Anthony 181, 186, 199
Hopper, Hedda 97, 132
Hostages 70
Hotel Berlin 122
Hotel Terminus: The Life and Times of Claus Barbie 189
The Hour Before the Dawn 99
The House I Live In 127
The House on 92nd Street 122–123
The House Un-American Activities Committee 148
How Green Was My Valley 36
Howard, Leslie 17, 31
Hudson, Rock 149, 171
The Human Comedy 73
Huston, John 2, 43, 81–82
Huston, Walter 72–73, 81, 104

I Am a Camera 153
I Love a Soldier 74
I Wanted Wings 34
I Was Monty's Double 156
Idiot's Delight 17
If I'm Lucky 105
Ike: Countdown to D-Day 199
The Immortal Sergeant 64
The Impatient Years 142
In Love and War 61
In the Meantime, Darling 106
In the Navy 35
In Which We Serve 54–55
Inside Fighting China 84
Inside Moves 146
Inside the Third Reich 186
International Lady 32
International Squadron 49
Invisible Agent 45
The Irving Thalberg Award 107, 147
Is Paris Burning? 170
It Can't Last 85
It Happened One Night 7, 81, 159

Joan of Paris 37
Joe Smith, American 51
Johnson, Van 40–41, 52, 69, 73, 103, 105, 132–133, 149, 163, 165, 173
Jolson, Al 88, 92, 94, 121
Jones, Jennifer 16, 78, 111–112
Journey for Margaret 52

Index

Journey Together 121
Judgment at Nuremberg 172
Jurassic Park 194

Keep 'Em Flying 35
Keep Your Powder Dry 125
Kelly, Gene 69–70, 78, 116
Kelly, Grace 183
Kennedy, John F. 119, 152
Kennedy, Robert F. 152
Kern, Jerome 37
Key to Rebecca 184
King, Martin Luther, Jr. 152
The King and I 97
Kings Go Forth 164
Kitty: Return to Auschwitz 183
Kramer, Stanley 135, 172

Ladd, Alan 46–47, 67, 76, 137
Ladies Courageous 68
Lady Be Good 37
The Lady Has Plans 46
The Lady Vanishes (1938) 12–13, 32, 36
The Lady Vanishes (1979) 13
Lake, Veronica 34, 46, 67, 76, 98–99, 126
Lamarr, Hedy 41, 57–58, 97, 116
Lamour, Dorothy 10, 36, 58, 62, 76, 124
Lancaster, Burt 153–154, 159, 172, 178
Lang, Fritz 30, 31, 70, 100, 137
Lansbury, Angela 13, 182
Lassie 121
Lassie Come Home 121
The Last Blitzkrieg 165
The Last Bridge 158
The Last Days 196–197
The Last Escape 184
The Last Metro 187
The Last Train from Madrid 10
Lawrence of Arabia 170
The League of Nations 42
Leigh, Vivien 17, 19
Lemmon, Jack 163
Lennon, John 183
Let There Be Light 82
A Letter from Bataan 85
A Letter to Three Wives 133
Letters from Iwo Jima 201
Life Is Beautiful 194
Life Line 85
Lifeboat 101
Lili Marleen 178
Lindbergh, Col. Charles 20
The Lion Has Wings 18
The Little Foxes 144
Little Tokyo U.S.A. 44
Lombard, Carole 2, 7, 16, 19, 38–39, 156
The Longest Day 169–170, 181
Loren, Sophia 172

The Lost Weekend 127
Love Under Fire 10, 11
Lubitsch, Ernst 38
Lucky Jordan 46
Lukas, Paul 12–13, 70, 72, 78, 99, 150

MacArthur, Gen. Douglas 40, 97, 114, 181
MacArthur's Children 181
MacMurray, Fred 34, 38, 41, 61, 76, 108, 126–128
Madame Spy 45
The Magic Face 158
The Maltese Falcon 42–43
Man Hunt 31
The Man I Married 26
The Man Who Never Was 156–157
Manila Calling 43
Mao Tse Tung 84
March, Fredric 30, 38–39, 108, 145, 147
The Marshall Plan 131
Mason, James 41, 98–99, 156–158, 191
Massacre in Rome 177
The Master Race 102
Mayer, Louis B. 16, 133, 167
McCarthy, Joseph 148, 153
McCrea, Joel 18, 24, 75
McDaniel, Hattie 17
The McKenzie Break 182
McQueen, Steve 166, 168
A Medal for Benny 124
Meet John Doe 81
Meet the People 104
The Memphis Belle (1943) 82
The Memphis Belle (1990) 83
The Men 143
Midway 178, 180
Mildred Pierce 127
Milland, Ray 22, 26, 34, 41, 46–47, 76, 100, 127, 151
Miller, Glenn 92, 101
Ministry of Fear 99–100
Minnelli, Liza 132, 175–176
The Miracle of Morgan's Creek 110
Les Misérables 195
The Misfits 142
Mission to Moscow 73
Mr. Deeds Goes to Town 81
Mr. Lucky 69
Mister Roberts 163
Mr. Smith Goes to Washington 81
Mr. Winkle Goes to War 63
Mitchell, Margaret 2, 16, 19
Mitchum, Robert 51, 73, 103, 143–144, 159, 169, 178, 180, 192
Monroe, Marilyn 142
Montgomery, Gen. Bernard 41, 64, 156, 171
Montgomery, Robert 17, 41, 119, 132, 150
The Moon Is Down 71–72

The More the Merrier 74–75, 108
The Mortal Storm 23–24
Moscow Strikes Back 83–84
The Motion Picture Industry War Activities Committee 120
Mrs. Miniver 48, 52–55
Murphy, Audie 165, 173
Murphy, George 51, 65, 76, 97, 133
Murphy's War 182
Murrow, Edward R. 20, 52
Mussolini, Benito 8, 26, 58, 115, 198
Mussolini and I 198
Mutiny on the Bounty 7
My Favorite Blonde 46

The Naked and the Dead 161
The Nasty Girl 194
National Socialist Party 9, 42
National World War II Museum 198, 205
The Navy Comes Through 51
Nazi Agent 44
Neeson, Liam 195–196
The Negro Soldier 82
Never So Few 165
New York Film Critics Award 101, 147, 195
Newman, Paul 165
A Night in Casablanca 150
Night of the Generals 173
Night Train to Munich 25
Niven, David 30, 101, 151, 169, 178, 189
Nixon, Richard M. 177
None But the Lonely Heart 113
None Shall Escape 99
The North Star (aka *Armored Attack*) 71–72
Northern Pursuit 7
Notorious 138
Nuremberg Trials 131, 203

Objective Burma 119
O'Brien, Margaret 52
Office of Strategic Services (OSS) 137
Olivier, Lawrence 17–18, 22, 31, 181
Once Upon a Honeymoon 48
One of Our Aircraft Is Missing 48
Open City 135–136
Operation Petticoat 164
O.S.S. 137
Over 21 125

Paisan 135–136
Paradise Road 193
Paris After Dark 60
Paris Calling 39
Paris Underground 121
Parsons, Louella 97, 132
Passport to Destiny 102
The Password Is Courage 168
Pastor Hall 23

Patriotic Pooches 87
Patton 178
Pearl Harbor 204
Peck, Gregory 58, 135, 169, 180, 189, 191
Pétain, Marshal Henri 182
The Petrified Forest 122
The Philadelphia Story 22, 27
Pickford, Mary 2, 26
Pidgeon, Walter 24, 31, 36, 53–54, 149
The Pied Piper 47
Pillow to Post 125
Pilot #5 70
Pimpernel Smith 31
Pin-Up Girl 104
Pinocchio 49
Playing for Time 188
Power, Tyrone 33, 41, 63, 132, 141
The Price of Victory 84
Pride of the Marines 124
The Purple Heart 102–103, 107
Pursuit of the Graf Spee (aka *Battle of the River Plate*) 155
Pyle, Ernie 117–119

Q Planes (aka *Clouds Over Europe*) 18
Quinn, Anthony 11, 68, 120, 129

The Raid 201
Raid on Rommel 177
Raiders of the Lost Ark 185, 194
Rathbone, Basil 22, 32, 39, 45, 61–62
Raye, Martha 35, 92, 94, 104–105
The Reader 203
Reagan, Nancy Davis 22, 165–166
Reagan, Ronald 22, 41, 49, 56, 76, 83, 85, 97, 150, 165–166, 183
The Rear Gunner 85
Rebecca 27
Red Ball Express 165
Redford, Robert 181
Reds 185
Remarque, Erich Maria 11–12, 30, 149, 158–159
Report from the Aleutians 82
Resisting Enemy Interrogation 83
Reunion in France 47
Rhapsody in August 196
Riefenstahl, Leni 80–81
The Ritchie Boys 200
Robinson, Edward G. 13–14, 41, 63, 101, 121, 138
The Rocketeer 196
Rodgers and Hammerstein 163
Rogers, Ginger 7, 48, 58, 74
Rogues Regiment 150
Rommel, Field Marshal Erwin 32, 40, 60–61, 64, 96, 157–158, 171, 177, 184
Rooney, Mickey 35, 73, 78

Roosevelt, Franklin D. 7, 14, 16, 21, 27–29, 36 57–58, 82, 97, 114–115, 179, 191
Rosie the Riveter 189
Rossellini, Roberto 135–136
Reuben James 29
Run Silent, Run Deep 159
Russell, Harold 145–147

Saboteur 45
Saboteur: Code Name Morituri 167
Safe Conduct 202
Sahara 64
Saludos Amigos 86
Salute to the Marines 65
Sanders, George 13, 24, 31, 59–60, 71, 99
Sands of Iwo Jima 132, 134
Santa Fe Trail 49
Saving Private Ryan 196
The Scarlet and the Black 191
The Scarlet Pimpernel 31
Schickelgruber Doing the Lambeth Walk 88
Schindler's List 194–195
Scott, George C. 178
Screen Actor's Guild 97
The Sea Chase 160–161
The Sea Shall Not Have Us 160
The Sea Wolves 189
Sealed Cargo 165
The Search 136
Secret Agent of Japan 42
Secret Command 100
See Here, Private Hargrove 104
Selznick, David 1, 16–17, 19, 57, 75, 111, 139
September 1939 83
Sergeant York 36
Sherlock Holmes and the Secret Weapon 46
Sherlock Holmes and the Voice of Terror 45
Sherlock Holmes in Washington 62
Sherman, Gen. William Tecumseh 2, 19
Shining Through 196
Ship Ahoy 44
Ships with Wings 51
Shirer, William L. 20, 158
Shrine Auditorium 147
Simpson, Walis Warfield 8
Sinatra, Frank 45, 88, 91, 126–127, 153–154, 164, 166, 172
Since You Went Away 111–112, 143–144
The Sky's the Limit 75
So Ends Our Night 30
So Proudly We Hail 67, 99
Something for the Boys 105
Son of Lassie 121
The Song of Bernadette 78
Song of Victory 87
The Sorrow and the Pity 181–182
The Sound of Music 173–174
South Pacific 163

Spanish Civil War 10–11, 59, 61
Special Services Film Production Unit 81–82
Spielberg, Steven 185, 194–197, 199
Stage Door Canteen (film) 77, 92, 106
Stagecoach 119
Stairway to Heaven (aka *A Matter of Life and Death*) 151
Stalag 17 164
Stalin, Joseph 15, 19, 58, 114–115, 152, 191
Stallone, Sylvester 185, 189
Stand by for Action 63
Standing Room Only 108
Star Spangled Rhythm 76
State Fair 76
Stella Dallas 144
Stevens, George 2, 75, 83, 187
Stewart, James 23, 27, 36, 39, 41, 128, 132
The Stillwell Road 83
The Story of G.I. Joe 117–118
The Strange Death of Adolf Hitler 158
The Stranger 138
Street Scene 144
A Streetcar Named Desire 143
Sturgis, Preston 109–110
Submarine Raider 43
Submarine X-1 168
Sunday Dinner for a Soldier 110–111
Sundown 32
Suspicion 36
Swing Shift 190
Swing Shift Cinderella 88
Swing Shift Maisie 190
Swing Time 37
Swooner Crooner 88

Tag der Freiheit (*Day of Freedom*) 80
Tampico 101
Target for Tonight 34
Taylor, Robert 11, 24, 41, 63, 65–66, 132, 170
Tea with Mussolini 193
Temple, Shirley 111–112, 116, 134
Ten Days in Paris (aka *Spy in the Pantry* and *Missing Ten Days*) 18
Tender Comrade 74
Thank Your Lucky Stars 77
They Came to Blow Up America 59
They Got Me Covered 62
They Were Expendable 119
The Thin Man 7
The Thin Red Line 173
The Third Man 139
13 Rue Madeleine 137–138
Thirty Seconds Over Tokyo 40, 103
This Above All 141
This Gun for Hire 46
This Is the Army 76, 78

This Land Is Mine 71
Those Endearing Young Charms 124
Thousands Cheer 78
Three Caballeros 86
Three Came Home 165
Three Comrades 11–12
The Three Little Pigs 86
Tibbets, Col. Paul W., Jr. 192
Till the End of Time 143–144
Till We Meet Again 47
A Time to Love and a Time to Die 159
To Be or Not to Be (1942) 38–39
To Be or Not to Be (1983) 186
To Have and Have Not 98
To Hell and Back 165
To the Shores of Tripoli 67
Tobruk 171, 177
Togo, Gen. Hideki 29
Tomorrow the World 108
Tone, Franchot 11, 22, 26, 60–61, 70, 76, 99
Tonight and Every Night 126
Tonight We Raid Calais 62
Too Late the Hero 181
Tora! Tora! Tora! 178–179
Torpedo Run 160
Tracy, Spencer 40–41, 69, 103, 124, 172
Treaty of Versailles 8
Triple Cross 168
Triumph of the Will 80–81
The True Glory 83
Truman, Harry S 115, 135, 181, 192
Twelve O'Clock High 135
Two Girls and a Sailor 95, 105–106
Two Women 112

Uncertain Glory 72
Underground 32
United Nations 97, 114, 131
United Service Organization (USO) 2, 41–42, 91–92
U.S. News Review Issue #2 85
United We Stand 42
Until They Sail 165
Up Periscope 160

Valkyrie 202
Venice Film Festival 202
Victory 185
The Voice of the Turtle 150
Von Ryan's Express 172

Wake Island 50
A Walk in the Sun 132–134

The Wall 188
Wallace, Henry 84
Wallenberg: A Hero's Story 184
The Wannsee Conference 188
The War Against Mrs. Hadley 52
War and Remembrance 191
War Crimes Commission 138
The War Department Report 83
The War Speeds Up 85
Warner, Jack 13, 73 127, 163, 167
Washington, George 16
Watch on the Rhine 78–79
The Way Ahead 101
Wayne, John 47, 49, 92–93, 103, 119–120, 134, 160–161, 169
Welles, Orson 16, 36, 58, 107, 138–139, 170
What Next, Corporal Hargrove 105
When Willie Comes Marching Home 109
Where Do We Go from Here? 126, 128
Where Eagles Dare 173
The White Cliffs of Dover 101
The White Rose 194
Why We Fight Series 81–82, 84
Wilder, Billy 30, 61, 127, 136
Willis, Bruce 202
Wilson (film) 99, 107, 110
Wilson, Woodrow 99
The Winds of War 191
Wing and a Prayer 107
Winged Victory 107
Wings 112
Winslet, Kate 200, 203
The Wizard of Oz 23
Words and Music 106
Wuthering Heights 144
Wyler, William 2, 54, 82–83, 145, 147
Wyman, Jane 22, 41, 106, 108

Yamamoto, Adm. Isoroko 179–180
A Yank in the RAF 32–33
A Yank on the Burma Road 50
Yankee Doodle Dandy 48, 116
Yankee Doodle Swing Shift 88
Yanks 178
You Came Along 124
You Can't Take It with You 81
Young, Loretta 11, 17, 67–68, 138
Young, Robert 11, 23, 51–52, 124
The Young Lions 166
Your Hit Parade 92

Zanuck, Daryl F. 19, 26, 32, 72, 82, 102, 107, 169

www.ingramcontent.com/pod-product-compliance
Ingram Content Group UK Ltd.
Pitfield, Milton Keynes, MK11 3LW, UK
UKHW041955140426
5217IPUK00015B/816